LOVE
BEGAN IN
LAOS

THE STORY OF AN EXTRAORDINARY LIFE

PENELOPE KHOUNTA

PBK PRESS
WALNUT CREEK, CALIFORNIA

PBK PRESS
1565 Rockledge Lane, #1
Walnut Creek, California 94595

Cover design and interior formatting by Ruth Schwartz, mybookmidwife.com
Cover image: Pha That Luang, Vientiane, Laos, Penelope Khounta
Author photograph: Patricia Deverson

Ordering Information:
Quantity sales. Special discounts are available on quantity purchases by corporations, associations, and others. For details, contact the "Special Sales Department" at the address above.

Publisher's Cataloging-in-Publication Data
provided by Five Rainbows Cataloging Services

Names: Khounta, Penelope.
Title: Love began in Laos : the story of an extraordinary life / Penelope Khounta.
Description: Walnut Creek, CA: PBK Press, 2017.
Identifiers: LCCN 2017950571 | ISBN 978-0-6929272-9-8 (pbk.)
Subjects: LCSH: Intercountry marriage. | Laos—Social life and customs. |
    Culture shock. | Autobiography--Women authors. | Women—Biography. |
    BISAC: BIOGRAPHY & AUTOBIOGRAPHY / Personal Memoirs. | BIOGRAPHY
    & AUTOBIOGRAPHY / Women. | FAMILY & RELATIONSHIPS / Marriage &
    Long-Term Relationships.
Classification: LCC DS555.86.K56 2017 (print) | LCC DS555.86.K56 (ebook) | DDC
    959.4/092--dc23.

In loving memory of
Khounta, Mama, and Pa

Contents

Preface

Dear Peter and Alice,

Grown-up children may think they know all about their parents because they lived with them, but they know very little. First, they cannot remember much from before the age of four. Then for the next few years, they are centered on themselves and their wants and toys. Those years are followed by a period of discovering more about their surroundings, school, and friends. But they don't think about their parents unless they are intrusive in their play. Parents are just there. The teenage years are wicked. Teenagers usually don't want to acknowledge that they have parents, let alone the ones they have. In any case, during all those years, they have no idea of what is going on in the lives and heads of their parents, the why and what of their actions. In many ways, it is all too adult for them, and they do not need to know.

It is only later that some children become curious and have questions, especially after their parents can no longer remember themselves or have left this earth. Then there are no answers.

For you, I have written these answers to questions you someday may want to ask or do not know to ask.

I hope you find the photos interesting and that they bring back happy memories.

Love,
Mom

P.S. To the rest of you who pick up this memoir, I wrote it for you. It tells something about events in Laos, Iran, Spain and being in America, but it is not a history book. It is stories about incidents that occurred in my life and everyday living. Enjoy!

PART 1

CHAPTER 1
A New Beginning

In 1992, Khounta, who was living in France at the time, decided to move back to Vientiane and build a house. When we had lived there, it was the Royal Kingdom of Laos, but in 1975, it became the Lao People's Democratic Republic (PDR), a communist state.

He wrote me from Vientiane in November urgently asking me to send him five thousand dollars. That letter was the first I had heard from him in fifteen months. It was so imperative that he had written in English, a first. All his other letters, since the first postcard in 1965, had been in French. Moreover, he was asking for money, another first. I borrowed from my life insurance and sent the amount immediately with the help of my Lao cousin, your sister Air. He didn't say what he wanted the money for. He rarely gave his reasons for anything. However, just the action of asking was a gift to me. It was perhaps the beginning of a phase of greater communication in our lives. The last time we had spent time together was in California in August 1991 when he came from France to help us prepare the garden at the Piedmont house for the celebration of Pa's life.

However, this was a new beginning, so let's go back to the start.

CHAPTER 2

The Starting Point: 1962

My grown-up life began when I joined the United States Peace Corps in November 1962. I was twenty-one years old, a little overweight and I had just graduated from university with a degree in philosophy. My group trained at the University of Washington in Seattle, and we arrived in Thailand in February. My assignment was to teach English as a second language at a boys' secondary school in a remote, northeastern Thai town, Nakorn Panom, situated on the Mekong River, bordering with Laos.

From Nakorn Panom, open wooden buses sped down dusty, red dirt roads to smaller replicas of our town hours away. So Priscilla Spires, the only other Peace Corps Volunteer, and I never left the town's paved streets unless it was on official business to Bangkok, and to go meant a miserable, dirty, sweaty, scary eight-hour bus ride just to get to the train station in Udorn Thani or Ubol Rachathani. Then it was another twelve hours on the overnight train on second-class, blue padded benches with padded backs.

The only place that it was relatively easy to travel to was Thakhek, a ferryboat ride across the river. There, in Thakhek, the romance with Laos began.

At two p.m. the streets of Thakhek were still. The air was hot and stifling. One walked up the right side of the street and back down on the left. In the wide market strip between them, used banana leaf wrappings, spoiled vegetable scraps, and fruit peelings from the morning trading gave off an odor of decay. After lunch, the buyers and sellers were gone. The streets, the stalls, the buildings, the people, the animals were immersed in their siesta.

There were only a couple of shops open on the block-long street, which began at the riverbank with the river flowing by fifty meters below. The other buildings had their green, wooden, accordion doors closed against the heat. Those that stood ajar exposed a silent darkness. Nothing moved. Flies lazily buzzed from one sleeping dog lying in the dust to another. In Thakhek in 1963, we were the interlopers: Thais and Americans, coming across the Mekong River by ferryboat from Thailand, moving to a different timetable.

There was nothing to buy except 555 cigarettes in yellow wrappers, Gauloise in blue, bottles of Dubonnet or Algerian wine, and dusty boxes of California raisins or prunes in their metallic red and gold wrappers. The shops had an old wood, dust, and cement smell, void of cooking odors. It felt almost cool to stand in the small, dim, one-room, family-run businesses. We always bought an obligatory box of raisins, although I am not fond of them. One had to buy something, after all. The raisins were prized presents and exotica not available across the river where we lived in Nakorn Panom, our town in Thailand.

For us, the ride across the river was an exciting break in our routine life of teaching and enduring the heat. It was the only easy place to go. Pris and I went with Thai friends two or three times that first year. It was always the same. Everything closed up, nothing new to buy. No place to get anything to eat or drink. Had we crossed only a few hours earlier or later, women shopping for live ducks, chickens, eels, frogs, and pigs, blue-jacketed and capped *samlor* (pedicab) drivers transporting goods and people, and children playing games in the street would have given life to the town. We would have learned that farther down the road and on a cross street were a couple of soup shops and the town's only two restaurants, both serving French food.

Then one day in 1964, I spotted a slim, blond man crossing the street from the immigration office in Nakorn Panom. A foreigner was such an unusual sight that I approached him and learned that he lived across the river in Thakhek and had come to Thailand to mail his letters. He said he felt the post was more reliable on our side. I could not even recall a post office in Thakhek.

He wondered who I was and where I had sprung from, and I told him about Pris and our teaching assignments as Peace Corps Volunteers. I learned that his name was Brian Hackman, that he was British, and that he was a doctor with the Colombo Plan working at the hospital in Thakhek. He invited us to visit him. We could stay overnight in his house if we wished.

That was the beginning of many weekends spent in that unknown, remote, sleepy, small town where Royal Air Lao landed occasionally, and Thais came across the Mekong River for raisins or prunes. The town was more isolated than Nakorn Panom because the old, red dirt road going north to Vientiane and south to Savannakhet was in shambles and no longer secure from Vietnamese infiltration and Pathet Lao ambushes.

Slowly and unnoticed by me, each trip drew me closer to the town, jungle, people, and country. Away from the formal, explicit rules of behavior, dress, language, and food that I had to follow on the Thai side, I gradually realized I breathed differently on the Lao side. Nakorn Panom was the provincial capital, but the only foreigners who ever lived there were old missionaries. We were curiosities. We lived in a fish bowl under scrutiny for proprieties. Kids shouted at us every day, "*Farang, farang,*" which means "a foreigner, a foreigner." But in Thakhek, no one was watching to see if we knew how to behave or comment on what we did. It did not matter whether we could eat Thai food or not. The Lao were accustomed to occidentals in Thakhek. Laos had been a French protectorate, part of Indochina since 1893 until its independence in 1954. Frenchmen had been teaching in the middle school and running the tin mines in the nearby mountains for forty years.

In Thailand, I had to behave like a proper Thai teacher. I had to dress a certain way, cross my legs a certain way, eat a certain way, speak a certain way, and ride a bicycle a certain way. To the Thai, Western habits were impolite or wrong. Independent thinking and expression were discouraged. The response to un-Thai behavior was laughter that sounded like ridicule, but perhaps was only embarrassment or real amusement. This constant scrutiny created the necessity to be on guard at all times, a subliminal stress.

In Thakhek, I could be myself. I could drink a glass of wine or smoke a cigarette in public. A feeling of comfortable freedom came to permeate my whole being. No one was watching. Simple choices. That is why I came to love being there and was determined to live in Laos.

A couple of months later, two more English-speaking people came to live in Thakhek, Dottie and Al Bashor. International Voluntary Services (IVS) had sent them to work in rural development for the United States Agency for International Development (USAID). Then another IVSer, Dee Dick, a nurse, came from Vientiane in the summer break to teach a first aid course to schoolteachers. She had written a first aid book for the Lao, and USAID had it translated and printed.

Pris and I continued our routine with Brian, and they joined us. We added late night games of liars dice and pinochle, day-trips to visit caves and villages, and swimming in the rivers in the countryside to our weekend play activities. My two years with Peace Corps would finish in December, and they knew I wanted to come to Laos to work. They assured me that I could get a job teaching English as a second language with International Voluntary Services.

CHAPTER 3

The Knocking

Pris and I went to stay with Brian every weekend. One afternoon we had a curious experience, which further intensified my feelings for Laos. Living there is very comfortable and relaxing. Bizarre incidents do occur. They are explained by *phii,* that is, good and bad spirits cause inexplicable phenomena.

Brian and I were dozing under the mosquito net in his bedroom. We were stretched out on a rough, pink and blue flowered cotton cloth thrown over the kapok-filled mattress. The wooden shutters near the head of the bed were closed to make it dark and create an illusion of coolness, but a thin line of heated yellow light leaked in at the top and between the shutters. It was sweaty lying there in the semi-darkness. The dust motes barely moved in the sunlight. Pris was stretched out on the bed in the next room. We were taking our regular afternoon siesta after our usual five-course meal at one of the two French restaurants in Thakhek, both run by Frenchmen married to Vietnamese women, not wanting to return home after the fall of Dien Bien Phu. It was the quiet time for napping before afternoon tea with milk and sugar, to be followed by the "cocktail hour" — Pimm's or whiskey with tepid water. Later, it would be time to drive the Land Rover the few blocks to the other French restaurant for dinner before going to the Cercle Sportif to play boules and have a *digestif.*

It was very quiet. Then there came a loud, urgent, repetitive knock on the front door. The wooden doors banged together. The noise stirred us to semi-wakefulness, but we were enervated and too hot to move. Maybe they will go away, I thought. The knocking came again, louder and more demanding. I said, "Brian, you'd better go."

He groaned, lifted the mosquito net, and wrapped a sarong around his waist. I closed my eyes again. "There was no one there," he said when he came back. "I looked up and down the street, and it's deserted."

"We both heard the knocking," I said. "It woke us up. Someone was there. There had to be."

"They couldn't have gotten away in such a hurry that I wouldn't have seen them. There was no one anywhere on the street or under the house." We contemplated in silence. "Since I'm up now, I'll go over to the hospital and check on the patients," he sighed. It was about two o'clock, and as the British Colombo Plan doctor at the only hospital in town, he had to do his rounds at 2:30 in any case. He put on his usual rolled-up long sleeve white shirt and khaki trousers, stuffed his can of Players cigarettes in his pocket, and left. Pris went with him. I went back to dozing.

After about fifteen minutes, Pris was back. "What's your blood type?" she asked.

"B positive," I said.

"Brian wants you to come right over to the hospital to give a transfusion. A man has been lying on the operating table since eleven o'clock with blood dripping from his leg. His jeep hit a land mine on the road this morning."

Brian had understood that the *médicine chef* was going to operate, but for some unknown reason, he had not. The man had lain there as we leisurely ate our lunch and napped. I went immediately to the hospital. Brian took a pint of blood from my arm and put it directly into the man's arm. Then he began to operate. The man himself was too far-gone to have any anesthetic for the operation. Brian sewed as many of the shattered vessels together as he could and snipped off the rest. Pris began to feel faint watching the cutting and the blood, and I did, too, so we left. Brian finished sewing up the man's leg and swathed it in bandages. The day then proceeded as usual.

I saw the man a few weeks later lying in his hospital bed. His wife was also there, bringing him food. Hospitals then and now do not provide food. Brian said he was uncomfortable from the itching of the maggots eating the dead debris under the bandages. I was horrified, but he said it was an acceptable way to clean a wound under the circumstances. It was the same practice followed in the world wars. Eventually, the man walked away from the hospital.

We never learned what caused the knocking, but I believe it was the man's spirit, his *phii*, calling to us.

I liked the mystery in Laos.

CHAPTER 4

Vacation: December 1964

When I finished my Peace Corps tour in December, I went on a trip with Brian. We were good friends and enjoyed each other's company. We traveled first to Angkor Wat. It was my second visit, so I knew the route. First, one typically took the train from Bangkok to Aranyaprathet on the Thai border. It was a simple matter to be stamped out of Thailand, and a short walk from the immigration office to the Cambodian border Poipet, which was marked by a deserted, single-lane, wooden bridge over a ravine. There was never any water under the bridge the times I crossed, albeit always during the dry season. To walk across the bridge on a hot, dry, dusty day from one small village to another seemed uncanny. In my experience, I had only flown into an airport, taken a ferryboat or driven into another country, but to walk and carry my suitcase felt very strange. It was always still and the heat simmered in the air.

From the immigration office in Poipet, we walked into the village to get a bus to Siem Reap. The trick was to catch a bus early enough so that it would not be necessary to spend the night in an even smaller village along the way. The small villages had no accommodations for travelers. In the '60s, buses were wooden, and the shuttered windows did not close. The seats were narrow, and the distance between them was not adequate if one was more than five feet tall.

We got to Siem Reap the same day and found a room in one of the two or three Chinese hotels that foreigners stayed in. The rooms were clean but basic, no chairs or desks or pictures on the walls. For the next couple of days, we rented a motorized pedicab to get around the temples that make up the vast complex that includes Angkor Wat. We climbed to the tops of the temples and admired the bas-relief carvings on the walls, the overgrowth on the temples, and the grandeur and silence of the jungle. Usually, the driver would drop us at the entrance or exit of an immense temple and then drive around to where we would come out. In the shade of the giant overgrowth of trees, we walked along the path and into the temples where we would wander about and take photographs for hours. It was silent and crisp in the temples. One never saw any other visitors. We occasionally saw children digging for large, edible beetles or a man selling a mouth harp, a piece of bamboo with a hole in it that he blew on and strummed with a finger. It was peaceful and mysterious to walk in the now deserted temples that had been built and used by hundreds of people centuries before.

I had my birthday for the second year in a French outdoor restaurant near the main post office. I had been there the year before with Pris and a couple of other PCVs. The ground was swept bare and tall trees sprawled branches against the sun. Dappled light gave elegance to the setting of dilapidated wooden tables and chairs.

We took another bus from Siem Reap to Phnom Penh. I found the buses extraordinary. I had never seen any like them before or since. The buses had doors down one side, one for each row of seats. Five or six people would sit in a row. The ride, aside from being hot, was pleasant through the countryside to the great Tonle Sap, the largest freshwater lake in South East Asia, famous because it changes direction twice a year and expands and contracts according to the seasons.

One always knew when one was nearing Phnom Penh because there were large factories making fish sauce from the great harvest of fish from the lake opposite the capital. Once over the bridge, it was a short way to the bus terminal and another Chinese hotel. The two times I stayed overnight in the city I stayed at the Hawaii Hotel. The name has always amused me. It was a four or five story hotel with darkish rooms and shared bathrooms. Downstairs was a noisy restaurant.

We visited the King's palace, saw his white elephant, and watched river life along the Mekong.

The next stop was Saigon, to which we flew. It was still early in the Indochina war. Brian seemed to know where to go, and he directed a taxi to Cholon, the Chinese district. The front of this hotel, like all the hotels, had great rolls of barbed wire around the entrance and armed soldiers outside.

In Thakhek, Brian had spent many months talking with the Frenchmen teaching there to improve his French, so he was looking forward to using it in Saigon. Unfortunately, he was very disappointed. In the restaurants, the waitresses and others spoke a bastardized American English that they had learned from the American soldiers. Almost no one spoke French.

We made two memorable visits. The first was to a big maternity hospital. Brian is an ob-gyn doctor, and he had been invited to observe their procedures. I had never been in such a hospital. In one long room were twelve beds occupied with women in various stages of labor. As delivery became imminent, their bed would be rolled into the delivery room, and another bed and woman would take its place. Privacy was non-existent. The birth rate was terrific.

The second visit was to the zoo and surrounding gardens. It was like being in an oasis. The city was a din of vehicles, soldiers, sellers, and touts, but here was peace. Wide walks with beautiful, large metal cages meandered through well-kept gardens. Flowering plants and shrubs surrounded fountains and ponds. My favorite animal was a handsome African lion. For a few coins, a man would write your name on a strip of paper and decorate it with flowers and birds. Brian and I each got our names written. I rolled mine up, and it gave me pleasure for years until one day my cat was angry with me and destroyed it.

From Saigon, we flew to Singapore. It was Christmas time, and I was confident that, because this had been a former British colony, I would find something to mark Christmas, perhaps a bakery with Christmas cookies or a store with some decorations. There was nothing! It was simply a not-very-interesting, small town with lots of things for sale, particularly watches, jewelry, and cameras. I was glad to continue our trip, which we did by bus to Kuala Lumpur in Malaysia. We did not stay there for more than an hour but went directly by bus to Malacca. This city with its temples and old buildings was much more engaging than Singapore. We visited a statue of St. Francis Xavier on a hill overlooking the Strait of Malacca. For a few weeks in 1553, he was buried in a grave at St Paul's church atop the hill. Then the body was transported to Goa where it rests in the Basilica of Bom Jesus.

We continued to Penang by bus. One day we traveled back to mainland Malaysia to an old rubber plantation still in operation by some British people that Brian had been put in contact with. The manager was very cordial; he showed us around and invited us for lunch. It was fun to imagine oneself back in the colonial period in this perfect colonial setting, a lovely house surrounded by lawn and rubber trees in rows as far as the eye could see. I did not know such a place still existed!

Back in Penang, we took a trip around most of the island. We stopped at a temple famous for having many pit vipers in residence. That is to say; the temple is filled with the poisonous creatures, drugged by the incense that is always burning. They hang from candelabra on the altar and doze in every nook and cranny. I have an extreme fear of snakes, but in an attempt to overcome it, I touched the belly of one of the scaly reptiles. It was mostly a stupid thing to do, and I am still afraid when I think of it now.

From Penang, we took the train to Bangkok. It was a very long and uncomfortable two-day journey in second-class seats. A European man made it worse by taking up all the floor space between the seats as his bed.

We arrived in Bangkok in time for Christmas Eve, which I spent in a Gaysorn district nightclub dancing to "Joy to the World" and other carols. What a gas! It has been particularly memorable for me because, although I was twenty-four years old, I had never been to a nightclub.

CHAPTER 5

Vientiane to Thakhet: January 1965

Cambodia, Vietnam, Singapore, Malaysia. It had been fun. Pris was back in California with her boyfriend, and Brian had taken up residence in Vientiane. It was time to get a job. On January 2, 1965, I was in Vientiane, hoping for an interview with Bernie Wilder, the Chief of Party for IVS/Education. Unfortunately, he was motoring in Cambodia with his wife and three children and would not be back for at least a week. What could I do but wait for his return?

In 1961 in his "Special Message to the Congress on Foreign Aid," President Kennedy stated that it was the moral, economic and political obligation of the United States to help poorer countries. USAID was in Laos to raise the country from its level of poverty through programs in education, rural development, health, and infrastructure development. Also, the dominant belief at the time was the domino theory. The U.S. felt that if Laos fell to the Communists, Thailand would be next and eventually all of Southeast Asia.

The IVS crowd took me in. They lived in a row of one-story apartments within walking distance of the Naihaidio Compound, the name commonly used for the USAID headquarters due to its being located in Naihaidio village. At this time, Peace Corps Volunteers (PCVs) from Indonesia were coming to Vientiane looking for work. Sukarno was tightening his reins. Because it was not safe for PCVs to work there, the Peace Corps withdrew from the country. USAID began hiring them to work in rural development. USAID's hiring PCVs was good for me because when I was looking for Bernie, I was introduced to Dick Costantino, who worked in the USAID Education Division. Because he knew I had been a PCV in Thailand, he asked me if I would be interested in working for USAID. I said yes immediately. It would be so nice to be paid for a job similar to the one I would get with IVS yet not have to live on volunteer wages!

USAID, however, did not want to pay the same salary to Education Division personnel that they offered to the former PCVs hired by the Rural Development Division. The Education Division took umbrage, believing that since all the former PCVs had similar educational backgrounds, training and job experience, they should be paid the same. Furthermore, since I had been overseas for two years already, I did not want a two-year contract. I wanted one for eighteen months so that I could go to graduate school when it began in September 1966. Dick began dogged negotiations, and I flew on Air America to Thakhek to stay with Dottie and Al until the contract conditions were resolved. Brian hadn't come back to Thakhek, having been transferred to Vientiane.

Finally, at the end of January, I heard that the proposed terms had been agreed to and I should return to Vientiane to sign the contract and begin work. I took an Air America flight back.

The airport in Thakhek was nothing more than a dirt strip in the jungle. Almost the only planes landing there then or since were Air America planes in support of USAID personnel and projects. These were not scheduled flights but stops made as required. Al, as the USAID contact person, would be notified by radio of the day and approximate time of arrival. Then we would listen for the airplane. When we heard it, we jumped in the jeep and drove to the landing strip, usually arriving at the same time it did. Going to meet the plane was exciting. We drove as fast as the dusty, bumpy dirt road permitted. Would we arrive to catch the plane and greet the crew in time? Maybe there would be mail. It was a little like Santa's sled coming with a bag of surprises. Who or what might be in the bag? It was usually nothing more than parts for a generator or perhaps food from the commissary. But oh, the anticipation!

CHAPTER 6

Back to Vientiane: February 1965

When I arrived in Vientiane, I went to stay with my IVS friends again. Howie Lewin had tapes of the Beatles, a new group in England. We loved listening to them. One evening I had a date with a Lao police officer. When he said good night, he said I wouldn't see him for a couple of days. It was dark on my doorstep, and he told me in hushed tones that his boss was General Siho and that something was being planned. He would have to work. I was glad that he would not be back soon because he was pushy in his amorous advances. I hoped to be gone before he came back.

The next day I went to the Education Division Office to sign my contract, but unbeknownst to me at the time, because certain USAID personnel knew a coup d'état was being planned in Vientiane, the people I needed to see were not available. In fact, no USAID employees had come to the Education Office. I had a good Agatha Christie mystery, so I settled down to it. Galen Beery, who worked for IVS, came by. He said the city was preparing for battle, Did I want to see? "Of course!"

I rode on the back of his Lambretta motor scooter. Soldiers, wearing either a yellow or a pale blue scarf around their neck, were digging in. There were several emplacements manned by a couple of troops at the

Victory Monument, a massive, unfinished cement arch begun in 1957 and modeled on the Arc de Triomphe in Paris. (The gossip was that General Phoumi Nosavan had commandeered cement donated by USAID for the runway at the Vientiane airport to help build it, and so we called it the vertical runway.) We rode down to the Mekong River. Families with their bundles and pushcarts full of belongings were streaming towards Thailand across the giant sandbar, which is always exposed during the dry season. Galen explained that it had been announced on the radio that there would be a battle.

The next morning I went to the Education Division office again. Still, no one was there. It gave me a strange, hollow feeling. Nevertheless, I found a comfortable place to sit while I waited and kept reading my murder mystery. Then I heard gunfire. Army General Phoumi Nosavan began the fight against the Lao government headed by Prince Souvanna Phouma. The battle raged. I read my Agatha Christie. Around noon, people at work got hungry, but the Lao employees had known better than to come to work, so there was no kitchen staff. I went to work in the American Community Association (ACA) restaurant making peanut butter and jelly sandwiches for whoever wanted one.

The fighting continued all afternoon. The Naihaidio Compound was one street away from the Monument and bullets flew overhead. I stayed inside and resumed reading my exciting murder mystery. Night fell, and the gunfire stopped except for sporadic bursts. The IVS personnel decided it was probably safe enough to walk back to their apartments in Tong Toum District. The road was unpaved and lacked street lamps. I felt a thrill walking along in the dark, not knowing if there were dangerous soldiers hidden in the buildings and behind bushes. It reminded me of night games of kick-the-can when I was a child, the suspense, the daring, the fear of being caught. It was late when we got back, and I went to bed.

During the night, I heard a tremendous boom and found myself on the floor beside the bed. I ran to the louvered, wooden shutters at the back of the apartment and peered through. I saw flames in the distance. I learned the next day that an ammunition dump had been blown up.

Some soldiers, policemen, and civilians had been killed or wounded, the fire station and a fire truck in the city center burned, and bullet holes scarred many buildings, but the coup failed. General Phoumi had lost his bid for power and had gone with his family and bodyguards into exile in Thailand. General Phoumi's house was a bombed out shell. The General had been a colorful man, and he and his wife would be missed on the social scene. General Siho of the National Police also went into exile in Thailand although he had not joined forces with General Phoumi. I never saw the policeman again.

The next day people came back to town and picked up where they had left off as if nothing had happened. In July, the neutralist Prince Souvanna Phouma was returned to power as prime minister.

Some years later, Khounta told me that he had been caught close to his office in an area near the Monument and that Phoumi's men were trying to kill him. He hid out all night and did not get home until morning. He never explained why. Then, many years after Khounta had passed away, I learned that he had once dated Phoumi's younger sister. It had not worked out, and there was a loss of face.

I have always felt I missed the emotional trauma of the attempted coup, except for the few events I outlined. During that day, I read my whodunit, and it engrossed me. So much so that the gunfire, which was constant, did not distract or upset me. It was like being in a room where a child is being born and taking a nap instead of watching the birth. I wish now that I had looked for my friends and spent the time with them while history was being made, and lives and careers were irreversibly lost or changed. I didn't think about it then, but now when events occur, I recognize that the world is changing and relish being present.

CHAPTER 7
Savannakhet: 1965

After I had signed my contract, I was assigned to a technical school in Savannakhet, a town on the Mekong River south of Thakhek. I was glad to be out of Vientiane, where USAID employees lived in a compound six kilometers out of the city, and the air was always full of dust.

I flew to Savannakhet on an Air America flight. A USAID driver met the plane and drove me to the office. I met Aubrey Elliot, the Area Coordinator (AC), and Leontine "Lee" Engler, the Education Officer. In those years, USAID divided the Kingdom of Laos into fiefs, each with its ruler. No American moved without the knowledge and permission of the AC, other than the occasional hippie or world traveler, who perhaps came to Savannakhet by ferryboat across the Mekong River from Mukdahan, the Thai border town.

The AC was not prepared for me. That is to say, my house and vehicle were not ready. But he had arranged for me to live with Joe from the Bureau of Public Roads and his wife and small daughter. I was delighted to find myself living with an American family and eating American food. They had a square, two-story house in a four-house compound occupied by other Americans. I had a room upstairs.

The day after moving to Joe's, Lee Engler took me to meet the director of the Ecole Technique. He was a tall, ruddy-faced Frenchman with a lovely smile. He was married to a Lao lady and had lived in Laos for many years. Unfortunately, I could not speak French, so I never got to know him. My job was to teach English for two hours to each of the ten classes in the school. Forty to fifty teenage boys filled each classroom. The students were very polite and cooperative. I had great fun teaching them. I made charts with stick figure characters to go with the English book I had to teach. The book began teaching English with sentences with can: I can swim, I can dance, I can sing. It was all very easy, and we laughed a lot.

In those days, the dress code was a skirt, a blouse and high heels with pointy toes. For the first few weeks, I rode a bicycle to school. I almost had a head-on collision the second time I went out because I totally forgot that people drive on the opposite side of the road from Thailand. It had taken about five seconds before I realized why the car in front of me was in my lane. I cannot forget the fright I caused myself.

After three weeks, my house was ready: a brand new two-story brick and stucco house with three air-conditioned bedrooms and two bathrooms. It was at an intersection and rain ditches bordered the roads on each side. There was a big, barren, hard-dirt yard with a front gate on the corner, but no fence surrounded it. USAID employees had all their homes fully furnished, so I had a handsome rattan living room set with cushions, a dining room table for six, side tables, lamps, and other furniture. I felt peculiar. It was too much house, and I never got used to it. In Thailand, I had a two-story, two-room wooden house with no furniture, except for a coffee table, and a single wooden bed upstairs that my school had made for me. I had mats and cushions on the floor downstairs, a one-burner kerosene stovetop about the size of a hibachi, a water-seal squat toilet, and no running water. I was told that USAID employees must live in houses that represent how Americans live in the United States.

I had a houseboy. He was a man in his late thirties with a family. He cleaned the house and did my washing and ironing. He even ironed my underwear, which to me was a very novel thing to do. I only saw him on payday.

After a few more weeks I was also given a jeep, but I continued to ride my bicycle to school. The school was on the other side of town, and it was always fun and interesting to go by bike. There was almost no traffic, and people drove slowly. There were not any stop signs and certainly no traffic lights. I taught in the mornings and on the way home would stop at one of the two French restaurants for a long lunch. It was always three courses and delicious. I became acquainted with calf brains sautéed in butter, which I adore to this day, but don't eat anymore because I am afraid of mad cow disease and toxins that can accumulate in such tissues.

I had decided that I should learn French and engaged the 14-year old son of one of the French teachers as a tutor in the afternoons. That lasted about two weeks. What was more interesting was to visit Paul Altemus, the American IVS teacher teaching English at the lycée (high school). I liked him. He was my age, smoked a pipe and seemed to be lecturing in a college auditorium when he spoke. What he had to say was interesting, but too seriously delivered for my taste. Later he joined the United States Information Service and came back to work for it in Vientiane.

At least once a week we would go to the banks of the swift and mighty Mekong River and swim out to a long island. We would start up river opposite its middle and swim for about ten minutes before reaching shore near the bottom end. Then we would walk to the top of the island before starting back in the interest of ending up where we had begun. Another afternoon pastime was to go to the beauty salon for a hair wash and set. The hairdressers knew I swam in the river, especially since no one else did, and they would always question and advise me not to do so because of the crocodiles and the river dragons. I assured them that I had never seen any and that I was not afraid. Ignorance was beneficial because I otherwise would not have had the relief of a cool, invigorating swim. There are giant, two-ton catfish in the river, but they are rare. People also get caught in whirlpools and are found days later one or two miles downstream. The townspeople had good reason not to swim, but I thought they did not swim because they didn't know how, which is true, and because the women would never expose their thighs. All shore bathing was done in a sarong.

The rest of my free time was spent reading novels. I didn't have a radio or stereo and to this day enjoy the quiet, never having developed the habit of constant TV or music playing. I went to bed early and was never bored.

I wrote my mother and father every Sunday. By this time, they were supportive of my staying in Asia although they missed me terribly. Then in March, my mother wrote me that my father was trying to sell her house, the house in Piedmont that I grew up in. I was very angry. This information was very upsetting. Where would my mother and brother go to live? Besides, I loved the house and garden and did not want it sold. My father never wrote anything about it. I wrote him to please not proceed with selling the house and said that if he needed money, I would give it to him. He never wrote back, and due to this unfortunate lack of communication, we remained estranged for many years.

My parents were divorced in the early '50s. My mother had always told us, my sister, brother and I, that the house was hers. What I learned twenty-six years later when I went to the Alameda County Courthouse in Oakland and got a copy of the divorce decree was that the house was half my father's and that it was to be sold when my brother turned twenty-one in 1964. The proceeds were to be divided between them. The house was not sold, but my father visited it frequently to take care of the garden, which he loved. His coming by infuriated my mother because she felt trapped in the house when he was there, but she never said anything.

Two months after arriving, Aubrey Elliot asked to see me. He told me that his Vietnamese secretary was going to Saigon to visit her relatives, and a temporary replacement was coming from Vientiane. He had been expecting an American but had just learned that it was to be a young Lao woman. It would not be appropriate for her to stay in a local hotel. Could she stay at my house?

I was delighted. It was a wonderful opportunity to meet a Lao female that I could talk to. The Technical School was all men and boys, and the language was French. There was no way for me to meet an educated person my age.

One afternoon in April, the height of the hot season, I came home from lunch, and Somsangouane was sitting in the corner of the rattan couch in the living room. She had her legs pulled up to her side under her *phasinh* (a traditional silk or cotton sarong worn by women in Laos) and she had pulled her blouse up exposing her midriff, which was equal to indecent exposure in those days. She wore her hair in the traditional Lao style, a bun on the back of her head. She was strikingly beautiful with a wonderful smile. We became very close friends, and she introduced me to a life I had missed in college.

Somsangouane was not a reader or swimmer. A Mekong River water skier, yes, and she spoke French. She immediately made friends with Pradit, a handsome Thai man about our age, who came across the river every morning to work for USIS. She flirted with him and learned that he was as bored as she was. After that, the three of us went out almost every evening. Pradit knew of a restaurant where they played dance music. There we took turns being twirled and dipped to tango music. We would cha-cha and mambo the evening away, thoroughly enjoying ourselves. We always had the restaurant to ourselves. No one else ever came in the evenings.

CHAPTER 8

The Scarf: April 1965

The year before, Dee Dick, the nurse that had come to Thakhek, invited me to go with her to Luang Prabang for Lao New Year's celebrations in April 1965. There was a school break, so I went. Luang Prabang is the former royal capital with a population of about 20,000 at that time. The King, Savang Wattana, sent his invitations, too. For this celebration, all the high Lao government officials, military officers, and foreign dignitaries booked every room in every hotel and descended on anybody they knew to put them up. Since the country's business transactions and governmental affairs took place in Vientiane, there were only two or three hotels. Luang Prabang was just a small town with two main streets and dozens of architecturally beautiful temples, magnificently painted and decorated with gold-leaf stencils or colored glass mosaics. The city, now a World Heritage Cultural site and overwhelmed with tourists, was a peaceful place with few motor vehicles. One would just wander about enjoying its beauty and serenity.

Dee and I had become good friends during her summer assignment to Thakhek. On the weekends, I would go with her and other friends to the villages outside Thakhek or she would come across the river to socialize with me in Nakorn Panom.

Dee had arranged with Betty, another IVS volunteer who was working in self-help for women in Luang Prabang, for us to stay with her. I took the milk run flight to Vientiane, and then Dee and I took another Air America flight to Luang Prabang.

The planes were usually C-123s, and we sat in canvas bucket seats down the sides. In front of us, down the belly of the aircraft tied under green tarpaulins, was the cargo. Often it would be piled so high that we could not see who was seated on the opposite side.

Sometimes the plane would stop at places with names such as Vang Vieng or Ban Houay Xay, but we could not get off. In fact, I never saw more than one or two men get on or off, and sometimes only a manila envelope would be passed from the airplane to someone on the ground. At that time, those were forbidden places, and unsafe to live in due to a potential enemy attack. All we could do was look out at the green vegetation or barren, dusty airfield and be pervaded with a feeling of secrecy. What was there? Who lived there? What were they doing? Even to go to Luang Prabang, we had had to ask permission from the American USAID Area Coordinator.

Betty lived upstairs in a small, wooden two-story house on the Mekong River not far from the palace. We saw little of her as she had her own circle of friends. We slept on mats on the floor.

From the moment we arrived, we were greeted with water and remained wet throughout the days of our stay. In Theravada Buddhist countries in Southeast Asia, New Year's is a time of cleansing, a fresh start for the New Year. The water ceremony can be done graciously with a small cup of water poured gently at the back of another person's neck with great decorum and blessings, but the weather is sweltering, and people get carried away.

In addition to water blessings for people, Buddha statues in temples have water poured over them ceremoniously. In homes, Buddha statues are washed and fresh white flowers, burning incense, and new candles are placed on the raised shelf built to hold them. These altars are always placed respectfully near the head of the bed.

One afternoon, when we were out throwing water and joining in the processions, we met a couple of fellow merrymakers, the two youngest sons of the King. They were just a few years older than we were. One prince was tall, dark and serious. I learned that he had just come home from studying abroad for many years. The other son was short and round with short spiky hair and glasses. We went with them to their big, nondescript white house on the Mekong River. No one was home. We sat in the living room, which was rather bare and austere, except for a beautiful Lao silk scarf on the coffee table in front of us. It was hand-woven in a traditional geometrical Lao pattern from silk produced and dyed locally. The end hanging off on the window side was slightly faded a lighter magenta from the sun.

The brothers offered us snacks of hard-boiled eggs. Then the dark prince left and came back with a bottle of clear liquid. He poured some into a liqueur glass and lit a match. He was delighted with the beautiful blue-white light with which it burned. He said he had made the *lao Lao* (Lao rice whiskey) himself. As we sat around talking and laughing, Dee remarked on the beautiful scarf. The round prince jumped up immediately and pulled it out from under a tarnished silver bowl and gave it to Dee. The Lao way is to give away whatever is admired. Dee objected and tried to refuse, but the prince insisted. He said it was an old piece, and since Dee liked it, she should have it.

Later that evening was the party at the King's palace. Dee knew several of the Lao generals and ministers, and through her, we had been invited to celebrate New Year's Eve at the Palace. At that time, it was usual for young volunteers and young unmarried women to socialize with high functionaries. Most of the leaders in the government and military had been educated in France. They were attracted to foreign women of the same educational background. Their Lao wives usually stayed at home with the children. Since there were few of them and few foreigners at social events, we gravitated together regardless of our jobs or positions in Laos.

We sat with other guests in the front row in the garden, our backs to the palace, looking towards Mt. Phousi. Mt. Phousi is one hundred meters high and is across the street from the palace. At the top is a beautiful, golden stupa that gleams in the sunlight. It is twenty-four meters tall and is visible from every point in the valley. After sitting in the warm darkness for a while, the King came followed by his wife. They shook hands with everyone in the front row. I was thrilled.

The entertainment began with a procession of small boys carrying candle-lit colored lanterns wending its way down the switchback stairs of the mountain accompanied by Lao musicians playing in the garden. It was led by a paper maché snake about 20 feet long, and by the time the snake entered the palace grounds, the last boys were leaving the top of the mountain, and so it looked like one long snake curling down.

A young girl carried in on a facsimile of a pig, which was the animal of the year, followed this. Men preceded her playing long drums, cymbals, and flutes. After her came rows of men dressed alike. When that procession left, three rows of girls in beautiful Lao costumes with gold headpieces danced in with silver bowls filled with flowers which they presented to the King and Queen.

Two columns of about twenty-five men each followed them. The men were dressed in black with red hats like skullcaps with four flaps. The men each carried two lanterns made of watermelon colored parchment made into a lotus shape. All the lights were turned off and they danced for at least twenty minutes in the classical style to the music of bells and xylophone. After the dance, we had an excerpt from the Ramayana for more than two hours. I loved it and felt very fortunate to see it. Some final dancing by about fifty to seventy-five girls followed this.

Finally, at about 12:30 we got to eat the food that had taken days to prepare. People ate, standing, grazing along the tables. My favorite was the coconut custard baked in little pumpkin-squash. The memories of warmth and waiting, the stream of moving candles descending into darkness, and the tinkle of Lao classical music still move me with a feeling of mystery and peace.

The Royal Palace in Luang Prabang is a museum now. The King, the Queen, the Crown Prince, and the dark Prince Sisavang were taken away in 1977 to a camp in the northeast where they silently passed away. The round Prince Sauryavong Savang lives in exile in Paris.

Like many Lao exiles and refugees, he, too, perhaps dreams of the way things were and would like to come back and live in peace. The frangipani trees, bearing the Lao national flower, have grown tall on the side of Mt. Phousi, hiding the stairway from view. Dee moved to Tennessee in 2001 and sent me the scarf to return to the palace, a request still in the planning stage.

Occasionally, I buy coconut custard baked in pumpkin-squash from a street cart and savor my memories.

A time gone by . . .

CHAPTER 9

The Blind Date: June 1965

The school year was coming to an end, and there would be nothing for me to do in Savannakhet until school opened again in September. The French went back to France or simply traveled for two months. I was not so lucky. The Education Division recalled me to Vientiane for the summer for which I received TDY (temporary duty with per diem and housing). Aubrey's secretary was not back from Saigon, so Somsangouane stayed on in my house. Before I left, however, she told me there was someone she wanted me to meet in Vientiane. I said "fine" and forgot all about it.

I went to Vientiane, where I was assigned to an apartment in the bachelor officer quarters (BOQs) at KM-6, the large, chain-link fence enclosed housing area for USAID employees and their families. In the end, that is, when the communists took over the country in 1975, the chain-link fence confined the Americans for the Pathet Lao forces very effectively. The fence is still there, but today it isolates the elite communist cadres that live within. The BOQs were four rows of six or eight one-story apartments for single employees. The IVS teachers lived there until a few years later when apartments were built for teachers at Dong Dok.

KM-6 describes where it was located, that is, six kilometers out of the city and into the countryside on the road to Luang Prabang. But,

of course, because of the war, no one could drive there. The road to
the entrance was between spacious, green rice paddies, but now it is
almost concealed by the International Convention Center on the left
and the Kaysone Phomvihane Museum on the right.

From KM-6, one could drive only another three kilometers to the
km-9 turnoff to Sisavangvong University in Dong Dok village. Because of the conflict in Laos between the Pathet Lao and the Royal Lao
government, it was not safe to drive farther into the countryside. Now
the university is called the National University of Laos. I worked at
Dong Dok, which is how we referred to the University, for the summer with four colleagues. We prepared materials for the English Section.

The road after the turnoff to Dong Dok was broad and as I was
told, the idea that if there were a state of emergency, it could be used
to evacuate the hundreds of men, women, and children living at KM-
6. In hindsight, it is amusing to imagine that anyone could have seriously considered it as an escape route. It offered no protection and
only small planes not carrying more than twenty people could land on
the road because of its length. Perhaps they were thinking more in
terms of helicopters? In any case, it was a comforting thought at the
time.

KM-6 was also six kilometers from the USAID Headquarters in
Naihaidio District in Vientiane. USAID shuttle buses took people back
and forth to work, the commissary, the Army Postal Service (APO)
and the American Community Association (ACA) with its bar, restaurant with American food and ice cream, swimming pool, and theater,
where a different movie could be seen nightly.

One day as I was leaving the Education Division office in
Naihaidio, Somsangouane hailed me. I didn't know she was back
from Savannakhet. She said she had planned a dinner for that night
for me to meet her friend. I said I was sorry, but that Hitchcock's *The
Birds* was showing at the theater, and I had been looking forward to
seeing it for many months. We argued back and forth, and she said I

had to go. It would be rude to stand up the high-ranking man she wanted me to meet. I finally agreed.

We met at the Tan Dao Vieng Restaurant, the place of choice for the *phu jai* (literally big people) meaning individuals of high rank in the military and within the Lao civil service, to dine. It had the best Chinese food in town. It was up a narrow staircase, and dividers of wooden frames with cloth curtains were placed around one's table to ensure privacy. There were six of us: me, my blind date Khounta seated on my right, and our chaperones—my girlfriend Dee Dick on my left, Somsangouane on Khounta's right, Somsangouane's brother Somsanuk, and his wife, Chanpheng.

Khounta did not say much, but he was very handsome. The rest of us laughed, talked, and had a grand time. After dinner, we went our separate ways.

The next day Somsangouane told me that Khounta's mother had been trying to match him up with girls for years, but he had rejected all of them. Since he was highly educated, Somsangouane thought he might like me. She was playing matchmaker, but I was not interested.

On a Saturday afternoon two weeks later, I saw Khounta's car, drive up the street towards the BOQs. Dee Dick lived in the row of apartments behind mine. I was watching a baseball game in the grassy field in front of the BOQs. As his car pulled up in front of my place, I took off running because my apartment was at a distance. I was afraid that he would find I wasn't home and leave. I wanted to get to know him better. He wore dark glasses and was dressed smartly in an aloha-style shirt and trousers. I could see him better than at the restaurant and found him very attractive with a fun-loving look in his eyes and a lovely smile, which I fell in love with. He drove a very distinctive little Mercedes 190SL, a hardtop convertible that he usually drove with the top off. It was a beautiful gray blue. There were only two in the country. Bob Ware, a friend who worked for USAID, owned the other one.

Khounta had come to invite Dee and me to a party at the Lane Xang Hotel. Dee would be going with one of Khounta's friends.

Would I please ask her for him? Khounta said he would pick us up. I told Dee, and we were both very excited. It was common for unmarried foreign women to date Lao men. Most of the foreign men were married and the Lao, for the most part, were attractive and fun to be with. I was thrilled because the Lane Xang Hotel was the largest, most beautiful hotel in Vientiane, in all the country in fact, and all the major Lao functions and other important events were held there. Embassies usually held their national day celebrations at their residence. I would have to have something made to wear.

The party was splendid. The Lao women wore their most beautiful *phasinh*, a sarong made from hand-woven silk of designs often handed down from mother to daughter for generations and tailored with darts to fit and hooks on a waistband like a skirt. It hangs straight with a large piece of the material overlapping in the front. On the bottom is a five-inch silk border of intricate design, usually with gold threads. In the evenings, vivid colors are de rigueur. Black is only for funerals. The foreign women wore long gowns. Precious stones and gold glittered on the women's ears and around their necks. I wore a long green and white skirt of heavy cotton with a green floral design and a sleeveless, pale grass-green silk top. The civilian men wore tuxedos, and the military men wore their dress uniforms bedecked with ribbons. I took a photo of us together with my timer. We looked stunning. Brigadier General Kouprasith Abhay was celebrating the honor of being awarded a fifth star. He was the man who had defeated General Phoumi in February.

Every Lao minister, vice-minister and department head in the civil service, general and colonel in the army, and foreign ambassador and their spouse had been invited. Waiters in white uniforms circulated with trays of scotch, beer, soft drinks and delicious hors d'oeuvres. There was a band, and Dee and I danced throughout the evening with anyone who asked us. I had already met some of the generals and ministers at the New Year's activities in Luang Prabang the previous April. It felt strange but comfortable to be with the leaders of the country. We were accepted and welcomed.

There were not many single, young, foreign women in Vientiane, so we had not been singled out; we just happened to be a couple of the only ones. If the royal kingdom had been larger, we probably would not have been there. It did make one feel very special and privileged nonetheless.

The next Saturday afternoon, Khounta came again. He was fluent in French, but my French is limited. However, we managed to communicate with his limited English and the French dictionary. We tried Lao, but that was hopeless. In the beginning, I thought I would be able to learn Lao fluently. Isn't that the way you learn a language well—with your boyfriend? Khounta refused to speak Lao with me or listen to me when I tried to say something. He said he wasn't a teacher and that he had the wrong accent in any case. He said he had a Vientiane accent and the best accent, according to him, was the one spoken in Thakhek. Not being able to speak Lao together was always a big disappointment to me. To know a person well, I strongly felt that it was necessary to communicate in his or her native tongue. Much of a person's culture and many of their beliefs are contained in the language. Because things do not translate precisely, I believed you couldn't understand a person's core nature unless you could speak to them in their mother tongue. That is not true for everyone, of course, but I think that because of this and Khounta's non-communicative nature, he was always for me a mystery man. We only ever spoke English together, but he always spoke French with my French-speaking friends.

Khounta invited Dee and me to a local nightclub, the Vieng Ratry. It was the "in" place to go for people of Khounta's age and government position. Somsangouane had told me that he was the Director General of the Ministry of Public Works and Transportation and that he was thirty-eight years old. Dee's date would be Samlit, the same man she went to the five-star party with. He was the Director of the Ministry of Information. The Vieng Ratry was off the Rue Circulaire, now called Khou Vieng Road. The Rue Circulaire was built on top of the inner city wall, which was constructed 200 years ago with a moat on the outer side. The French had lined both sides of the road with trees decades before. The trees grew and formed a canopy over the road, making it the most beautiful and shady street in the city. It was also very narrow with hardly enough room for two cars to pass each other. Bicycles, pedicabs, and salespeople with their inventory in two baskets hanging from a bamboo stick on their shoulder always thronged the way. It was like driving through an obstacle course. One had to go very slowly. I avoided it altogether. When the road was widened in 1996, the trees on the moat side had to be cut down to make a two-lane road with a sidewalk. The destruction of so many beautiful giants was sad to witness.

The Vieng Ratry was down a dirt road, at a level about ten feet below the Rue Circulaire on the city side. It was a two-story building with a restaurant upstairs and a nightclub on the ground floor. The restaurant had curtained rooms. It reminded me of the Chinese restaurants my parents had taken us to as children in Oakland and San Francisco. Later, Khounta and I ate there frequently. He always ordered *mii fukian*, that is, fried egg noodles with shrimp, chicken, pork, and vegetables. He would make a show of squeezing limes for juice and putting *nam siracha* (chili sauce) on it. I can still see and savor the delicious flavor when I close my eyes. I have never had it served so deliciously since.

The nightclub was a dark and smoky place. Everyone smoked in the sixties and even if you didn't, you had to light up for self-protection. After a while, your eyes would begin to water. The drink of choice was Scotch, usually just one. People went to dance and socialize, not to drink. The clientele were young unmarried men and married men without their wives. I didn't know it at the time, but it was not the custom for wives to go to nightclubs. We usually sat alone. There were many dance hostesses, and I loved to watch them dance. There was a Filipino band. Samlit would often sing Lao songs at the mike. The most frequently performed song was "Your Cheatin' Heart." It was sung two or three times every evening. Khounta and I two-stepped to the slow music. He didn't know any fast dances. We danced decorously with Khounta's right hand on my shoulder and his left hand holding mine. He was only three or four inches taller than me, so he was comfortable to dance with. My neck was never strained. My nose came just below his ear, and I loved the smell of his French cologne. He told me I was the perfect height to dance with.

My hair was long, and I wore it in a French roll, the style of the times, which necessitated twice-weekly trips to the beauty parlor. I went to Queen's Beauty Salon at the Nam Phu Circle. Saysamone did my hair and her sister Syri made my clothes. I wore cotton mini-skirt sheaths and pointy-toe heels. I bought material for my dresses at the Shinawatra cotton factory in Bangkok. The plant produced beautiful fabric in original Thai patterns and designs in every possible color.

The next weekend Khounta came again on a Saturday afternoon and took me on a date without Dee. We went to Samlit's house, where I met his wife and several of his children. It hadn't occurred to me that he was married. I played Scrabble with two of the kids. I asked Khounta later about Samlit's going out with Dee when he was already married. Why didn't he take his wife? Khounta explained to me that a wife stays home and protects the house and takes care of the children. She is the only person a husband can trust with certainty. Besides, it would not be appropriate for his wife to go to a nightclub, which is a place for single people, men, dance hostesses and illicit liaisons. That lesson went into my store of interesting Lao customs, unaware that it would ever mean anything for me.

Khounta and I began to go out in the evenings for dinner and a movie or to the Vieng Ratry unchaperoned.

One night going back to the BOQs he stopped the car, and we sat in the dark. Then he kissed me. It was only a couple of kisses, and then we continued to my place. I had not been expecting or anticipating any amorous advances. Neither romance nor sex had occurred to me. I was not interested. I purely enjoyed his companionship— playing badminton, eating out, dancing, and listening to music.

CHAPTER 10

Dating Continues: September 1965

September came, and Dick Costantino decided I should stay in Vientiane and teach at Sisavangvong University. An English Section began that year, and I taught ESL. The students, teenagers, were selected from all over Laos to become English teachers. They lived in dormitories at the University and studied English for thirty hours a week.

My status was permanently changed, and I moved to a duplex in Rainbow Village, which was about five kilometers from Vientiane. There were ten duplexes in this USAID compound, most of which were occupied by single employees. They had two bedrooms, two bathrooms, and they were fully furnished, including air conditioning and free utilities. I had no expenses other than food, clothes, film, and amusements. I bought a two-year-old light green Volkswagen from a secretary who was leaving Vientiane. My drive to school was about five kilometers.

Khounta was handsome, debonair, dressed smartly, without pretension, and had an impressive car. We enjoyed the same things—food, music, picnics, dancing. He had a beautiful smile and was very attentive. He would, if things continued in the same pattern, take me out every evening and weekend. He was someone with whom I could relax and have fun. Life was delightful.

My permanent move to Vientiane changed things. We became lovers. We never spoke of how we felt. But, does one spend one's free time with someone he finds unattractive and a bore? We liked each other and enjoyed our time together.

In September, Khounta had to go on a study tour to Europe. Before he left, I went to Bangkok and stayed in the Vieng Tai Hotel. Khounta stayed there, too. He suggested we go to the beach at Pattaya. That sounded exciting. Khounta rented a car and driver, and we went and stayed in the best hotel. It had a swimming pool, but we lay on the beach. When we were at dinner in the hotel, Mrs. Sally Mann, the wife of the Director of USAID, saw Khounta, came over and said good evening. I believe her curiosity rather than politeness prompted her. She looked me up and down. Who was I anyhow? She didn't know me. We stayed one night because Khounta was leaving the next day. When it came time for him to go to the airport, he would not let me go with him, which I wanted to do.

While he was away, he sent me a postcard from Brussels with the famous statue of a naked boy peeing in a fountain. On his return, he brought me three gifts: a long-sleeve, flowered black top, a yellow leather handbag, and a Persian miniature in an inlaid frame. They were precious to me, and I still have them.

At the time, I thought I was very lucky to have a handsome escort to fancy parties and nightclub dancing. I might as well enjoy myself. It never occurred to me that the relationship might be anything more than a good time during my year in Vientiane.

I had lived in Thailand and had had a good view of the stereotypical married Thai male. He drank Mekong whiskey after work every night and got drunk, had a girlfriend or a minor wife besides his lawful wife, and got home well after midnight. I assumed Lao men must be just like the Thai. They looked the same to me; they spoke almost the same language. I had had my eyes opened, and I was not interested in that kind of relationship. Nevertheless, I could date and have fun.

In Nakorn Panom, I had lived with the family of the provincial education officer. He was my *Khun Paw* (father), and his wife was my

Khun Mae (mother). At my arrival dinner, with my ears still blocked from not popping after the plane landed, he boasted of having fourteen children. I counted three and wondered where the others were. After some months, I learned that only the two oldest in the house belonged to *Khun Mae*. The younger teenage boy was the son of *Khun Paw's* minor wife who was the niece of his first wife. *Khun Mae* had had nine children, and they were all grown up, married, and lived in other towns, except for the two at home, one son who became a monk and one daughter who worked at a bank.

Khun Paw's job was to work in the countryside to strengthen the education of the youth so that the Communist recruiters from across the Mekong River in Laos could not lure them away. It was a serious problem. The province was very, very poor and just a little money could entice boys to leave school.

When *Khun Paw* came home after a week or two away, he would have his hair touched up with black dye. He came to the dinner table before the final rinse. After dinner, he left to visit his second wife. I never met her or any of his other children, except one teenage son who lived with us. *Khun Mae* would tell me of her disappointment and loneliness. I was shocked, as none of my Peace Corps training had prepared me for this cultural tradition. At least *Khun Paw* did not drink, but other husbands did. I knew many unhappy wives. I liked *Khun Paw*, a kind, gentle man with a lovely smile, but I did not agree with men having minor wives.

Khounta and I had wonderful, fun times together. He was charming, highly educated, and knowledgeable of Western philosophy, art, music, literature, and manners. He had lived in Paris for almost seven years studying to become a civil engineer. We enjoyed the same things and went out every night. First, we went to dinner. I learned about many new restaurants and dishes. The restaurants had open fronts, and he always sat with his back to the street so that no one would recognize him. I asked him why, and he said he was out to dinner with me, and he was not interested in satisfying his friends' curiosity. Afterwards, we went dancing at the Vieng Ratry, visited our

Lao or American friends, or saw a movie at the ACA. Khounta loved
movies, even the bad ones where I had to walk out and wait in the
lobby. We usually discussed them later, and he would tell me that the
protagonist, man or woman, was wrong or right for what was done or
said. We often disagreed. He had a very rigid moral sense about what
was correct, whereas I felt that what people did was up to them as
long as they were not hurting others, that there was no absolute right
or wrong, just differences. He had a code of behavior that I never figured out. I remember one night at the Vieng Ratry when he said,
"Let's go," and since I was having a good time I said, "Let's stay." So
he sat down, and after a few minutes, I noticed that most people were
gone. I hadn't realized that it was closing time, and soon only a few
hostesses and the cleaners were left. I said, "The place is closed. Let's
go," but he just sat at the table for another ten minutes, not saying a
word. I felt quite stupid sitting there. Why hadn't he told me that the
place was closing? I will never know or understand his reasoning, but
I realized, after we were married, that he had been angry with me. I
had had no experience of this silent form of punishment.

The ACA was a large building, halfway down on the right-hand
side of the road in the USAID compound. Behind the ACA was an APO
from which one could send and receive mail with a San Francisco address. One did not pay overseas postage. Also, a commissary sold
American food, laundry products, cosmetics, clothes and other items,
mostly not available locally, at below stateside retail prices. Americans
living in Vientiane never had to go to the local markets, and some of
them never did, except for perhaps a sightseeing expedition. Most people had a well-stocked liquor cabinet with a large assortment of after
dinner drinks to offer guests. We ordered glassware and china from
PACEX (Pacific Exchange) in Japan. Two or three times I went with a
couple of friends as "crew" on the Air America planes going to Taipei
to be overhauled. We stopped for fuel in Danang and stayed in Hong
Kong until the plane returned a few days later and took us back to
Vientiane. On the last trip that I took to Hong Kong, we could not stop
in Danang because of fierce fighting in the area. These free flights were

lots of fun, a time for shopping, eating, and exploring Kowloon and Hong Kong Island.

On the weekends, Khounta and I played badminton on the court behind my duplex and listened to music. We both had Akai M-8 reel-to-reel tape recorders and spent a lot of time copying tapes from friends. Our favorite pastime was to pack up American hot dogs, buns, and condiments and drive to a nearby rice paddy of dry stubble in a secluded area. We would spread the mats. Khounta would make a fire, and we would roast the hot dogs, play a game of dominos, take a siesta or read. Khounta always had his *Paris Match* for his weekend reading, and some of the articles led to an interesting exchange of ideas.

In November, American turkeys were available from the commissary. I looked forward to my favorite holiday. I hadn't had a home-cooked Thanksgiving dinner for three years, and I love turkey. I invited Khounta, and I prepared a traditional dinner with turkey, stuffing, mashed potatoes, gravy, cranberry sauce and all the other trimmings. It was his first Thanksgiving. I got a bottle of champagne to celebrate, and Khounta brought one, too. I set the table with candles, and we sat down and began to make toasts and take photographs and enjoy the bubbly. We began with his champagne and continued with mine. Then we both fell asleep on my bed and missed dinner. We had Thanksgiving the next night but without the champagne.

In December was my twenty-fifth birthday. Khounta told me that it was a significant milestone in France. He invited our good friends, Dorothy and Alan Bashor with whom we had shared many good times and experiences and me out to dinner. I had my hair done and wore the blouse Khounta had brought me from Europe. Before dinner, Al and Dottie surprised us by taking us to Venus Photo on the corner of SamSenThai and Chanthakoummane Streets to have our pictures taken. Those black and white photos are among my most precious possessions. I have one up in my house to this day. I love that picture and look back with tears of sadness and happiness to see us so young, smiling, and happy to be together.

In December, USAID had pine trees cut upcountry and brought down for Christmas. I enjoyed being able to have a real tree. In Nakorn Panom, I had cut one out of green paper and pasted it up with sticky rice on the wall in my room over my bed.

One weekend we went with some of Khounta's relatives on a buffalo hunt. We drove out into the bush to shoot a water buffalo that had gone wild. I took along a couple of hot dogs in case we got hungry. We started in the morning; by noon, the hunters still had not found the buffalo. We were hungry. The men captured a beautiful, green parrot-like bird and barbecued it over an open fire. The grownups ate it, two small bites each, while I gave the children the hot dogs. The day was hot, and it was boring just standing around. Finally, the hunters found the unfortunate animal. They shot her, and she ran into a grove of bamboo and collapsed. The location was not good because she was not readily accessible. I got there to find her on her side and the hunters beginning to cut her up. The first thing they did was to fashion a bamboo tube to collect the blood for later consumption. They would usually have eaten the liver while it was still warm inside the animal, but it was getting late. Besides, on cutting her open, we saw she was with calf, which they hadn't known. A mountain of green grass filled her stomach. Now that the hunters had been successful, we could go home. It was all a horrible experience, never to be repeated. The next night Khounta proudly came over with two buffalo steaks, the best ones. I fixed some salad and broiled the steaks. At least something good would come from the terrible day. We sat down to eat. I cut a bite. It smelled wonderful. I put it in my mouth and immediately spit it out. It tasted awful. Khounta figured out that the bladder had leaked all over the meat. Ugh. Neither of us could eat it. He took the meat home with him. He said his relatives would appreciate it.

All the months we were playing and having fun together, Khounta was in turmoil at his office. I knew he was the Director General of the Ministry of Public Works and Transportation, and he had mentioned that things were changing; he did not seem very busy. However, we never talked about our jobs, so that was all I knew.

Khounta had earned his engineering degree from the Ecole Spécial des Travaux Publics in Paris, and he had been promoted to his position by working his way up in the system. His was not a political appointment as an appointment to minister usually was. As I understand it, the problem was that a man, Mr. Phonekeo, wanted to marry the prime minister's daughter, but he didn't have a prestigious post in the government. The prime minister was looking for a suitable position to give the man so he would have high enough status to marry his daughter. In the end, he gave Mr. Phonekeo Khounta's position. Sometime later in 1966, the position of Inspector General was created in the Ministry, and Khounta was appointed to it. The prime minister's daughter had never wanted to marry Mr. Phonekeo. She was in love with an American Francophile whom she married a few years later, and they moved away. As it turned out, it was a lot of string pulling, pain, and intrigue for nothing.

In December of 1965, Khounta suggested we drive to Cambodia in April over the New Year holidays to visit Angkor Wat and to see his relatives in Phnom Penh.

CHAPTER 11

Cambodia: April 1966

In April, Khounta and I took advantage of the New Year holidays, as he had suggested, that is, drive to Phnom Penh and the beach via Bangkok, Aranyaprathet, and Angkor Wat. When he had suggested that we go, I was excited by the thought of a secret, romantic adventure. I told no one because, of course, it was improper to go off unchaperoned. In the end, a secret was all it was. The magnificence of Angkor and Sihanoukville remain ingrained in my memory, but so do the feelings of frustration and disappointment.

After a couple of nights in Bangkok and three nights in Siem Reap to visit Angkor Wat, we arrived in Phnom Penh. We drove to the house of Khounta's father who had passed away in 1962. Khounta led me up the front stairs to the main room of the big two-story house to show me a large framed photograph of his father surrounded by a black ribbon. In a case below it were his awards and other memorabilia. Khounta explained to me that his father had been like James Bond—a 007— meaning that he could have killed with impunity because he had been the Minister of Interior in Cambodia, which controls the police.

At the house, I saw some of Khounta's half-siblings from the major wife and some minor wives, one of whom I was introduced to, and some beautiful big-eyed nieces. I knew from living in Thailand and Laos that it was normal for men who could afford it to have more than one wife. Remember, the father in the family I lived with in Thailand had a minor wife. I was very surprised to learn about the custom at the time, but I was used to the idea now. The minor wives were not legally married to their husband. They usually lived in different towns and attained some security from the man, although they saw him infrequently. According to Khounta, the man was helping them in the sense that they might not have married otherwise, or the husband might not have been a good provider.

Khounta's father Prak Praproeung was a Cambodian from a noble Phnom Penh family. He completed high school in Phnom Penh and went to law school in Hanoi. He was a civil servant in the French administration that sent him to Laos where he worked in the French Sureté in the 1920s and '30s. Khounta's mother was his second wife. Praproeung would visit his family in Cambodia from time to time, and sometimes he took Khounta to visit with him.

In 1934 on Praproeung's visit to Cambodia to see his dying mother, his mother entrusted him and his three siblings to her sister and demanded the hand of her sister's daughter Mlle Tep Srey Mom for her son. Mlle Tep, who was one of the ladies-in-waiting to the queen, became pregnant by him. It was not obvious, however, until some months later after he had returned to Vientiane. Khounta's mother had also become pregnant again. Mlle Tep's son Prak Chanbona was born in June 1935. Prak Praproeung's family demanded that he return to Cambodia and marry Mlle Tep, which he did that September. He never returned to Laos. Prakelie, Khounta's sister, was born in December of the same year.

Khounta chatted with his half-sister and her husband and then asked them and a half-brother to go with us to the beach. I was surprised because we had not discussed inviting them. What was happening to our private getaway? The family readily agreed. They had been talking in French for hours, and I had not understood more than two words. There had been no effort to include me in the conversation. I might as well have been a wooden post. However, the thought of our soon being alone, swimming and sunbathing, had kept me smiling politely and trying to look interested.

Khounta told me later that he was very annoyed with talking to his brother-in-law because he was so opinionated, but knew nothing. No outside news was allowed into the country, and people were not permitted to leave. What irritated him most was that his brother would not believe him about the dangerous political situation in Indochina, and kept spouting what was broadcast on the government-controlled radio and published in the government-controlled press. This brother and all the Cambodian family perished in the killing fields or Tuol Sleng Prison when Cambodia was overthrown April 13, 1975, except Prak Chanbona and his family who had left several years before for medical treatment in France and Prak Pramon who was studying in East Germany and still lives somewhere there.

When we arrived at the exclusive beach resort area at Kep on the southern coast of the Gulf of Siam, we stopped, stretched and looked at it. Then we continued up a nearby hill that overlooked the beach at Sihanoukville where we sat around on mats in the shade. Khounta and his relatives discussed politics in French. Again, I was very bored and wondered why we were sitting there. With each passing minute, my anticipation of enjoying the beach increased. When the sun began to go down, and the mosquitoes came out, we got in the car and drove to the summer house in the hills of Kampot about five kilometers from Kep. I was confused. I asked about the beach. Khounta told me it was too late to go.

As children, his half-brothers and sisters were unhappy that their father had built on the side of a hill instead of on the beach at Kep, as he could have done. After having seen how exceedingly uninterested they were in the flawless sand and skin-darkening sun, it was easy for me to understand how years ago when the choice of land was made their parents had chosen the hills for coolness, trees, and shade.

The summer house was a simple, rectangular block of dirty white concrete containing four rooms. We ate a picnic dinner on the floor in the living room. I was given one of the rooms, bare, other than for a mattress on the floor and a mosquito net. It was sweltering. I lay there feeling lonely and sorry for myself. Later, when the house was silent,

Khounta came to slip under the net. I was angry and said, "Shhh. Talking will bother the people trying to sleep," and waved him away. I didn't want his relatives to know we were sleeping together. They appeared to be very judgmental and censorious.

In the morning, Khounta told me we would be going back to Phnom Penh. I asked, "What about the beach? We came here to go to the beach." He explained that since we had invited his family to join us, they were our guests, and they were not interested. I was almost in tears. I had barely spoken to anyone in twenty-four hours, had endured being a silent outsider with the saving thought that soon we would be going to the beach. Now we were not going! I had seen the water, smelled the air, had my swimsuit in my bag, but touching the sand or water was not to be? I was bewildered and hurt. The beach was why we had come to Cambodia. At last, Khounta relented and spoke to his relatives. He did not like asking them to wait for his girlfriend, and they did not like waiting. At least that is how they made me feel.

Dazzling, magnificent, alluring: it was the most exquisite beach I had ever seen. Beautiful, white sand spread from the beach onto the side of the road. Azure water gently caressed the sand, and when I walked into the water, it felt perfectly refreshing. Looking down, through the clean, transparent water up to my neck, I could see my feet on the white sand. Gazing out to sea to the edge of the earth, I saw sparkling blue water. Glancing back to the beach, I saw where vibrant green jungle met the white sand about fifty meters away. It was quiet, other than the slight shush of water against the sand. The beach was pristine. There were no people, no hawkers or touts, no mats or towels, no beach umbrellas, no papers, bottles or plastic bags. Nature had made this beautiful place, and no one visited it except to look at it from a distance. I thought this is where I want to honeymoon, Sihanoukville. It's perfect.

On the other hand, in my private world, since I was about nine years old, I had dreamed of marrying and having children. In my teens, people in their twenties appeared to be ancient. I decided then that the deadline for the dream to be realized was no later than age twenty-five. I was an introverted, reserved person and, if unsuccessful in my goal, I believed I should end my life. I still held that belief. My twenty-sixth birthday was looming, and I was not married yet. I thought this would be a beautiful place to stop growing older. Here is where I could walk into the water and swim until utterly exhausted and then sink below the surface with the sun shining on my back and the water embracing me. No one would think it was anything but an accident.

I could have thirty minutes at the beach. It was just enough time to get in my swimsuit, walk up the beach out of sight of the others, swim a little bit, and walk back to the car and change. At least Khounta came with me. He liked the water as much as I did. We splashed and laughed and drank in the surrounding beauty for barely ten minutes and then went back to Khounta's siblings, waiting in their long sleeves and hats, holding their umbrellas against the sun.

On the way back to Phnom Penh, Khounta whispered in English that if I wanted, we could go back to the beach after we dropped his relatives off. His offer touched me, but I said no. It was a long way, and we already had a lengthy drive ahead of us.

CHAPTER 12

The Accident: July 1966

When I returned to Vientiane, I had to think of my future. My USAID contract was up in mid-August. I needed to apply to graduate school. My mother had a very good college friend Shen Yao, a professor of English at the University of Hawaii, and she suggested I apply there. I applied and was accepted into the M.A. program. I wanted a degree in Teaching English as a Second Language (TESL) because I wanted to return to Laos and teach at Dong Dok. I wanted to be able to create an aptitude test for Lao wishing to learn English. With Shen's, help I received a Graduate Assistantship at the English Language Institute (ELI) at the University. My inadequate-money situation was solved.

Hawaii was the perfect place for me to go because of the climate. The other excellent university I could have applied to was the University of Michigan, but it was cold in Ann Arbor and had lots of snow in winter. I would have had to buy a new wardrobe, and the weather would have made me miserable. Besides, Shen, whom I knew, was in Honolulu.

I didn't have to be in Hawaii to begin my M.A. program until mid-September. I gave my mother a round-the-world ticket to visit me before I left Vientiane. She organized her trip with her friend Esther Madsen. I would meet them in Bangkok, and we would drive to Angkor Wat together, totally ignoring the fact that the border with Thailand was closed.

It had only been closed for a few weeks, but I believed it would be open by the time I wanted to go.

Khounta invited my mother and Esther to stay with him in Ban Khoua Luang, a village in Vientiane. The city is made up of hundreds of adjacent villages called bans, and each village has its *wat* (temple) after which the village is named. Khounta's father named him after the village of his first Lao wife who had died because he never wanted to forget her.

Khounta's house was the most modern in Vientiane. He had designed it himself with sliding glass windows in wooden frames, five bedrooms with built in closets in two of them, three bathrooms with bathtubs and bidets, one with built in closets. The electrical wiring was inside the walls. I never saw another house in Laos with hidden wiring. All the houses had ribbons of wires from one to seven strands wide tacked along the edge of the ceilings and doorframes running from electrical outlets to little switch boxes with porcelain fuses and switches to turn the power on and off, a practice still followed today. The standard feature in California of built-in closets was almost unknown. Because of the French influence, a bidet in the master bathroom was usual, but this house had one in each bathroom.

On the tile floor in the living room was a large oriental carpet, another first in Laos. The sofas and chairs, stylish in the France of the 1950s, were stuffed and covered with vinyl, rather than the typical rattan furniture with cushions found in other foreigners' homes. The dining room table sat ten. It was a European-style house even to having a kitchen inside the house instead of in a detached building. In the master bedroom, on the wall at the end of the king-sized bed hung a full-length oil painting of a reclining nude that Khounta had brought from Paris. She had bobbed, blond hair and she lay on a brightly colored cloth of red, green and yellow.

I had some vacation due me from USAID from mid-July onwards. Over the weekend, July 16-17, I packed my household goods from my duplex for mailing through the Army Post Office. I was entitled to the shipment of my household effects back to my point of hire, which was

Thakhek, not the USA. I wanted them to go to California, so I had to take care of them myself. To mail to the USA, I would have to send them from the APO in Udorn Thani, Thailand because the boxes were too large for the APO in Vientiane. In Udorn was a huge U.S. military base for making bombing sorties over Hanoi and the Ho Chi Minh trail. The bombs not dropped were released over the Lao countryside many miles from Vientiane, so that there would be no danger of a devastating accident when the planes landed in Udorn.

On Monday morning, I drove my loaded pale green 1963 Volkswagen to the APO in Udorn. While I was waiting my turn in line, I felt as if I would faint. I had never felt that way before. I sat on one of the boxes and leaned over, putting my head between my knees. After a few minutes, I felt better. I mailed the boxes of stereo equipment, speakers, amplifier, tapes, kitchenware, and keepsakes and drove back to the border town of Nong Khai. I parked my car in the safety of a hotel garage and took the ferryboat back across the river to Laos.

The dizziness in Udorn had frightened me, so I went to see Dr. Pfenemuller at the American Clinic in Vientiane. He assured me that my feeling faint was just due to excitement over the upcoming trip to meet my mother, and he gave me some medicine for heart palpitations. I had never been dizzy before, nor was I the sort to be dizzy about seeing my mother, but I took the pills anyway.

I spent the night at Khounta's because I wanted to get off to an early start the next morning. That was why I had taken the car across the river the day before and stored it there, but I overslept. Something was wrong with me. Khounta drove me to the border at eight a.m. instead of six a.m. I sat beside him as we drove down Sethathirath Street, thinking how beautifully the trees on both sides shaded the street, letting in only small slivers of yellow light. I also felt very annoyed with myself and wondered why Khounta had not wakened me. I knew he was a little worried, as I had never driven to Bangkok alone. He also thought it ill-considered because the Cambodian border was closed and we would not be able to continue to Angkor.

In Nong Khai, I got my car and drove a mile or two only to have a flat tire. Some passing motorists helped me change it, but then I had to stop in Udorn to have it patched. Finally, I was on my way. After a couple of hours, I began to feel sleepy. What was wrong with me? I had overslept, and now, still morning, I was sleepy. My adrenaline at the excitement of my adventure should be keeping me on the edge of my seat. I opened a can of corn chips. I lit a cigarette. I figured activity would keep me focused. I promised myself a wake-up Pepsi when I reached Korat. I continued to speed down the recently completed Friendship Highway through the silent, flat, barren countryside.

The next thing I heard was someone screaming in pain. I felt my body being held in someone's arms and I opened my eyes to see a truck stopped up the road; then blackness. My next memory is of lying on a hard bed with several people with scissors bending over me cutting my clothes; then again, blackness. Then I felt someone pushing at my face, and I opened my eyes to see three or four people looking at me. Someone explained that the nurse was trying to insert a stomach pump so I would not vomit. It must have been a subliminal suggestion because I immediately vomited and passed out. Later I came to, and the nurse explained that they needed to take some x-rays. I was wheeled into a room and placed on a table that moved from a horizontal to a vertical position. As it did so, my legs collapsed like toweling. I could not stand up, and the x-ray could not be taken. Had I broken my neck or my back or both?

My last memory in that hospital was when I opened my eyes and saw a nurse in the light of the doorway. She was my guard. I was the only female patient in the hospital at the U.S. military base in Korat. A plane was on its way from Vientiane to take me to Bangkok. Dr. Pat McCreedy of the USAID Public Health Division was coming to accompany me. I asked for painkillers. I remember nothing of the trip except for a few moments when I was unloaded onto the tarmac at Don Muang Airport. I came to again as a doctor in the Seventh Day Adventist Hospital was examining me. He declared me a healthy, young female with nothing more than severe contusions.

In the wee hours of the fourth day, I awoke in the darkness, except for a small light from the hallway, to find my mother and Esther peering down at me in relief. My friends in Vientiane had told USAID that I was on my way to meet my mother in Bangkok, and the message had been sent to the USAID office there. The office manager graciously met my mother's plane. He was not a native speaker of English and his words of introduction, "I knew your daughter," surprised my mother. Although it was after two a.m., she calmly took what he said and reserved any outward emotion until she could see me for herself. They stayed looking at me matter-of-factly for a few minutes, long enough to ascertain that I was not in the past tense, then left.

The next morning I slowly eased my hand up to feel my face and hair. They were caked with mud. Why hadn't someone at least washed my face? My mind was awake, but my internal systems were still unconscious. All the usual needles and tubes were stuck in me to keep the juices flowing. Very luckily, I had not broken any bones, but I hurt so much I could not move.

The next day Khounta and Somsangouane astonished me with their presence. Khounta looked at me gravely and said little. He was a man of great privacy who never told anyone what he was feeling, including me. It was only at Somsangouane's insistence that he drove down from Vientiane, an eight to nine-hour trip. This act of caring, more than any other, showed me how he felt. After the one visit of not more than ten minutes, they did not come again although I know they stayed in Bangkok for several days. I could never understand why they didn't visit me again, but as I learned through the years, it was a pattern of Khounta's. He did not like visiting hospitals or being visited in one himself. It seemed to embarrass him. This behavior, so contrary to my feelings and desires, bewildered and hurt me. I was glad to learn from my mother that he took her and Esther to eat at our favorite seafood restaurant.

After a few more days, my body was pretty much sorted, and one week to the day after the accident, I walked away from the hospital. My mother and Esther got sleeping berths on the overnight train to

Nong Khai. I was still so bruised that I had to take a reclining chair. If I lay down, I could not get up. Khounta met us at the train station and drove us to his house.

My mother and I shared the master bedroom. One time Khounta walked in without knocking, as we were resting. He was terribly embarrassed, and so was I. I thought he had forgotten my mother was with me. I wondered what my mother thought.

Khounta showed my mother and Esther around Vientiane and took them out to dinner, but I stayed at the house because the roads were so rough and potholed that it was painful to ride around in the car. After a few days, it was time for them to leave. Since my car had been in an accident, I could not drive them to Angkor Wat. I would not have been able to in any case because the border was still closed. In my own perversely optimistic and confident way, I had honestly believed that the border would reopen when I was ready to cross.

I borrowed Khounta's car to take them to the ferryboat. As we were driving along my mother surprised me by asking, "Why don't you marry Khounta?" Had I heard my mother correctly? It was a typical, bright, warm sunny day. The paddy fields lay unmoving. Where had her question come from? The idea was against all she had taught me. "Don't marry," she had told me, "someone of a different culture. Marriage is difficult enough to complicate with a labyrinth of unknown beliefs and practices." This advice was the result of my being at a university where there had been many international students. She had gone to an all women's college. Obviously, she had been concerned. However, now she was suggesting marriage to an older man of a different ethnicity, religion, and country. She knew I was leaving to go to graduate school in a week. Perhaps she felt it safe to ask. Had she been thinking about it all week, or did the idea just pop into her head? She knew Khounta liked me, and I must like him as I was staying in his house. I was stunned into silence, and I felt embarrassed, partly because my mother had never asked me a personal question before, especially of such significant magnitude. If she had asked, "Are you going to marry Khounta?" I might have said yes, but I never answered her. A one-word response is easier than a long explanation to a negative question. I had not seen or spoken to my mother for three and a half years (we had communicated by aerogram every week), and now after ten days, she asked this question. Maybe I was annoyed that she had seen the obvious without my telling her, but there was no reason to be annoyed. I adored Khounta. A naive, inexperienced girl of twenty-five cannot conceal such an aura. What inhibition would not let me share my exciting news with my own mother? But then, we never shared our feelings, hers with me nor mine with her. Of what were we afraid?

Khounta had asked me to move in with him on several occasions, but this was the mid-60s. Nice girls did not do that, especially in a small, closed, gossipy community. Then one day, in June, driving home from a picnic in the rice paddies, he asked me to marry him. I said, "What?" I had heard him, but I was so startled that I could not be sure I had heard correctly. I had never given marriage to him a thought. He was someone I liked to be with, party with, eat and dance with, picnic and read with, but marry? He did not repeat his proposal. He was a one-time-opportunity man, and one had to be quick. I didn't say no, and I didn't say yes. I had to think. Did I love him? Did I want to spend my life in Laos, a place most of the world had never heard of? After a week, I realized that I had become accustomed to him and that I wanted to be with him, just as I had fallen in love with Laos and not realized it at first. I did not want to leave him. Since I did not stop seeing him, he understood that we were engaged, but neither of us told anyone. I didn't tell anyone because I was shy and didn't want to be the center of attention, and I was a little unsure, too, what if he changed his mind? I didn't know I should have told my mother and that she would have made the announcement. I lived in a cocoon where feelings were not shared. Happily, I don't live there anymore.

Now I didn't want to go to Hawaii to get my M.A. I wanted to stay in Laos and get married, but it was very important to Khounta that I get my Master's degree. He could see into the future, or so it seemed, that I would need it in my career for obtaining a good job and salary and for status in my field and the community. He was right about it and me. He knew I needed to keep my mind engaged and challenged, and I needed the degree to have TESL credibility. We would be married when I returned.

Two weeks after my mother and Esther left, I felt well enough to go to Korat and find out about the accident and my car. I flew to Bangkok and took the train to Korat. I learned that I had fallen asleep. It was eleven o'clock in the morning! While asleep, I drove past a police box, across the highway into a rice field, and hit a log that had rolled off a truck traveling on a diagonal road. On impact, I had been thrown ten feet out of the car, landing face down in the mud. I am still missing hair from my eyebrows where my glasses frame scrapped off the skin. The car engine went twenty feet out the back of the car. The policemen had been watching my car, and they ran and pulled me out of the mud. Their quick action probably saved me from suffocating. Then they flagged down a passing truck whose driver took me to the local hospital, where, luckily for me, two Peace Corps Volunteers were working. They saved me from a horse serum tetanus shot and later told me that I spoke to them in Thai. They called the district Peace Corps Director, Scott Duncan, with whom I had trained and served in the Peace Corps. He got me transferred to the American military base hospital.

I went to see my wrecked car. The night of the accident two policemen had guarded my car, but all the tires disappeared anyway. The battery had burst open, and acid was eating the seat upholstery and whatever else it touched. People were amazed after looking at the car to see me walking around. I took the nurses to lunch in appreciation for their taking care of me and returned to Vientiane.

Although I had bought 100% comprehensive insurance and complete medical coverage for the trip before I left Laos, I left a day early and so I was not covered, but the car was. Frank Manley of Manley Enterprises made sure I got a check for the value of my car.

For many years afterwards, I wondered why I fell asleep. The hospital had tested me for malaria, but they found no trace. The bigger question for me was why hadn't I been killed? I could have hit an oncoming vehicle, smashed my head on pavement, or suffocated in the rice paddy. Most troubling was the fact that I would have been dead with no warning, an instant, painless death. I decided God had saved me for a purpose that would be revealed to me.

CHAPTER 13

Leaving Laos: August 1966

August is a pleasant month to be in Vientiane, although some afternoons can be too hot. It is normally sunny all day. It is still the rainy season, but it usually only rains at night. That is good because Vientiane is a very, very dusty city and the rain subdues the dust for the start of a new day. There is almost no wind at this time of year, but with the roosters' crow, the trucks and cars blow up the dirt on the roads. This is as true today as it was in 1966. In that year, apart from a few paved cross streets in the downtown area and in the residential areas where foreigners lived, the only paved roads were one that went west to the airport, one that went east to the ferryboat at Thadeua, and one in front of the morning market up to the Monument where it divided into two roads, one that went to That Luang, and one that went to Sisavangvong University, renamed the National University of Laos. Moreover, there were no curbs and no sidewalks. Along the sides of some of the roads were open ditches for runoff that were usually filled with a nauseating-looking black sludge.

During the final week before I left for Hawaii, I sat around the house with nowhere to go and nothing to do. Besides, my rib cage was so bruised I could hardly move. The Mekong River was rising, so Khounta, in his position as the Director General of the Ministry of

Public Works, was busy directing the building of dikes to keep the water from coming into the city. However, he could call upon very few trucks or earth-moving machines. While I was there, he mostly checked the level of the water in Luang Prabang, a town 136 miles up the river, which is an indication of how much higher the water will rise in Vientiane. Vientiane, which is situated in a bowl-shaped area beside the riverbank, had never flooded in anyone's memory. But the water kept rising.

The night before I left, Khounta drove us to Somsangouane's in his yellow Bureau of Public Roads car. The car was at his disposal for business because of his position. Somsangouane's house was a typical, little, wooden one-story rectangle on one-meter stilts on the way to the airport. We parked in the grassy area in front of the house. Inside it was dark with just one low-watt bulb burning. Lao houses do not usually have chairs because people sit on mats on the floor. But the floor is hard, so the three of us stretched out on Somsangouane's bed with Khounta in the middle. The two of them lay there whispering in Lao and giggling. I didn't want to be there. This was my last night. I did not want to spend it with a third person, especially her. Why we went there is an unanswered question. Perhaps Khounta, in his way, was being polite. After all, she had introduced us and I should, exhibiting good manners, come to see her and thank her before I left.

With my Western cultural, romantic dreams, I wanted to be at home whispering words of undying love and enjoying long kisses, embraces, and periods of comfortable silence. After endless boring hours for me (I think I even fell asleep), Khounta decided it was time to leave. We went to the door and opened it. In front of us was a river of water. Almost a foot of water had silently covered the road, and it was moving with great speed and force towards town. We leapt from the steps of her porch to the car and took off slowly down the middle of the road. The only light came from our headlights. The river kept rising and swirled around and passed us. We were afraid the car would stall. It did! Khounta tried to start it over and over again. He became frustrated and impatient. A few cars came along making waves and spraying us. Khounta was furious that no one stopped to help him. He expected them to, although I am not sure if he would have dared stop to help anyone himself.

After ten minutes, the car started unexpectedly, and we made it to the house. Thankfully, there was electricity. With the flooding, there was no clean water for bathing, and the septic tanks were full. We could not even flush the toilet. We did not talk much, but I knew Khounta's mind was occupied with the flood. But my mind was occupied thinking that this was our last night together for two years. We lay on the bed in the upstairs guest room, thinking our separate thoughts. I still wanted him to ask me to stay and not go to Hawaii.

In the morning, we got ready to go to the train station. As I was closing my suitcase, Khounta stood in front of me. Holding his most sacred and precious possession—his gold chain with Buddhist amulets that he always wore, he asked, "Do you want this?" I was overwhelmed that he would make such an offer. After his 190SL Mercedes, his three most prized possessions were his Rolex watch, his gold ID bracelet, and the gold chain with the Buddha images.

I should have said yes and let him put it over my head, but the polite American in me said, "Are you sure?" Mistake. He immediately withdrew the chain and put it back over his head. I had learned a valuable lesson. Of course, he was sure. He was careful and thoughtful about everything he did. He had decided to give me a farewell gift, and I had questioned him. He made a personal and cultural decision, and I made a natural and spontaneous Western response of care and respect. With Khounta, I was learning one got only one chance, and one did not ask for repetitions. I tried never to question him again, which led to a torturous guessing-game life: What did he want? What did he mean? What were the rules?

We left for the train station early because we didn't know the extent of the flooding. Was Thadeua Road passable? Fortunately, there was only an inch or so of water running over the road in a few places. Khounta had a lot of work to do to try to save the city. We took the ferry across the Mekong River. There was about an inch of water at the train station, too, but the train was there. It was August 30, 1966, and the Mekong River was rising. It would cause the worst flood in Vientiane history. We were both close to tears. No embrace. No kiss. I got on the train. We waved good-bye.

I stayed in Bangkok for a couple of days and then flew to Honolulu with a plane change in Taipei, which necessitated a stopover. I put up in a small, quiet hotel. The desk manager could see how sad I was, and the following morning he took me for a ride on his motorcycle into the countryside to cheer me up. I did feel happier with the wind blowing through my hair and making my eyes water.

CHAPTER 14
University and Post Cards: September 1966

Richard "Dick" Sittler, the head of the TESOL Department and the ELI at the University, met my plane in Honolulu and helped me through customs. When we reached the parking lot, we saw that a hit-run driver had crushed the left rear fender of his red sports car. I felt terrible and somehow responsible.

Driving from the airport, Dick told me about a new ELI instructor, Eileen Streich, who had just arrived from New York and was looking for a roommate. He had suggested to her that we might room together, so he dropped me at her apartment. I thought how well everything was working out! However, Eileen had met someone on the bus that morning and had invited her to be her roommate. Mary was beginning an M.A. in ethnomusicology. Oh, well. We asked if there was another vacancy in the same building and there was. I moved in.

The apartment rent was more than I wished to spend, but I saved money by buying ten pounds of apples and a pound of cheese a week for my meals at home. I wanted to live on the money I received as a graduate assistant and reserve my savings for travel. I began by riding the local bus to school, but after a few months, I bought a bicycle and saved on bus fare.

As a graduate assistant (GA) my assignment was to teach one course each semester. I learned as much from the teaching as I did from my studies. Seven GAs taught at the ELI in addition to the regular instructors. Besides teaching, we had some other small duties at registration and in test administration. Four of us were former Peace Corps Volunteer teachers, and we shared an office in Kuykendall Hall. It was very convenient because the TESL Office was on the same floor and we could study there in the evenings.

On the weekends, Eileen and I would spend time wandering around in the Ala Moana shopping mall, which was the largest one in the world at the time. It was just down the street from our apartment. Delicious curry puffs and other tasty foods were available. We usually went to the Chinese restaurant down the street for a food splurge once a week. Then, of course, there was the beach. In the beginning, we found it difficult to lie in the sun for hours. We were not used to such inactivity, but after a few month's practice, we became expert at it and could even sleep for hours. Other people's conversations and their music lulled us insensible.

I was used to having my hair washed and put up in a French roll twice a week, but now I let my long hair hang straight. I had worn a skirt and blouse or a dress and heels or sandals with heels for more than three years. Giving up my usual dress was more difficult. I went to flats quickly, but stayed in my dresses, chiefly because I taught every day. I felt professional and comfortable in them.

On a personal level, after having been away from studying, I could not concentrate for more than a minute whether I was trying to read text or write a paper. Lectures were easier because they required active note taking. After a couple of months, I worked up to five minutes of sustained concentration. The problem was that I was always thinking of Khounta. Every day after classes, I would rush back to the apartment to check the mailbox only to be disappointed. At last in October, after the floodwaters in Vientiane had receded, I received three postcards in one week. I was ecstatic. They were all in French because he didn't know how to write in English. With my college French, I was able to decipher most of his messages and his handwriting. I wrote every week, pouring out my thoughts in simple English, using words I thought he would know. And, like Pavlov's dog, I continued to race home every day expecting more postcards or a letter, but I didn't receive any.

In December, I went home to Piedmont, California for Christmas. I was miserable. Why had I not heard from Khounta? I knew he loved me, and I hung on to that. I went back to Hawaii to celebrate New Year's Eve. I joined Eileen's sister Ursel and her husband Gunter, who was teaching geography at the University, and a friend of theirs from McGill University. I thought of Khounta the entire time and jumped convulsively when firecrackers, like bombs, went off, which was often because that is one of the ways the New Year is greeted in Hawaii. Ursel told me later that their friend was interested in me. I was "so nice and quiet" he had told her. Little did he know why!

A school break was coming up at the end of January 1967. I confided in Eileen about Khounta, and she confided in me about one of her students at NYU whom she married later in the year.

Not hearing from Khounta was torture. I could not endure it, and I secretly booked myself on Pan Am Flight One. Telephoning was not an option. I never thought about it. I didn't even call California from Hawaii. It was expensive, and so in my family, we never made long distance calls. Cell phones, Skype, and the Internet didn't exist.

Pan American Airways International went bankrupt in the 1980s, but then it ruled the skies. It went around the world in both directions every day: San Francisco to Honolulu to Tokyo to Hong Kong to Bangkok and on. On the plane, I found myself sitting next to a USAID secretary whom I recognized from Vientiane. Would she say anything when she got back? I wondered. I learned with relief that she was on her way to Saigon and was more concerned with the situation there than to wonder why I was on the plane.

From Bangkok, I took the train to Nong Khai and then the ferryboat across the Mekong River to Thadeua. A taxi took me to Khounta's front door. It was Tuesday morning, and he was home. He was surprised to see me. He was on his way to the airport to meet his minister Ngon Sananikone, for a trip to Savannakhet. I was disappointed, but he would be back in a couple of days. I was just happy to be back.

He left for the airport, and I took one of our reclining picnic chairs into the front yard and grabbed an orange soda and my book. January weather in Vientiane is very pleasant, not hot. The sun was shining. This time of year is called either the dry season or the cold season. I had just settled down when Khounta came back. "Did you forget something?" I asked.

"No, I told Ngon I wasn't feeling well, and he told me to go home." I was very surprised at his lie and very pleased.

I had not told Dee or any of my friends that I was coming for a visit. When later that day she came over and was shouting Khounta's name and I appeared from upstairs, she was astonished. When, what, where, why—the questions bubbled forth. It was so good to see another familiar face.

One day we went for a picnic on the porch of General Kouprasith Abhay's uncle's country house, about 80 kilometers from Vientiane. I had never been there before. It was in the jungle under some shady trees. After lunch, a water buffalo wandered into the yard. I asked Khounta if I could get on it while he took a photo. He said yes. I set him up with my camera and asked him how to get on the buffalo. He said to grab hold of the buffalo's tail and pull myself on. I didn't see how that would work, and I had never seen any of the little boys that rode them get on one. I needed a bench or tall stool, but there wasn't one. Finally, I pulled myself up one side and was sitting on its back when it bucked. I fell in the dust, and the buffalo ran off. I was shaken, but unhurt. Luckily, Khounta had taken a photo before I was thrown, but none afterwards. It had all happened so fast that he could only watch in alarm. I've never tried to get on a buffalo again. Some Lao had told me before to be careful of water buffalo, as they don't like the smell of foreigners. That was why I had asked Khounta in the first place, but perhaps he hadn't heard me or was only concentrating on the mechanics of taking a photo. Our concerns were different, and I didn't communicate mine.

One evening we drove out to Dong Dok to make a surprise visit on Bernie and Shirley Wilder, but other than that, we didn't go out.

When it came time to leave, I flew from Wattay International Airport. That building is now the domestic airport. As we turned to go upstairs to wait for the plane, I beseeched him to write me, and he promised he would, but he never did.

I continued to write every week and checked the mailbox daily. What did it mean when I received nothing?

CHAPTER 15

Return to Vientiane: June 1968

The graduate assistantship was for two years, the length of the M.A. TESL program. I missed Khounta so much that I finished it in one and a half years, in January 1968, and planned to return to Vientiane immediately. However, I was offered a TESL job in Hilo, Hawaii, preparing a Peace Corps group going to Thailand. The position was for three months. It was an excellent opportunity, and the work experience proved to be invaluable. Finally, I left in May for Vientiane.

On the way, I visited friends in Japan, Okinawa, Taiwan, South Korea, the Philippines, and Cambodia, including Khounta's family whom I had met in April 1966. Then I was in Bangkok. My cold feet got colder. If we had announced our engagement, I wouldn't have been so apprehensive. In any case, I was traveling on a round-the-world ticket. I didn't have enough confidence to arrive in Vientiane after a year and a half of silence from Khounta without having an onward backup. I stayed off Sukhumvit Road on Soi 15 with the Mosteller's. They were a Southern Baptist Missionary family whom I had first been introduced to by Larry Smith in Haadyai in the south of Thailand.

Mrs. Mosteller was a warm and peaceful person. She took me in without question and soothed my disquiet with her intelligent way of handling her family and getting on with her life. I don't know if Larry had told her anything about Khounta, but I did not confide in her. I had the feeling that she knew and was being considerate of my reticence and anxiety. I got my train ticket to Nong Khai and even stayed on in their house for two days to build my courage after they had gone on vacation. I had already decided that if Khounta were not at the train station to meet me, I would return to Bangkok directly. I'd written to him every week for eighteen months, so he knew I would be arriving on the morning train on 12 June. He waved to me from the platform when the train pulled into the station. What a relief!

We took a pedicab, then the ferryboat across the Mekong River to Laos and Khounta drove the twenty kilometers to Vientiane. He pulled in at the Lane Xang Hotel. I was surprised because I had expected to go back to his house. I wondered why he was taking me to a hotel. When we got to the room, I wanted to throw myself in his arms, hug him, and kiss him. I had dreamed of this moment for months, but he made no motion whatsoever to touch me, and I respected his lead. But I was puzzled. He said he thought I must be tired and stayed just long enough to put my suitcase down.

I didn't receive a warm embrace or even a welcoming kiss. It is impolite in Lao and Thai culture to make any outward display of affection in public but behind a closed door? I thought perhaps he was watching his reputation or mine or not daring to tempt his emotions. We went downstairs, and he left for work.

I went back to my room. The narrow windows opened onto the Mekong River across the street. The room was small, the bed was narrow, the lighting dim, and there were no decorations on the white walls. I felt deflated, lonely, and bewildered, and the room offered no comfort. The Lane Xang Hotel was the finest hotel in Vientiane, built in 1962 on the site of the Auguste Pavie Plaza. Auguste Pavie was the first French vice-consul in Luang Prabang in 1886. The bronze statue of Pavie was relocated from the plaza to the garden of the French Embassy and the accompanying statues of a boy and girl offering him flowers decorate the grounds at the Museum of Religious Art (Haw Pha Kaew).

For the first couple of days, I stayed in the room. Khounta came, and we went to lunch. Then he went to his house for a nap. He would come again for dinner and then go home. Everything was at arm's length. I couldn't understand. He had been amorous before, and now he was merely polite as if I were a visiting guest he was forced to entertain. Finally, he explained that his mother's house had been torn down, and she was living with him. Why he didn't tell me when I arrived is an unanswered question. I didn't ask him how she felt about us. Feelings were not something I talked about with my mother or other family members and never with Khounta. I didn't know how. Feelings were a scary, foreign and dangerous territory to venture into. Even the thought of asking personal questions was stressful. I was unhappy, disappointed and lonely in the barren time we spent together. Why did he have to go home for a nap? Why didn't he spend the time with me? My notions of how a man in love with a woman acted were being bombarded.

Feeling isolated, I went to look for my good friends Ron and June Pulcini whom I had met in Savannakhet when they had visited as IVS Volunteers. When June had stepped off the plane at the Savannakhet Airport and vomited, it was her first inkling that she was pregnant. Being the mid-60s, it was a no-no for IVS couples to have children, but the Lao loved it. They love babies, and if you do not produce one in the first year of marriage, they want to help you and tell you how. But IVS terminated their contracts. They had already served many months in South Vietnam and Cambodia. This posting was their third, but the rule had been broken. They liked Laos, however, and stayed. Ron and I had taught English together at Dong Dok. In the months I had been away, June had graciously included Khounta in events at her house and teased him about me. I found her at home. Believe me; she was startled to see me as I had not told anyone I was coming. At last, a warm and friendly welcome!

I told her where I was staying, and she invited me to stay with her and Ron in the room next to their baby's. I readily accepted and moved in the next day.

CHAPTER 16

The New Car: July 1968

It was Saturday and a beautiful July morning in Vientiane. The sky was blue, and the air was fresh from pre-dawn rains. I had been back only a month. I was jittery in anticipation of my coming marriage to Khounta. Two days before, he had gone to Bangkok to get his new car and was due back today. How could I contain my excitement? What could I do with myself? I knew: I would surprise him and meet him at Thanalang. I put on my white dress with big red and blue polka dots that my sister had made for me. It was collarless, sleeveless and cut in gores from neck to hemline. It was fitted without a belt. The material had body and hung great. I knew I looked good in it.

I estimated that Khounta would be crossing sometime soon, so I drove to the car ferry. (There was no bridge across the Mekong River until 1994.) I arrived at about ten o'clock, parked my car, and went to an area above where the ferry docked. I sat on a low wall at the top of the riverbank near the fence. I had a lovely view up, down, and across the river. It was getting hot. The sparse leaves on the tree above me gave little protection. I had brought a book with me because there is always a wait no matter what you do in Laos.

The hours went by, but no Khounta. I read and waited, but I was getting bored and stiff from sitting so long. Lunchtime came and went, but I was so excited about surprising Khounta that I didn't feel hungry. I had a bottle of water with me, and I took a few sips. The temperature continued to rise.

A couple of hours into the afternoon the ferryman asked me for whom I was waiting, and I explained. He said that Khounta had come across the day before. I was sure he was mistaken, and I continued to wait. From under the tree, I watched the sky turning gray, and then a few drops of rain fell. I waited. Suddenly, drops the size of cherries fell in a deluge.

I ran for the car, but the dirt pathway now shined a glossy burnt orange from the crashing water. As I streaked for the car, I slipped. Now, not only was my hair disheveled and my face and limbs streaked with rivulets of water, but my hands and knees were muddy, and my dress had a big red stain down one side. I made it to the car and cleaned myself up wondering where Khounta could be. I was worried. I decided to go to his house to see if there was a message.

I drove the twenty kilometers back to town. The rain and dark clouds had brought evening on. It was five o'clock by the time I arrived. The guard opened the gate, and I drove in. I saw the new car. I was stunned. How did I miss him? I burst into the house without knocking. Khounta and his mother Nang Im were sitting calmly at the dining room table eating dinner. They turned and stared. I was stricken with shock. How could this be? I saw them see me. The air tensed with their combined thoughts, who and what is she doing here? I gasped and sobbed. I was wet and dirty and crying uncontrollably. I had never met Khounta's mother. Khounta looked alarmed and jumped up from the table. "Where were you?" I stammered. "I waited for you all day at Thanalang." Khounta's prime concern seemed to be to get me out of sight of his mother who was sitting and watching the spectacle. He came and guided me to a chair in the living room where his mother could only get a profile view. I learned that he had returned the day before and had driven directly to his friend Laurent's house. His other cronies and their wives had shown up later, and after admiring the car, they had played cards half the night.

Knowing where Khounta had been made me feel worse than not knowing. Questions coursed through my mind. Why does he show the car to his friends before me? I'm going to be his wife. Don't I come first? I didn't understand. It was Saturday. Where was he all day? What was he doing? Why didn't he look for me today? Khounta offered to take me to dinner, but inside I hurt too much. He didn't introduce me to his mother. I returned to the Pulcini's house, went quickly up the stairs out of sight, and got out of my sodden clothes. I felt too humiliated to tell June and Ron about my day. When I saw them later, I let them believe I had spent the day with Khounta. I smiled and told them how beautiful the new car was.

CHAPTER 17

The Summer and Autumn Months: Paris 1968

During the summer months, Khounta visited me in the evenings after dinner at the Pulcini's, and we would go for a drive. On the weekends, we went on picnics and sometimes we went to dinner, but we never went to his house or out to lunch, and he never showed any feelings of affection. He didn't seem interested in spending much time with me. His nap was always more important than being with me. I had been thinking about Khounta every day for eighteen months and never heard from him. Now I was near him, and he didn't touch me. What was going on? I reached out to him once in the Pulcini's driveway as he was leaving, but he angrily pushed me away. I asked what was wrong, but he didn't answer. He was so upset that he appeared to be straining to control himself. Without speaking, he got into his car and drove away. He was a stranger to me, but I had made a decision, just as he had: to marry. Was he testing me — or himself in some way? I will never know.

Khounta helped me buy a white Volkswagen bug to get around in. I wished he would loan me his sports car. He wasn't using it, but I didn't ask him. If he wanted to lend it to me, he would offer.

In July, I got a job through June Pulcini. She was working at USIS with the American Field Service (AFS), placing American teenagers with Lao families for a month. Through the Cultural Affairs Office, she knew that the Director of Courses, a USIS employee, at the Lao American Association (LAA), had not returned from her vacation as expected and someone was needed to step in. An interview was arranged for me with the LAA director Richard Hughes, and he hired me. My experience with the Peace Corps training program had been a useful stepping-stone. After a month, Perry Stieglitz, the Cultural Affairs Officer, came to see me. Would I be interested in a Fulbright-Hayes Grant to teach at the Lycée de Vientiane for the 1968-69 school year? Yes, of course. Did I speak French? No, I didn't. Could I resurrect my high school French and learn to converse by the start of school in September? I said I would get a teacher immediately. I told Khounta, and he said one of his secretaries could tutor me. We could never arrange a time.

One weekend in early August, Khounta took me for a drive for some serious talk. Was I sure I still wanted to marry him, considering all the differences in our backgrounds? We weren't talking about our families or prior experiences because we had never shared what our lives had been like before we met. I said yes, I was sure. He was hesitant. He told me I was nervous. I had never considered myself nervous, but now my nerve endings were exposed, and he was bruising them with his change in behavior. I, who never cried, would become teary, something he had never experienced. He said, "You think too much." I think, I was and am a typical American, who likes to hear words of appreciation, compliments, and reassurance of love and affection. Khounta, on the other hand, as I came to learn, said something once and saw no reason to repeat it. He knew he did good work and looked well turned out and was not interested in other people's comments. He believed he knew the correct way of doing things and acted accordingly. It was an enduring problem for me to learn his code of fused family, Lao and French morés, which he did not reveal unless a rule was transgressed.

He told me that while I was away, he had been offered two study tours, one to France and another to England. They would begin in September and finish in January. I thought this is mad. I have been away for almost two years. I have come back to get married, and he is going away for four months! How could he do this and just tell me now? Then he suggested we get married in Europe during the Christmas school break. I was so relieved to hear that, after months of getting the cold shoulder, he wanted to be wed in Paris.

I left for California in mid-September, before Khounta left for Europe so that my place-of-hire for the Fulbright at the lycée would be the United States, rather than locally. Being hired in the U.S. entitled me to a round-trip ticket to Laos. At home, I told my mother I was marrying Khounta. She was not surprised.

Mama and I went shopping for a mini-skirt wedding dress, white stockings, and a garter to throw at the reception. She made me a veil. I bought a negligee for the wedding night. She said, "What do you want that for? You won't be wearing it." Her words made me feel embarrassed, and of course, she was right, but all the magazine adver-tisements, books, and movie scenes made me believe I needed it. It is part of the romance. On the way back to Vientiane, I stopped in Hong Kong and had white lizard-skin shoes made with a clutch bag to match. I was ready, but I still had not told my friends. I guess I was secretive because I had been disappointed before, not with marriage, but other thwarted expectations, and I did not want the pain and em-barrassment of being stood up.

I told Mama we weren't going to be married in Laos, but probably in Paris. She wanted to come, but I said she couldn't. Khounta and I had never discussed it. When it came time to leave, she wept and sobbed, "I'll never see you again." Her tears and words tore at my heart. I can still visualize her standing in front of the doorway to my sister's bedroom next to the square piano, and hear her crying in pain. It brings tears to my eyes. I am sorry now. I would have liked her to have been with me

When I got back to Vientiane, Khounta was gone. I started at the lycée, where I taught the equivalent of ninth and tenth-grade students English from books written in French with British cultural subjects. I could not learn how to play cricket from the book any more than the students could.

Jennifer Johnsen, my roommate from UC Davis, her husband Dennis, and their three young children came to live off Phaholyothin Street in Bangkok. Dennis was a veterinary doctor doing his service with the U.S. Army. I went down several weekends to visit. We went swimming at the Florida Hotel near the Victory Monument. The U.S. Army had special arrangements for their troops and families to swim there. I went as Jennifer's guest, so it was free for me, too. One evening Jennifer and Dennis carefully inquired if I would like them to fix me up with someone so we could go out as a foursome. It was then that I told them about Khounta.

In November, I told June and Ron Pulcini that I was going to meet Khounta in France and that we were going to be married. They knew we would get married, but not when. They were very excited about being let in on the elopement. I didn't know where or how yet because in France it was necessary for the mayor in the town in which you were living to post banns of marriage and to live in the town for forty days beforehand. My mother, with the help of her friend Dottie Kendall at the Piedmont Community Church, had arranged for us to be married in a Protestant church in Greece because a time of residency and posting banns were not required. When I wrote Khounta, he said he would not be married in a church.

I looked for my round-the-world ticket to fly to Paris. I had carefully put it away in my room so I would not lose it, but I couldn't find it. I had to buy a new round-trip ticket. A voice in my head nagged at me, asking if Khounta should buy the ticket. It reasoned he wants you to come to Paris; he should provide you the ticket. But, I argued, I agreed to go to Paris, I want to go to Paris, I had a ticket I needed to use, and Khounta doesn't know that I have misplaced it. He probably doesn't have the money to buy me one anyway. Then Khounta wrote that he couldn't meet me on my scheduled arrival date in Paris because he would still be on his study tour in Reims, but he would arrive a day later. So, I changed my ticket to include a day in Greece and sent Khounta a telegram to let him know.

The stopover in Athens was wonderful. It was my first trip to Europe. The air was sharp, the pale sunlight distant, and the city new and intriguing. I stood in line and was able to get tickets for my favorite opera *Carmen* for that evening. The next day on the plane, I sat between two very charming men. On the window-side was a very handsome young Greek from one of the islands. He loved my name, Penelope, because its origin is Greek. His mother knitted beautiful sweaters and sold them to tourists. He wanted me to visit him. I told him I was going to get married in Paris. On the aisle-side was an Italian with a bandage on his head. He had been in the opera the night before, and when the set was being changed in the dark, he had banged his head. We had a fun time on the plane. It was the Greek's first visit to Paris, too, and he wanted the three of us to get together for a drink when we landed. I told him I was going to meet my fiancé. That was agreeable to him, and he wanted all of us to go together. I did too. He looked very disappointed when I walked away with Khounta.

We gathered my suitcase and took the Metro back to Khounta's hotel. Walking to catch the Metro, he told me he had borrowed his friend's car and come to meet the plane the day before. When I hadn't arrived, he didn't know what to think. He couldn't borrow his friend's car again in case I had changed my mind and wasn't coming. I said I had sent a telegram, but I am not sure he believed me. He found it stuck up behind the telephone on the wall in the hotel lobby when we got there. He took it with an annoyed look, irritated that it hadn't been delivered to him.

We went to our tiny room. Khounta opened the bottle of champagne he had left chilling on the windowsill and poured two crystal flutes of greeting and relief. We were together at last and, after more than two years of being separated and secretly engaged, we really were going to be married.

Khounta's Chansomphou family, back row: Khounta, Uncles Noukham, Khamsouk, Mong, and Nouum; front row: cousin Bounluang, Aunt Chansy, Khounta's mother Im, Khounta's brother Prakan, Grandfather Bounmy, Khounta's sister Prakel "Kellie," Great Grandmother Kham (Bouaphan's mother), unknown, Grandmother Bouaphan, cousin Sounthorn, Aunt Chantay, cousin Oudone, circa 1938.

Khounta and his father Prak Praproeung, Vientiane, Laos, January 8, 1928.

Nang Im with her children *(left to right)* Prakel, Prakan, and Khounta,
Vientiane, Laos, circa 1937.

With Somsangouane, Savannakhet, May 1965.

With Dee Dick and Khounta's Mercedes 190SL in front of my house in Rainbow Village, Vientiane, 1966.

VW wreck by the side of the Friendship Highway, outside Korat, Thailand, August 1966.

My 25th Birthday photo with Khounta and Dottie and Al Bashor,
Vientiane, December 7, 1965. *(Venus Photo)*

PART 2

CHAPTER 18

Married in Paris

New Year's Eve 1968

The room was on the top floor of a five-story hotel. Students and Lao army officers taking advanced courses lodged there. The elevator went only to the fourth floor. From there, we walked up two short flights of stairs to our small, and, I thought, romantic garret at the head of the stairs. The hall light came in from the stairwell window and dimly exposed the doors to the rooms on either side of ours.

On entering our room, my eyes were always drawn to the changing picture composed in the window opposite. It was often snow flying or bouncing gently, or a pale yellow winter light, straining to be visible. Usually, it was simply a shade of gray. In addition to champagne, we placed oranges and cheese on the outside ledge to keep them cold. The double bed was just to the right of the entrance against the wall and filled most of the room. In the corner at the end of the bed was a sink with a fold-up bidet in a cabinet underneath. A thin carpet covered only the narrow aisle from the door to the window. The bare wooden floor at the end of the bed was cold to walk on.

The toilet was down the stairs, on the landing between floors. The people on the fourth floor had to walk up, and the people on the fifth floor had to walk down. The walls were thin, and every cough and shuffle could be heard. Fortunately, on our floor, it was usually silent because the single occupants on either side of us were often out. The walls were an aged yellow, and the ceiling over the bed sloped into the room. In the corner, opposite the sink was a chair that served as our closet, leaving only the bed to sit on.

"Get up. We get married today," Khounta said one gray morning after ten days in Paris.

What had I heard? "No, you promised me you'd tell me the day before so I could go to the hairdresser."

"Get up. Get dressed," he said.

I was angry. "We can get married another day."

"It's now or no time."

I rolled over and faced the wall. I could not believe what I had heard. I didn't want to get married with five minutes notice. I brooded for a while. Then I got up in anger and resignation. I loved Khounta. I did want to get married.

I couldn't even consider a shower. They were available on the first floor, but you had to sign up a day in advance and pay extra for hot water.

I began to put on my ivory wedding dress, sleeveless, hem above the knees and a wide attached belt, chilly for December in Paris, but useful for special occasions in Vientiane.

"You don't need to wear that," Khounta said.

The time to wear my wedding dress is at my wedding, I thought stubbornly and continued dressing. Long white gloves with buttons at the wrist kept my arms warm, and I had a very smart, gray, flared wool coat to keep out the cold. Sheer stockings and the white lizard-skin shoes and handbag completed my outfit. I skipped my mother's veil and left the white garter in my suitcase.

I asked about flowers, but he said, "Later."

We took a taxi to the Lao Consulate. Inside it was murky as if they were saving on electricity. The Consul was a short, plump man with porcine eyes in a fat round face. His oily, black hair was slicked over his pate. His black eyes darted back and forth from me to Khounta, and he smirked in a gloating way. Only he could marry us in France.

Khounta acted as if he wanted to leave as quickly as possible. We followed the Consul from the vestibule through a gloomy corridor to his dim, cheerless high-ceilinged room. He and Khounta spoke in Lao. I understood nothing. I felt embarrassed. The Consul teasingly smiled at me and asked in English, "Do you love Khounta?"

"Yes," I said. No other questions. No vows. No kiss. Only infants and small children are shown affection in public in Lao culture.

We had bought wide-band gold wedding rings at a jewelry store the day before. Khounta got them out of his pocket, and we put them on. We signed multiple copies of the marriage certificate and left. No one else was there. There was nothing more to do.

On the way back to our attic room Khounta directed the taxi to a flower shop where he dashed in and purchased a pot of white azaleas. I was surprised and amused. What a funny wedding bouquet! I smiled my thanks to Khounta and thought, how strange. Together we would enjoy the blossoms against the backdrop of falling snow outside our hotel window.

I asked Khounta about witnesses, and he said he would get someone in the hotel to sign in a couple of days. I never did meet the Lao army officers whose names are on the certificates. Though Khounta pointed them out to me later, I doubt if I could have recognized them if I had ever seen them again.

To celebrate our marriage, Khounta chose the romantic Rotisserie Perigourdine Restaurant de tradition at 2, Place St-Michel on the Seine with picture windows of Notre Dame Cathedral. The view, the white tablecloths, the uniformed waiters, the light, the warmth, the elegance, and the exquisite food made it a fairy-tale banquet that surpassed my romantic fantasies. The restaurant had a postcard, which captured the essence of its interior with a view of the cathedral. I sent it to several of my friends to announce the exciting news.

After a slowly unfolding lunch of many house specialties, we went back to the hotel to rest and prepare for New Year's Eve. The Lao Consul had invited us to his house to welcome in 1969. My idea of New Year's in Paris was a noisy, happy, festive bar or restaurant filled with people eating,

laughing, blowing horns, throwing streamers, drinking champagne, dancing, talking and singing. Or, at the very least, since it was also our wedding
day, a luxurious night in the Hilton Hotel.

I said I didn't want to go. Khounta said we had to go to be polite
because the Consul had done him a favor by marrying us. I went with
poor grace. The sight of the bottle of champagne we took with us
cheered me slightly. The Consul lived far from our hotel.

A couple that knew the way picked us up. When we arrived, the
other two or three people at the party inspected me, or so I felt. I was
self-conscious and tongue-tied. If the other guests spoke English, they
did not let on. We sat around the dining room table for a quick bite,
just to get the eating out of the way for the evening pastime: Cards. I
was excluded. The adults, as I thought of them, were gambling. They
played a Lao card game for a limited number of players, and there
was no place for me. Besides, I didn't know how to play. The fact that
it was our wedding day and night meant nothing to them. They had
been married for years, and they had grown children. Like Khounta,
they were members of the wealthy and politically influential class in
Laos; however, they weren't people with whom he ever chose to
spend time. He found their supercilious airs distasteful and silly.
Khounta liked to play cards for fun.

I sat in the darkened living room that opened off the dining room
and watched television. The card playing proceeded in Lao. The TV
yammered in French. I was totally ignored and isolated. I wanted to
see Paris shouting in the New Year. At midnight, Khounta stopped
the card playing just long enough to open the champagne and pour it
around. I got a glassful as, what seemed to me, an afterthought. The
card players were not interested in the date, the time or the drink, only the cards.

Khounta wanted me to go upstairs and go to bed. He reasoned I
must be tired sitting around in front of a flickering black and white
TV unable to understand anything. I was probably seen as an unso-
ciable detraction, too. The card playing was intense. I was too angry to
be pushed out of the way. I sat in the next room and contemplated

going out and finding my way to the Champs-Elysées and some action, but I was torn between doing what Khounta wanted and my fear of getting lost. I was too meek. Today, I would just go.

I sat in the next room until morning light slipped in the windows. People smiled and stretched. It was time to go home. We took a taxi back. Khounta was tired. I asked him how much he had lost. "$100."

I thought how thoughtless and mean his friends were to him on his wedding day. I wondered, who is this man who lets his friends do this to him, who feels that paying the debt of receiving a favor is more important than this momentous day?

The taxi let us off in front of our hotel. I told Khounta I wanted to get a newspaper and would be right up.

The first morning of 1969 was cold, damp and gray. The black, wet streets were empty of activity. The revelers of the night before were all in bed. I walked the kilometer to the Hilton Hotel. I checked the price of a room. $100. The exact amount Khounta had lost at cards. I went to the bar. There was only the bartender. I ordered a brandy Alexander and sat at a little round table along the back wall. I felt dreadfully sorry for myself and humiliated, but the drink gave me some peace. I actually felt relieved sitting there by myself. It was quiet. I could focus on the evening that had just passed. I asked myself, do I really want to be married to Khounta? Is this what life will be like? No communication? No consideration? Misunderstandings? Being ignored? Being isolated?

There had been no witnesses at the Embassy. The certificates were not signed. It was not yet final. I had another drink. I was calm. It was time to go.

I walked back to the hotel. Out front, Khounta was pacing the sidewalk alarmed that I had been gone so long. I said nothing.

The Honeymoon: January 1969

It was evening when we left for Orly Airport. Khounta's study tour continued in England, so it became part of our honeymoon. At the airport, Khounta checked in, but he didn't have a ticket for me, and the plane was full. What to do? As I stood at the departure gate, he said we would meet up in London and waved good-bye. My mind raced in dismay, how will I find him? I don't know his hotel. How will I get to the hotel? Will I get a ticket? How will I get a ticket? My mind stopped, overloaded, and I stared at his back as he walked toward the lounge door. He's leaving me! I stood there. People moved around me. Then an airline attendant in a dark blue uniform with a white blouse came toward me, waving a ticket. They had found a seat. I went to the lounge and found Khounta. He smiled and looked relieved, but at the same time grave and concerned. "They don't know about you," he said. He was worried about my arrival in England being an inconvenience. His thoughtfulness for his hosts was admirable, but what about me?

I thought, so what? We'll just pay the difference for a larger room and a second breakfast. But I saw that Khounta would have liked to have arrived alone, as planned. My presence embarrassed him. He didn't like to ask for help or favors.

At Heathrow, the officials meeting the plane were surprised but recovered graciously. They were concerned about not having a plan to keep me occupied while Khounta was visiting roads and bridges or having events planned for us in the evening. I would have loved to have seen Margot Fontaine and Rudolf Nureyev dance, but it was too late to get tickets. I assured them that I could entertain myself. I think they were inwardly grateful that I spoke English. An American bride was easier to deal with than a Lao bride who only spoke Lao. Khounta had a French interpreter.

London was gray and rainy. Every day after an English breakfast selected from the full range of British breakfast fare, an assortment, and quantity far exceeding the American Breakfast, Khounta would be picked up for the day. I entertained myself first with a bus tour that included the Tower of London to see the crown jewels. They were spectacular, so many and so full of light. I went to the Tate Gallery and the Victoria and Albert Museum. I wandered the main shopping streets and went to Harrods and Marks & Spencer.

In the evenings, Khounta and I looked for a place to have typical, local food, but were at a loss. What was typical? We thought it would probably be boiled. We went to an attractive place with white table-cloths but found the food bland and expensive. After that, we stuck to street kiosks selling hot-dog-like fare. One night we went to the movies and saw Disney's *Chitty Chitty Bang Bang.* We found the title reflected our mood and we laughed and laughed. For the rest of the trip when something amused us, we would say "chitty chitty, bang bang" and laugh.

Our planned honeymoon was in Greece, and after four days in London, we flew to Athens. We stayed in a comfortable pension with a room next to the reception desk. Khounta had brought a bottle of champagne with him, and I was looking forward to a romantic evening, just the two of us, but surprise, he invited the woman proprietor of the hotel to join us. I was miffed but didn't want to appear ungracious, so I said nothing. I asked myself why he had invited her. It was as if he wanted to share our good fortune with others. I thought this must be the Lao way.

One night, after drinking retsina at a little café, I wanted to walk up to the Acropolis and view it by moonlight. I imagined it would be very romantic, but Khounta got mad and told me that if I wanted to go, go ahead. He was not going. Maybe he was tired and didn't want to walk up the hill, or maybe he was afraid of what might be hidden in the dark. Fine. He didn't want to go, but why not tell me the reason? His sudden anger puzzled me.

During the day, we took bus tours to view ancient ruins, including the Acropolis. We especially liked the theater at Epidaurus. The acoustics are phenomenal. The limestone tiers of seats resonate and amplify the sound magnificently. We stood in the center of the stage, and without projecting our voices, they carried up and around to the top rows.

We had a wonderful time in Greece, eating in little restaurants and drinking raki, but, all too soon, we had to return to Vientiane. I had already missed the first two weeks of school. I had sent a telegram to the director telling him that I had married in Paris and advising him when I would be back.

The airplane landed at Wattay Airport. June Pulcini and some other friends met us at the airport. I felt like my wide, gold wedding band was flashing like a giant neon sign saying, "Stare here, she's a new bride." I was glad my friends met us, but we didn't know what to do. Should we invite everyone over for a drink? We didn't have anything planned or on hand. It was a little awkward, but finally, we all went our separate ways.

I wished I could ease back into the community as if nothing had changed, but this is what happens when one elopes. People want to look at the anomaly, and they wonder, why did they do that? It is a good question. We did it because Khounta wanted to, but I don't know why he felt that way. I wanted to get married, and I was happy to elope. I expected a *baci* (Lao ceremony) later. I came to learn that he generally did not ask me what I wanted, and I rarely spoke up.

CHAPTER 19

The First Year: 1969

Back Home, Settling In

We went to Khounta's house, now my new home. His mother and sister Nang Kellie, but not his brother Prakan, were waiting for us. They all spoke together in Lao and smiled a lot, but I didn't understand the conversation and Khounta didn't translate. I assumed they were congratulating us, but who told them we were coming? I smiled back and wondered what was expected of me. After a while, they left. Khounta told me his mother was unwell and that she was going to move in with Kellie and her family at Ban Phone Sa'at, that his mother said she would live with us later. I wondered to myself if I was the cause of her feeling unwell. Khounta's mother had been trying to marry him to a Lao woman for years. And what did he do? He married a foreigner! I got the feeling she did not like the idea. She had married a Cambodian, and he had left her with three young children.

Also waiting at the house was Khounta's wedding gift to me; his most loved and prized possession, his 1952 Mercedes 190SL sports car. He had it painted white for me while he was away. I loved the car, but I couldn't possibly feel the depth of meaning of this gift because I didn't think about it. It is only in retrospect that I appreciate how heartfelt the giving was. Cars were never important to me. They are something that takes one from point A to point B. I know they are important to some people. My mother always had her Cadillac, and Khounta had an elegant car. It was his trademark. In comparison, my gift to him was small. I didn't know I was supposed to give one until my mother told me it was traditional for a new wife to give her husband a gift. We had gone to Shreve & Co. in San Francisco, and I had chosen a small sterling silver case from which a nail file and scissors could be swiveled out. From that day on, he always carried it in his pocket.

June Pulcini had a lovely bridal shower for me in February. My friends from LAA, Betty Polak, Narumon, Claire Laubis, Patti Mathisen and others, came. We dressed in our Thai silk dresses. June had a beautiful, single-layer cake with a tall, decorative white bell on it. For me, it was the wedding cake that I hadn't had. She took photos while I ceremoniously cut the cake, just like at a wedding reception, albeit without the groom. The conversation and laughter were warm and generous.

Our first public exposure as newlyweds was later in the month when Arthur Ashe came to Vientiane. He was on the United States Davis Cup team, and the USA won in 1968. Ashe was on an Asian tour giving exhibition games. The game was held on the grass court behind the Service Géographique building near the Monument. Chansamone Voravong had gone to university in Paris, where his love for tennis matured. When he returned to Laos and became the Director of the Service, he had a grass court built behind his office building, the only grass court in the country.

It was a beautiful, sunny day and I felt my wedding band was radiating signals again, "Look. Newlyweds." I would be under inspection by Khounta's friends and colleagues, who were all delighted and relieved that he was finally married, especially the men. He was, after all, forty-two years old and had been flirting with their wives for years. Now they could breathe easier. After their scrutiny, I could too.

Going back to the lycée was simple. The students easily switched from Miss Breuer, which was difficult for them to pronounce, to Mrs. Khounta.

Khounta went back to work on a new vehicle registration project at the Ministry of Public Works and Transportation. He arranged for traffic nets. The police stopped every motorbike, car, and truck to see if the driver had a license and if the vehicle had a registration paper, neither one of which ever expired. If either were missing, the vehicle was confiscated and parked in a barbed wire enclosure at the That Luang fairgrounds until the documentation was completed. Some vehicles were there for many months and even years.

The House

I had always admired the house for its size and modern touches. The kitchen, however, was different. In a Lao home, the cooking is done in a detached space or room behind the house. If the house is on stilts, the kitchen is separated by a platform or is on the ground level. People cook on little hibachi-like wood or coal burning clay stoves. Food preparation takes place squatting or sitting on the wooden, dirt or cement floor. Some women sit on a small, little wooden bench or a rattan and bamboo seat the size of a footstool.

We had a large kitchen in our house, but no one had ever used it. One entered it from the door in the hallway at the bottom of the staircase, the dining room, or the back door. It had a long, very low counter with cupboards underneath. Four-inch-square, smooth, white tiles covered the counter and cabinets. The wooden doors were painted white and opened to a dark, damp-looking space, where large brown cockroaches danced. After the first glance, I never looked inside again. Against the wall opposite the counter was a long, wooden sideboard with sliding doors that stuck (what havoc they would play!) for dishes and utensils, pots and pans. A sink built into the tile countertop and a refrigerator completed the kitchen. The room was always dark because the trees and the walkway roof shaded the only window, which was next to the back door. The single fluorescent tube barely punctured the gloom.

Khounta bought a round, one-burner kerosene stove, about 12″ x 12″, like the one I had had as a Peace Corps Volunteer in Nakorn

Panom. On it, I could make breakfast coffee and prepare our soft-boiled eggs. He also had an antique toaster. Only one side of the bread toasted at a time. It was necessary to watch closely, or the toast would burn. When one side was ready, you pushed a lever that moved the bread to be toasted to the other side. I made breakfast every morning and carried it upstairs on a wooden tray to the bedroom, where we would sit on the bed to eat. A morning breakfast tray was a habit we followed all our lives. We would eat and make plans for the day.

Lunch was at home. Several restaurants prepared take-away meals. We had French food, which the driver would pick up in a tiffin box (four round, stacking, enamel containers that slid onto metal side bars and locked at the top). An appetizer of pasta or something else, the main course of meat and vegetables, and a salad made up the meal. We had this at the dining room table if I got home in time. If not, I carried my lunch to the bedroom where Khounta always took a nap until he had to be back at work at two o'clock. Sometimes, I rested too. It depended on whether I was tired or if I had classes to prepare for. For dinner, we went to a restaurant.

We didn't have a cook, but we had a houseboy who was about thirty-five years old. His name was Chan. His job was to pick up our lunch, wash the cars, do the laundry, clean the house, and water the garden. He also had to patrol the neighborhood at night with three or four others when it was our household's turn to be on guard against enemy infiltrators. They usually carried rifles of some sort. People were afraid of enemy soldiers planting bombs or shooting fiery arrows onto the wooden roofs. I never heard of any incidents.

We didn't have any air conditioners. We had sliding glass windows in thick wooden frames on the inside and louvered shutters on the outside, but no screens, so we never opened them. The first couple of months, January and February, were still in the cold season, and not too bad. But by mid-March, it was unbearable in the bedroom, similar to being in a car in the hot sun with the windows rolled up. We moved outside to the covered side porch over the carport where we slept under a mosquito net and were exposed to the dusty street, noise, people, and cars passing. It was not romantic. At night, in my nightgown, I had to look swiftly out the door to see if anyone was around and then scurry and duck under the net. Our marriage was suffering from the hot weather and sleeping in public, but air conditioners were very expensive. I was finally able to get one tax-free from a good friend at USAID. If he had been found out selling one to non-USAID personnel, he could have gotten into a lot of trouble. We moved back inside. Saved! Connubial life resurrected.

Classes at the Lycée de Vientiane ended in June, and I developed a summer English language program to be held at the LAA for the best English students from the four high schools in Laos, one each in Pakse, Savannakhet, Luang Prabang and Vientiane. It was a smashing success, with classes in the morning and activities in the afternoon.

After the course ended, I still had time for a vacation. I had the remaining half of my round-the-world ticket from Hawaii. I hadn't used it to go to Paris because I had hidden it away in the bottom dresser drawer in my room at the Pulcini's house. In the move from there, I had found it. I needed to use it or lose it. My mother had loved seeing India. She had told me that I would have to wear blinkers to see and enjoy the beauty of India's artistic heritage, and not dwell on the condition of the poor people. I wanted to go and asked Khounta if he would go with me. He had been there before and said he never wanted to go again. It made him too sad to see the disease and poverty of the street people.

My good friend Patti Mathisen was visiting her parent's Art and Bobbie in New Delhi. I knew them from when they lived in Vientiane and Art had worked for USAID. He had transferred to New Delhi in 1968. I wrote Patti and asked her if she would be interested in going to Bombay to see the Ajanta and Ellora caves with me, and if she would go what I called Peace Corps style, that is trains, pedicabs, cheap hotels, and food. She agreed if I would travel to some other places with her first.

Yes! I would meet her in New Delhi.

My air ticket converted to a round-trip ticket from Bangkok to Bombay with a stopover in New Delhi. I took the train to Bangkok.

India Trip: September

When I arrived in New Delhi, Patti met me at the airport in her parent's chauffeured car and took me to their house. Bobbie had just come home from shopping and was waiting for someone to carry the groceries into the house. What followed would be my introduction to the strict separation of household duties in India. The cook was there, but carrying groceries was not his job. He only cooked. They were both waiting for the porter to come out of the house. He did the dishes, cleaning up after a meal and carrying things. You might wonder why Bobbie didn't carry the groceries in herself, but she was the memsahib. Her duty was to tell the employees what to do. Otherwise, she would lose face. If she didn't have her workers' respect, they wouldn't do what she told them to do. They had to have seven people working for them. Besides the dishes, the porter cleaned downstairs. The *dhobi's* sole task was to do the laundry. A little old man with a long white beard and turban who sat in the semi-darkness on the stairs between the main part of the house and the roof garden did the sewing. The gardener gardened. The security guard sat on the front porch with a big rifle from dusk till dawn and guarded. The driver drove and took care of the car. Having many servants was a reflection of the caste system.

We spent a couple of days getting train tickets and sightseeing in New Delhi. It was my first experience seeing sacred cows, of all colors, standing around in the streets. The cars drove around them. I loved seeing a cow harnessed to a lawn mower to cut the vast swathes of grassy areas found throughout the city. I thought it appropriate to buy a book on yoga, and I began to practice yoga breathing.

Patti wanted to go to Agra first to see the Taj Mahal and the Red Fort. I watched from the train window with interest as we rolled through the countryside. What fun to see a camel walking along, carrying its load just like any pickup truck speeding down the highway in America! The Taj looked beautiful, just like the photos. By the time we reached the Red Fort, the sun was intense. I had to go to the bathroom, and there was no place to go, other than behind the shrubs in the garden. I practiced yoga breaths in our hotel room.

From Agra, we went to Khajuraho, farther east along the railway line in Madhya Pradesh. I had never heard of it and had no idea what to expect. It was a quiet, dusty town with tree-lined roads. We stayed at a simple, one-story government guesthouse, which was within easy walking distance of what we had come to view, the temples dedicated to Shiva. In the bright, hot morning sun, I vividly remember walking around the temples trying to look casual as I stared at the art. We laughed, tickled by the startling postures, as we admired the relief carvings of one erotic scene after another. Patti walked on ahead of me and turned the corner. When she rejoined me, her face was red with a shimmer of perspiration, and her eyes were wide with alarm. "Oh, Penny, I'm so glad I found you. Some horrid boys were chasing me." I never saw them. We had lunch and took the next train to Benares.

Varanasi (Benares) is the most sacred place for Hindus in India. Here is the place on the Holy Ganges River where people come from all over India and abroad to take morning ablutions, drink the water, and collect water in containers to take home. People come here to die, and the dead are brought here to be burned at a cremation ghat not far from the river's edge.

It is also a holy place for Buddhists, and a large and important Buddhist school is here. Patti had heard that two Lao monks were studying there, so we looked them up. We found the school and one of the monks, but instead of orange robes, he was wearing street clothes. We wondered about that, and he explained that he had defrocked. We loved that word. He said he was not ready to lead a celibate life. He took us to see Buddha's footprint at Sarnath, the deer park where Gautama Buddha first taught the Dharma and where the Buddhist Sangha began. He offered to guide us to the Ganges to see the morning activities. He said we would see many Indian eagles, and smiled. We arranged for six a.m. the next morning and went to our hotel.

The room was a bit of a disaster, even by my standards. The bathroom was en suite, but there was water leaking everywhere. The whole place was filthy, mildew painted the walls, and the air was fusty. It was only for one night of sleeping, so we endured. I practiced yoga breathing.

The next morning the three of us took pedicabs to the Ganges where steps were leading into the river. We got a boat and went out on the gray, soupy water. Smoke was rising from funeral pyres, a dead cow floated by, as did little piles of charred wood and bodily remains. If a family did not have enough money for sufficient wood for a full cremation, whatever was left when the fire burned out went into the river. Our former-monk friend pointed out the Indian eagles. He used those words for the vultures that cleaned the river. They were everywhere, including on the cow's carcass. It was still early, but Patti and I had seen enough and went ashore to find a tasty breakfast.

It was a little drizzly, and the streets were under repair, making walking unpleasant. We felt ready to move on and decided to go to Jaipur, the famous red city. It would be an overnight train. We wanted a sleeping compartment to ourselves, one that we did not have to share with any men, and we wanted to be able to lock the door. Patti was very nervous about men getting into our compartment. The ride was without incident, but the train arrived at five a.m., and the city was not awake yet. It was the end of the line, and the train was not going anywhere for a while, so the conductor let us stay on board until six. Then we had to leave. We found a nearby railway hotel. It had a dormitory room with rope-strung beds and metal lockers to padlock our possessions in. We headed for the toilets. What relief after the long trip! I came out and looked at Patti. She appeared stricken. "Patti, what's wrong?" I asked.

"I can't squat," she replied. Such a predicament had not occurred to me. I'd lived with a squat toilet in Thailand for two years, and Patti had lived in Laos with her parents for several years. Of course, USAID houses only had western facilities, but the rest of the country, restaurants included, did not have them.

As the sun came up, we wandered around looking for a western toilet and breakfast. There were no people about yet. The morning light on the few red buildings we saw was beautiful and peaceful, but we had not done any homework on places to visit, and we had no guidebooks. We didn't know where to go.

The situation reminded me of how I had felt in 1964. After a long bus ride from Fort Benning in Georgia to Washington D.C. and followed by several days being a tourist in New York City, I went to Coney Island, but I had not considered when to go. I had taken an early morning train, and I arrived about eight a.m. The place appeared vacant. There were no crowds of fun-seeking people smiling or screaming on the roller coaster. I saw several men sleeping on benches with newspapers over their faces, and one man was hosing down the boardwalk. The rides, the hot dog stands, and other kiosks hadn't opened yet. It was too early. I went directly to a phone booth and telephoned my mother to tell her I was coming home.

In the same way, Patti and I were both feeling lonely, homesick and travel-tired. Over breakfast, we agreed to fly directly to New Delhi. As it was, our plane had a stopover in Agra. We spent another day in Delhi getting train and plane tickets for Kashmir. I practiced yoga breaths.

I felt fine when we boarded the night train from New Delhi to the end of the line in Jammu eleven hours away and still 211 miles from Srinagar. We had a compartment. I had the top berth, and she had the lower berth. It was stifling hot. Sometime in the night, Patti wanted to change because the fan was blowing on me and not her. I happily changed because although I was sweating profusely, I was getting chills and the fan was uncomfortable.

At last, the train arrived, and we could get into the open air. The train station was a blur of arms, legs, and bundles going in all directions. We got a pedicab to go to the airport, the type where one sits on a wooden bench behind the driver. When still in the station grounds, I leaned over the side and vomited a disgusting, bright yellow stream.

It shocked me, and I felt slightly embarrassed, especially for Patti, but I was too groggy to care very much. What was wrong with me?

When the pedicab stopped, we found we were not where the airport was! We had to take a very long bus ride. Patti negotiated it. I was walking comatose. We got seats somewhere in the middle of a crowded bus. She had me sit by the open window. I sat and swayed, seeing only the back of the seat in front of me. Patti told me later that I had continued to be sick out the window and complained loudly of the body odors on the bus. Fortunately, no one understood English. After an eternity, or so it seemed, the bus stopped. All the foreigners had to get out and walk to a visa checkpoint about 200 yards away across a hard, dirt field. I struggled to get up and started walking. Patti tried to help me, and people could see I wasn't going to make it. Somehow I was back on the bus, and Patti took care of our passports. After another eternity, we arrived at the airport. But by now it was afternoon and our morning flight was long gone. The afternoon flight was full. We sat in the airline manager's office, not knowing quite what to do. Should we get a hotel room? Did we need to buy new tickets? Would we forfeit the tickets we had? When could we get a flight?

Patti consulted, and I slept. By some means, she got us on the afternoon flight to Srinagar. At last, we arrived. Immediately upon leaving the airport building, we were set upon by boatmen wanting to show us their houseboat on Dal Lake. Patti asked me what we should do. She was tired of making all the decisions.

I looked and pointed my head in the direction of one man. He helped us with our bags to a small, motorized boat, which would take us to his houseboat. The houseboat was long and wide. In the front was a sitting space, separated by a half partition from an eating area complete with a table and chairs. Next was a walled-off bedroom with two beds and an attached bathroom that was reached by going along a walkway on the side of the boat. I lay down on the closest bed, said, "This is fine," and closed my eyes.

When I opened my eyes, the room was gray. A strip of bright light slanted in from the doorway. I didn't care. I closed my eyes. My clothes and the sheets were wet. During the night, I had wobbled into the bathroom to wring out my Indian cotton kurti several times. The mattress felt like it had lumps in it. My breathing was shallow, and I couldn't sleep on my right side facing the wall. It was too painful. I had to sleep looking towards the floor and the doorway, but it wasn't comfortable. I usually sleep on my right side. Patti's bed was at the end of the room at right angles to mine. I had to pass her to get to the bathroom.

I slept all afternoon, all night, the next day, and the next night. On the third day, the boatman came to our room in the morning and said, "I think your friend is sick. I have brought a doctor." In fact, Patti had gone with the boatman to town to find a doctor and bring him back to the houseboat. The doctor looked at me and prescribed Terramycin tablets after a glass of warm goat's milk, three times a day.

I thanked him. Patti went with the doctor, got the tablets and came back. The doctor asked her for help in getting to the United States to continue studying medicine. The boatman heated some goat's milk, and I took the tablets and fell asleep again.

In the afternoon, I heard some cloth hawkers ringing a bell and shouting their wares. Going boat to boat was a common way of selling. I struggled out of bed to tell them I was not interested and to please go away. There were two heavy-set men in white tunics with material stretched between their extended arms, shouting. A third man was steering their small boat, which sat low in the water. It was brimming with colorful lengths of cloth and clothing for sale. I tried to speak, but only strangled air came out of my mouth, and I was gasping for breath. Finally, I whispered, "Please go away." They got the message and moved on.

I went back to bed and tears ran from my eyes. I don't want to die in Kashmir, I thought. Not now. In the evening, I had another dose of goat's milk and tablets.

In the morning, I felt much better. Patti and the boatman were pleased. Patti had been lonely and bored not having a companion to be a tourist with. We rented a motorized water taxi and toured around the lake. Dal Lake is large and a beautiful blue. Along the shore, colorful houseboats were moored nearby the city. We visited some lovely hanging gardens across the lake from where we were staying. Patti had heard about a fortune-teller, so we went to see him. Our water taxi driver knew where to take us. We got out of the boat, took a bus and then walked up an exhausting gravel and rock trail to find him. When we arrived at his house, he was sitting in front on a mat under the roof overhang, counseling a couple whose son had been put in jail. We waited until they left, then we took off our shoes and sat in front of him. His English was minimal, and I was fading. His warm blue eyes stared into mine, and he spoke at great length. The boatman helped with a few words of translation. He told me I would begin having children when I was thirty and would have a total of nine if I didn't use contraceptives. He said my husband would go on a trip without me. He also said that Asia's fighting would be resolved within three years, unfavorably, and that I would have to leave Laos, and that Khounta would have to go too. We came away skeptical, but happy.

We went back to the boat, and I had some more milk and pills. For entertainment, the boatman brought out some Kashmiri traditional clothing, and Patti dressed up, and I took photos. Later we took another water taxi to the city for some souvenir shopping and bought airline tickets departing the next day to New Delhi and, for me, on to Bangkok and Vientiane.

The reason I had come to India was to visit the Allora and Ajanta Caves, and I would have gone, but the lack of breath and the pain prevented me. I couldn't carry my bags. My mother and Esther had gone there after they visited me in 1966, and Mama was always telling me, "You must go, Penelope. The drawings on the walls are beautiful and a wonder to see."

When I arrived in Bangkok, there wasn't a connecting flight to Vientiane, so I went to Jennifer's house. During the day, I had a check-up at the U.S. clinic. At night, I slept on a mattress on the floor next to her daughter, Cyndy, asleep in her crib. She was only three years old, and I was worried that I was contagious. In the morning, I had to roll onto my side and get on my hands and knees to stand up. There was a great heaviness in my chest.

When I arrived home, Khounta was surprised and delighted to see me. He hadn't expected me for another week, and I hadn't telephoned. One didn't. It was so difficult and expensive. I told him I had come home early because I was sick, but perhaps he didn't hear me. Besides, I looked and sounded all right. He was so happy to see me he said, "Let's go on a picnic," and, of course, we went. "You get the chairs," he directed. "I'll get the rest." The chaise lounges seemed heavy in my condition, but I managed. Being home was comforting. The picnic was fun and reassuring. I had not died in Kashmir.

The next day I went to the American Clinic. The X-ray report from Bangkok showed I had pneumonia. This time, tetracycline was prescribed, and I was ordered home for ten days of complete bed rest. I was not even to get up to eat. I was concerned about being ill as I had received a second Fulbright-Hayes teaching grant for 1969-70 and school was starting at the lycée in a week. I took the medical report to the school director and then went to see Bill Allard, the Cultural Affairs Officer at USIS. The USIS offices were on the second floor of the building next to the lycée. I struggled up the stairs and to his room at the opposite end of the building. His only response was, "Who's going to teach the class?" I couldn't believe he was so focused on the special after-school course he had arranged for the East-West Center candidates for the University of Hawaii. I felt appalled that he didn't think of me, but I just said I was sorry and went home to bed.

I told Khounta I had pneumonia. He asked, "What's that?" The French pronounce it differently, and we did not look it up in the English-French dictionary. He announced he had to go out-of-town with a consultant the next day and would be gone for ten days. I thought, how can you go away, but I just looked at him and went to sleep.

When he came back, he told me with some excitement that he and the consultant had cooled off in the Mekong River. I was surprised at his animation. It was as if he had never been in the river before. Perhaps he hadn't. He belonged to the elitist class, which did not bathe in the river, and it was not something inspector generals of ministries did. Then, with regret, he told me that he had lost his wedding ring in the water. "I said it was loose when we got it," he remarked. I felt sad, too. We had had matching wedding bands. He had also learned what pneumonia meant, and he was very concerned and apologetic. He nursed me until I was well.

With very deep breaths, my lungs continued to tweak for three years. I stopped yoga breathing in foreign lands.

Christmas at Sattahip: December

On Christmas Day, we drove the gold Mercedes 250s from Vientiane to Bangkok. It took about nine hours. Driving was difficult because our car was a left-hand drive for Laos, whereas in Thailand people drive on the opposite side. The Friendship Highway had two lanes, and I was the navigator, checking to see when it was safe to pass the large trucks transporting goods north.

We were excited to be joining Jennifer and Dennis Johnsen on a diving and fishing trip to Sattahip in the Gulf of Siam, 140 kilometers southeast of Bangkok. The Johnsens met Khounta for the first time when we visited them on our way to Pattaya in April. Khounta had given them a fast game of ping-pong, and we had had fun eating and discussing politics together.

The Thai military had an air base at U-Tapao near Sattahip, which the U.S. Air Force used during the Vietnam War for sorties into North Vietnam. Many American troops were stationed there. Dennis was a U.S. Army major doing research at the SEATO Medical Research Laboratory in Bangkok, and so we had access to the base for gasoline for the car and oxygen for the diving tanks. He'd arranged a bungalow in Sattahip for us and for his brother Patrick, who would join us for a few days.

Dennis drove us down from Bangkok, and we settled in. The next day we went to the harbor at Sattahip to rent a fishing boat. The wharf was strung with lines of cuttlefish drying in the sun, and the breeze filled the air with their pungent, but not unpleasant, smell. Dennis had fishing lines. He purchased bait and negotiated a boat with a driver. Khounta hesitated. He was worried on two counts. He remembered his sea voyage in 1946.

In March 1945 during World War II, the Japanese captured Vientiane and in April, they captured Luang Prabang. The king had to declare the end of Laos as a French protectorate. Khounta was eighteen years old, and he left Vientiane and crossed the river into Thailand with some of his friends. They stayed in the jungle as resistance fighters.

In fact, although short-lived, there were not many Japanese soldiers in Vientiane. Their strategy of fear kept them in control. They moved around a lot, so the Lao thought that there were many more troops than there were, and they were very much afraid. In August, the Prime Minister, Prince Phetsarath, wired the provinces that the Japanese had surrendered, and the king assured the French that they were still in control. But Prince Phetsarath disagreed with the king and refused to recognize French authority because he wanted independence for Laos. He formed the *Lao Issara* or Free Lao. Khounta joined them for a few months, but in 1946 when Laos came under French rule again, Khounta went back to Vientiane.

Education in Laos was very elitist. Less than 2% of school-age children were enrolled in school, and the language of instruction was French. It was the French education system and included primary and middle school, that is, the first nine years of schooling. Khounta attended the Collège Pavie, in central Vientiane, where the medical school is presently located. The Lao wanted to govern themselves, but very few Lao had the necessary schooling. The French, needing government administrators, were looking for young Lao that they could send to France for further education. Khounta had done well at school, and he was chosen as one of the first three students that the French sent to Paris. The French probably didn't know that he had been Lao Issara. The students went by ship. Khounta remembered being seasick below deck the entire trip, which in those days was many weeks. Consequently, he avoided sea vessels of all types.

Second, he didn't know how to swim. Living on the banks of a river is no guarantee of being able to swim. The Mekong River is very fast moving, has whirlpools, is opaque with eroded earth, and has a lot of fallen vegetation bobbing along in it. In the six-month rainy season, trees and logs are a serious threat to all water traffic. Also, the Lao believe there are Naga, mystical creatures, and other dragon-like creatures living in the river near Vientiane to protect it. When Khounta was a young boy and went by boat to visit his father in Phnom Penh, he would have seen baby crocodiles in the waters in the south, as well.

Nonetheless, we were in the Gulf of Siam for a water holiday. With trepidation, Khounta stepped into the boat, and it moved out onto the water. The boatman found a good fishing spot. We put three or four hooks on our line and were pulling in fish two and three at a time. Khounta sat without moving for an hour. He watched, found he felt okay and joined in the fun.

We kept only the larger fish, nine inches or more, and when we had about twenty, the boatman took us to a deserted island. We jumped into the waist-deep water and waded ashore. The boatman gathered sticks, started a fire, and began barbecuing the fish. Meanwhile, Khounta made a dip of fish sauce, garlic, chilies, lime juice, a little sugar, and water. As the fish came off the barbecue, Khounta would taste each fish and declare, "This is the best, better than the last one." We laughed and ate and then ate some more; sure that with each bite we had, we could not take another. Then Khounta would insist, "This is better. You must try this one," and we would eat more. We ate them all! In the beginning, we had figured the boatman would have a good catch of fish to take home, but he only got what he cooked, and we shared.

On the other days, Dennis and Jennifer would get their diving tanks refilled at the base, when necessary, and we would go to different islands to swim, dive and snorkel. Neither Khounta nor I knew how to dive, but we snorkeled. He had never seen under the water using a mask and snorkel before and laughed with joy at being able to see the colorful fish up close.

At night, we talked, laughed, and played Hearts. One night we went to the base to see *Ice Station Zebra* with Rock Hudson. We sat outdoors in the hot, humid weather watching the actors move around in an icy ocean at sub-zero temperatures. I was so engrossed in the film that I was surprised I could feel so hot when I was enveloped by ice and snow.

As a wedding anniversary and New Year's present, I gave Khounta a new, gold wedding band, a duplicate of the Parisian one, which I had ordered at the jewelry shop across from the Settha Palace Hotel in Vientiane. This one fit, and I had had it engraved with our initials on the inside. He was delighted to have a new ring.

After New Year's we drove back to Bangkok, arriving in the late afternoon. Cyndy was overjoyed to see her mother and began to snivel for attention. I remember Jennifer saying firmly, "Stop whining, Cyndy." I was put off balance by this adult treatment of, in my eyes, a baby. My inclination would have been to hug her rather than scold her. I was getting lessons in parenting.

On January 4, buoyed by our memories of fun with Jennifer, Dennis, and Patrick, we drove back to Vientiane ready for work the next day.

CHAPTER 20

The Second Year: 1970

Our first wedding anniversary came and went. It was still honeymoon time for me. I was as much in love and confused by Khounta as ever. Khounta was busy in his job at the ministry, and I was busy with my teaching at the lycée and USIS. We continued to have food brought in for lunch and went out to eat for dinner. One could hardly prepare a meal on a one-burner kerosene stove. Besides, I didn't have the time or inclination to cook.

Khounta played tennis for an hour after work at the court he had built in front of his office at the ministry. In the evenings, as usual, we often got together with Khounta's old friends Laurent, Boulom, Nyinera, and their wives and played cards. Sometimes Souriya, a member of the royal family, came to play too. They played a Lao game that I gradually learned how to play, but only four could play at a time. It was fun to play, but I usually had to watch, which became tedious. The spouses sat and watched or chatted, but I couldn't participate because I didn't understand Lao and was too shy to try. So, after many evenings of boredom, I began to take a nap. Of course, it would have been rude to do that if I had spoken Lao. After a while, I took along a book to read. I couldn't apologize for reading either, which I would have done if I could have. I'm sure they thought I had no manners. No one said anything. That is a Lao thing. If you are doing something that they consider impolite or wrong according to their culture, they won't tell you. Because you are a foreigner, you are excused, but not forgiven, which is to say, you will be gossiped about later. I hadn't lived with Lao people or socialized with them before. I had my slight knowledge of Thai etiquette, but beyond that, I was in no man's land. I didn't even realize how improper I was being. Khounta didn't apologize for me or inform me of Lao cultural etiquette and conventions, and that was wrong of him as his family and friends naturally thought he would do so. Consequently, when I did something culturally inappropriate, they thought, perhaps, that I did it to ignore their ways and was being ill-mannered deliberately. I realize now that Khounta was also embarrassed by my behavior, but maybe he thought I would change without him saying anything, through osmosis, I imagine.

Khounta firmly believed that he wasn't a teacher and couldn't bother to help me. I was unaware of this at the time, but I had experience with his way when trying to learn Lao. Khounta wanted me to speak Lao, but not to him, and he refused to help me. He would not listen to me. One time when we were driving along Sethathirath Street near Mahosot Hospital and Khounta spoke to me in English I answered in Lao. This exchange continued for about five minutes at which point he stopped talking to me. He was so angry he drove me home, dumped me, and took off again. I never tried to speak Lao with him again. He wanted to learn English, and so, selfishly I thought, that is all he would speak or allow me to speak. I was unhappy not to learn Lao with him. I wanted to be included when he met with his friends.

Soukwan and Baci

A *baci* ceremony can be held at any time for occasions such as a birth, a wedding, a trip overseas or any other event deemed worthy. A *soukwan* ceremony is similar to a *baci*, but it is more formal than a *baci*. Its purpose is the raising of the soul and the calling back of that which is lost, such as health or luck. When people or animals get sick, it is said, "We have lost spirit," or "Our spirit is weak." The person who officiates is called a *mo phon*. He is traditionally a monk, a former monk or a respected elder. He sits in front of the beautiful silver *baci* bowl with the participants sitting in a semi-circle around him. He chants details in Lao about the person or persons the ceremony is for, and then he chants blessings in Pali. At the end, he conveys good wishes in Lao, as appropriate, such as, may you be free from pain, may you live well and be healthy, may you be rich and win the lottery. Then people tie white strings around the wrists of the person for whom the *soukwan* is held to keep the good spirits in. People also tie strings around each other's wrists and wish them well.

Apart from different focuses the *soukwan* and *baci* ceremonies are essentially the same. A *baci* is usually for happy transitional events. It is particularly essential to mark a wedding. That is why I had a *baci* for my daughter and her husband when they got married in 1995.

Lao people have a way of often not giving invitations until the day before an event, and Khounta often carried it to the extreme of not telling me at all!

One ordinary day, indistinguishable from any other in the workweek, as unremarkable as a daily breakfast, I came home after school, parked my car in the carport next to the front door, gathered my books and purse, turned the doorknob, and went into the house. A beautiful and unexpected sight greeted me. Sitting on mats on the living room floor was a group of women, including Nang Im, gathered around a large, silver bowl holding a decoration of artfully rolled banana leaves with marigolds on them, white strings and candles. I had not expected my mother-in-law or her friends to be there. They were having a *baci* or *soukwan* ceremony in our house! I could not have been more surprised.

It was wonderful! I hurried upstairs to get my camera. When I came down, Khounta angrily told me to put my camera away and not to take any photos. "Later," he said. His manner and tone of voice hurt me. I went back upstairs to the bedroom, confused and bewildered. Why did he speak to me like that? What did I do wrong?

When I did not come back down, he came up and told me to come down. I was sitting on the end of the bed crying and said no. He left, and his sister came, distraught, and asked me to come. She said it was a ceremony for her mother, I think. My comprehension of Lao was minimal, and if I could have understood what she was saying, my life might have been very different. Unfortunately, I was stubborn and refused. Khounta had scolded me like a child in front of the guests.

When I had walked in the house, I didn't know if the ceremony was over or if they were waiting for me. I didn't know what the ceremony was for. Maybe it was for Nang Im because she had been ill, or, perhaps, for Khounta and me because we were newly married. Maybe it was to bless the house?

I stayed in the bedroom until the people left, and the living room was straightened up. We never spoke of that day. Khounta gave me no explanations, and I never asked him or anyone for them. He was angry, and I realize now that I had embarrassed him in front of his family and the elders. I knew of no Lao person I could ask for enlightenment. My friends and colleagues were all foreigners, primarily American and British. From that day on we never went to a *baci* or *soukwan* ceremony.

I knew it was the custom to have a marriage *baci*. I had been to one in northeast Thailand when some Peace Corps friends had married. I always wanted one and wondered why Khounta never mentioned our having one. I figured since we didn't go to any, he didn't want one himself. He didn't like crowds or to be obligated in any way. There is a Lao proverb that goes, "Eat the ghost's food, listen to the ghost's words," meaning accepting a gift obligates you to the giver. Besides, he was shy and didn't like being the focus of attention.

By not attending *bacis* we were out of mainstream Lao life. How many did we miss? What did I lose? Did it matter?

Penang at Pimay: April

At Lao New Year's in April, we went to Penang for ten days. We took the train as far as Bangkok and then flew the rest of the way. We had a hotel on the beach, but our room faced the mountains. I didn't think it was worth the additional cost to look at the ocean when we would be on the beach all day. Khounta was angry because I had agreed to the hotel clerk's offer of rooms. When I realized how he felt, I suggested changing rooms, but since a decision had been made, he refused to move. I believe he would have felt embarrassed.

There were only about three hotels on the beach at the time, and they were not more than ten stories high. The water was beautiful and calm. I was able to teach Khounta how to swim. At one point, however, he became irked with me. He wouldn't tell me why. I got the silent treatment for a few days. It was not fun, and I was feeling lonely. I had burned myself severely when I fell asleep on the beach with no one with me. I was so angry at his behavior that one morning I took a bus into Penang and went sightseeing alone. Then, luckily that evening at the hotel I met a friend. He worked in Vientiane and had been to Nepal. Khounta wanted to see Mt. Everest, and so he became civil to me again. My friend, who was cheerful and lots of fun, joined us for meals and chats. It was at this time we decided to go to Nepal over the Christmas break.

Nang Im Moves In

One day I came home to find that Nang Im had moved in with us. It was not a complete surprise because she had been living in the house with Khounta before we got married. While we were in Paris, she had become ill and had gone to live with her daughter, saying she would be back.

When I first met Khounta, he lived with his mother in her small, wooden one-story house on short, one-meter stilts on Khun Boulom Street, a very busy commercial street. His mother's house was the only one left on the road. All the other buildings were three-story shop fronts. While I was studying in Hawaii, his mother leased the property to a Chinese merchant for ten years. Her payment was the three-story, three-storefront, cement and brick building he was obligated to construct. This kind of agreement was a very common practice in Laos.

The Lao American Association building was a similar arrangement. The United States Information Service built a three-story building of classrooms, offices, and an auditorium on Royal Lao Government (RLG) land with no annual rent due. At the end of ten years, the land and structures reverted to the RLG unless a rental agreement could be negotiated should USIS want to continue to use the property. As it was, it was a moot point because USIS left after five years, the RLG was out, and the Lao PDR was in. The new government asked LAA to shut down its operation a month after it declared Lao National Day on December 2, 1975. The *Khaosan Pathet Lao* (KPL) is located there now next to Khop Chai Deu restaurant.

In the beginning, I was happy with Khounta's mother moving in. I wanted to get to know my mother-in-law. We ate lunch and dinner together every day. Nang Im and I tried to talk to each other, but my Lao was rudimentary, and Khounta wouldn't help by translating for her or me or by teaching me Lao. At the same time, he kept after me to talk to his mother. The Lao I got in language class was not helpful for family conversation. The only thing I understood from her was that there had been a fourth child, a girl that had died.

In the mornings, we had breakfast in bed, as usual. His mother, seemingly, became irate with me every morning and would shout at me. I couldn't understand what she was saying. However, one day, I finally got the gist, which was that I was too noisy because I slammed the sliding cupboard door. I tried not to, but it stuck. When it suddenly became unstuck, it would slide shut with a big bang before I could stop it. Then one day she shouted, "You think this is your house, but it isn't. It's mine." That was news to me.

I took the breakfast up to Khounta and told him what she had said and asked if it were true. He said to take it easy. "You don't understand what she's saying."

I said I knew. "*Khoy, khoy* means gently," referring to the banging. He said that was not what she meant. I demanded to know what she meant and whether or not it was her house. Earlier, when he had told me that he had built the house, I had understood that to mean that it was his house.

He never answered my questions. He just told me to take it easy, again. "You don't understand."

That, of course, just made me more angry and upset. "If I don't understand, please explain," I implored. He didn't say another word.

He finished his breakfast, got up and went to work.

Meanwhile, meal times with his mother were unraveling. We could not communicate. Khounta wouldn't help us, and so we ate in silence. Or Khounta and his mother talked and ignored me. I was missing our time together, and finally, I asked Khounta if we could have dinner out together some evenings. He said no. I did understand that that would be unkind to his mother, but I was not getting any time alone with Khounta. I still felt like a newlywed.

Visit to the USA: September

My Fulbright-Hayes teaching grant finished at the end of August, and I had agreed to accept the position of Director of Courses at the LAA beginning in October. For the summer months, I had been both Acting Director, while the director was on vacation, and Acting Director of Courses because USIS was downsizing and had eliminated the position. I made plans to visit my mother for the month of September in California. Family life was getting on my nerves. I asked Khounta if we could stay in a hotel and have dinner and be alone together the night before I left. He said no.

At breakfast the morning of the day I was to leave, I asked Khounta if we could have lunch out, just the two of us. He said no, and left for work. At that point, something snapped. As I lay on the bed, I began to scream, but it wasn't a high scream. It was more of a low guttural moan, a cry of pain from deep inside me. When I heard it, I was surprised, and I tried to make the sound louder and louder. Khounta was getting into his car, but he stopped, ran back upstairs, and told me to be quiet. I looked at him. I had no thoughts in my head. I kept screaming.

He gathered me off the bed, carried me into the bathroom, put me in the bathtub, and turned on the cold water. Even then I could not stop screaming. Finally, the cold water got to me, and I began to sob. He didn't put his arms around me or say anything comforting. I believe he was simply dumbfounded. I told him, "It's her or me."

At last, I got out of the bathtub. Khounta put a towel around me, and I went to bed. He went to work. He had had enough embarrassment for one day.

In the afternoon, he took me to the airport. My friend Patti Mathisen came to see me off. She looked at me with surprise and concern and asked, "What happened to your voice?"

My throat was raw from screaming, and my voice was low and raspy. I said, "I must be getting a cold."

I enjoyed my California stay. I didn't tell my mother or anyone how unhappy I was. I was too embarrassed about losing it. In any case, it was my problem. I loved Khounta, and he loved me. We just had clashing cultural and personal differences to work out. When I came back, everything went on as before. Neither of us ever mentioned my fit.

Khounta introduced me to the swimming pool in the compound of the EDL, Électricité du Lao, and its generating plant in Sokpaluang village. It was very special. The pool had been built by the Lao electricity company, which came under Khounta's jurisdiction in the Ministry of Public Works and Transportation. He said the water circulated through the electric power generating system to keep it cool. I noticed it had become a public pool when I returned in 1993, and later it was replaced by a big office building. We were the only ones who went there. It was like having a private pool. It was very large with a standard and a high-diving board. A grassy slope was on one side of it. It was delightful to put down my towel and stretch out in the sun. It was quiet, too, with no radios or boom boxes, no people talking or children running around. We went every weekend for months, Khounta with his *Paris Match* magazine and me with a novel. I was grateful to Khounta for finding this spot.

But I had to have something more to maintain my sanity. There were some apartments with private parking on SamSenThai Street above the shop fronts. One could drive down the one-way street, make a quick left into the tunnel between two offices and be secluded in the building courtyard. The parking area was always in shadow because of the angle of the sun and the height of the buildings. There was a vacant apartment overlooking the street, and I rented it. It was a small studio apartment, and the manager was an American friend who was like a doctor at keeping confidences. If it had been a Lao, all of Vientiane would have known overnight. Just knowing I had a place to go to be alone gave me a sense of freedom, air to breathe, and the strength to continue.

I never told Khounta. Patti agreed to say it was her apartment, and we shared the rent. Now I had a secret place to go to if things became too unbearable.

CHAPTER 21
The Third Year: 1971

The Move: January

"We're moving today," Khounta announced.

"What do you mean?" I asked.

"We're moving to another house. Get up. Get ready."

"You didn't tell me. I haven't packed anything," I said.

"Never mind," he replied. "You don't need to."

"Where are we moving to?" I asked.

"Put some things in your car. You can follow me," he directed. "We're moving."

"But I don't have any boxes to pack in."

"You don't need them."

This move was a total surprise. The curtains were closed, and the room was still dark. I sat up and tried to gather my thoughts. I could hardly grasp what I had just heard. Last year, many months ago, I had said, "Her or me." Now, in January, we were moving. He had heard me.

I could hear men's voices downstairs. I dressed and went down. Men were loading our furniture into a pickup truck. No rugs, towels, blankets or packing material of any kind was being used to protect the items from scratches, scrapes or gouges.

Khounta put a load in his car, and I followed with one in mine. The house was about ten minutes away. I learned later that the house was

Nang Kellie's. I assumed that it belonged to her because he had asked her to move out so that we could move in. I found out a few years later that in reality, the house belonged to her husband Phanh. I found it incomprehensible that he could ask his brother-in-law to move out, and that Phanh would do it. I didn't know at the time, but Lao culture is matrilineal in that way. When a boy marries, he moves into his wife's house. So having girls in Laos is good because you get to keep your daughters, and you get sons-in-law, too. Also, the boy pays the dowry. When the son-in-law can provide a house for his wife and family, they move out. What came into play here was that Khounta was the oldest son, and the Lao custom is that younger siblings should defer to older ones. Position in the family is what counts. Also, it is the daughter's duty to care for the parents.

The new house, like the house in Ban Khoua Luang, was on a red dirt road in Ban Phone Sa'at between the U.S. Marine House, where the U.S. Embassy guards lived, and a Lao police electrical repair facility. It backed on Silver City, a compound of houses for U.S. Embassy and USIS personnel. It was a typical Lao-style house, just one step beyond a wooden house on stilts. It was wood above, but the bottom area had been enclosed with bricks and cement. Downstairs were the living room, dining room, kitchen, guest bedroom, and bath. It was a squeeze to get all our furniture in. We lived upstairs where there was one long room next to a short hall leading directly to a bathroom. On the right was our bedroom and to the left a storage room. There was no inside stairway. The only way to get from one floor to the other was to go out the front or back door upstairs and go in the front or back door downstairs. The front door led onto a covered porch. The back stairs relied on the overhang from the roof for protection from the rain.

Months of preparation had obviously gone into fixing up the house and yard. Out the kitchen door, Khounta had an enclosed patio built where a new style of life began. We ate all our meals out there, except for breakfast in bed. Also, he had installed a carport next to the house, and a high wall at the end of the lawn where it met the road.

Even the lawn was new. The turf had been brought in and covered what had been hard, barren, red ground. In the wall, a sturdy gate had been built to keep our German Shepherds, Zorro and Sheena, in and unwanted dogs out.

I went back to the house for a second load. The pick-up truck was there, and men were throwing my books in helter-skelter along with the bookshelves. I cringed inside, but there was nothing I could do about it. After I had delivered my second load, I drove down SamSenThai Street and into the sheltered driveway. I went to the apartment to think and gather myself from the shock. I didn't turn the lights on but just sat there, numb. My biggest question was why didn't he tell me what he was doing? Why the surprise? Why not plan with me? Why not give me some warning of the move? Was this secrecy a Lao custom? It was mostly me, me, me-questions. I never gave a thought to Nang Kellie, Phanh Inthavong, and their five sons. Where had they been living while this work had been going on? What did it cost Khounta mentally and otherwise to conceive and implement this move? We never discussed it. It was a fait accompli.

We moved in one day, and Khounta's sister and her family were back with Nang Im. That was not going to be a blissful living arrangement: Nang Kellie's five obstreperous, young boys and Prakan's young son and daughter, who had been living in the servant's quarters at our house for several months, would be together with Grandma. And she thought I made too much noise!

When I met up with Khounta later in the day, he asked me where I had been. I said, "Just driving back and forth. We must have missed each other." We never went back to the house where we began our married life and the place I thought of as ours.

Family Visit: February

Surprisingly, all our belongings arrived in the new house intact. The books in the back of the truck were put in a pile upstairs, and I divided them into the four bookcases, none the worse for being manhandled.

A couple of weeks after we had settled in, Nang Kellie and Phanh came over. They had a look around and admired how agreeable everything looked. They had brought some treats, and I got everyone something to drink. We sat around the table on the patio. I was very pleased that they had come to visit us. We had never gotten together socially before. I had seen them, of course, at various formal functions. After chatting for a short time, a deck of cards appeared. We were going to play for a little while and then go swimming at the Sokpaluang pool. I enjoy playing cards, but when the cards were dealt, I wasn't dealt a hand. I was surprised. When we played cards with Khounta's friends, there were always four hands dealt. I asked Khounta why I didn't get to play. He said it was a game for three people only.

Well, play a game for three people, I thought, but I didn't comment. I sat and watched. They laughed and chatted in Lao and were having a great time. I wanted to join in the fun, but I was ignored. No one looked at me. No one spoke to me. Khounta would not even let me see his cards. Was this Lao custom? I thought that they didn't want me, that they wanted to play by themselves. They were being Lao, and I was thinking American, but wasn't it my husband's duty to help me adjust to his culture? I felt very hurt and left out, so I went into the living room to connect the record turntable to the stereo system. We had moved everything in and put it in place, but it was not all connected. I had a lot of trouble trying to get it to work and was concentrating so hard that I didn't mark the passage of time.

After a while, a short time, I thought, Khounta came in. I said, "Hi, are we going swimming now?"

He said, "They've left."

"I thought we were going swimming," I said.

Khounta was furious. He felt I had insulted his sister and Phanh. They had come to visit us with sweets, in their house, and I had rudely gone off by myself, ignoring them. He shouted that he had given up all his friends for me.

I could only stare at him. I was shocked. What was he talking about? Why had he given up his friends? I liked them. We had fun together.

Life with Khounta was like a huge lottery game, but you didn't know there was a prize to be lost instead of won. You usually only got one ticket, and my number always seemed to lose. Life was a guessing game for me.

What I became aware of over the following months and years were four things.

One was that Nang Kellie and Phanh never came to visit again, and we never visited them or invited them over.

The second thing was that Khounta never asked any of his friends over, and we never went to anyone's house to play cards again. I never enquired about this because I didn't notice it. I was busy thinking about my new LAA job and maybe having a baby.

The third was that we didn't go to the pool anymore. I missed that a lot. I loved to go there. I loved to jump off the ten-foot-high diving board. It was scary. Afterwards, I liked to sunbathe on the lawn and sleep or just smell the grass and feel it tickle me. It was the only place like it in Laos. Once when I asked to go, he said we needed photo ID cards. That didn't make sense to me. He was the Inspector General after all and could go anywhere. But I gave Khounta a photo. The cards for us never appeared. I drove to see the pool several times, and no one was ever there. Another time when I asked to go, he said that a New Year's party had been held there, and some people had gotten drunk and vomited in the pool. We couldn't go until it was cleaned. I waited and waited. I never asked again, and to my great disappointment, we never went. In my mind, I wondered if Khounta was punishing me because of the day with Nang Kellie and Phanh, but he was hurting himself, too. I couldn't understand.

The last thing I noticed was his tennis racket. When we had lived in Ban Khoua Luang, Khounta played almost daily with the men in his office. He loved tennis and was quite skilled. I asked Khounta to hit the ball with me, but I played so poorly, he wasn't interested and refused. I sometimes played with one of the Fulbright teachers at the lycée early in the morning. Now at the house in Ban Phone Sa'at, the racket sat on the bookcase in the upstairs room. I had bought it for him at the PX in Udorn on our way to Pattaya one day. The grip was too big, and he had to have it adjusted. Was there no place in Vientiane to have it done, or was it meant to be a reminder that he had given up everything for me? On the other hand, did I just have a fanciful imagination? As far as I know, he never played tennis again.

Life at Phone Sa'at

In our new life, Khounta came home every day at five o'clock and sat out back and talked with Suwan, a police officer married to Khounta's cousin Dam. They lived with their eight children in a house built directly behind our house on Phanh's property. Khounta would change into his Bermuda shorts, sit shirtless, laugh, and talk with Suwan until dinner was ready. I loved seeing them there. I had it in the back of my mind to learn Lao from his wife and children, but I never made the time.

We were both focused on our work. I was in the process of revising the English language program at LAA and enjoying it very much. Khounta was doing ministerial inspections. When we moved, Khounta got us a cook. Her specialty was baked duck. She would find plump ducks, soften them somehow, and cook them with herbs to make a gastronomic delight. We frequently invited our American friends for dinner, and we often had duck. About this time, we had taken an interest in learning bridge. Patti Mathisen, who had joined IVS, had married John, an IVS colleague, who was a fanatic about duplicate bridge, and he agreed to teach us contract bridge. We met once a week for dinner, lessons, and laughter.

An Encounter on the Friendship Highway

Two northeastern Thai farmers,
Standing under the trees, not two meters from where we are sitting,
Staring over us towards the highway,
Lined, darkly tanned, expressionless faces,

Standing, still and silent.
Worn, grayed shirts; dark, faded shorts,
Black and dirty-white checkered sashes around their waists.
Bare feet.
A bucket.
A long coiled rope over one man's shoulder.
Machetes.
One machete in a holder at the taller man's waist.
The other man's dangling from his hand.
Machetes.
Wooden handles. Long, gray blades beginning narrowly at the
handle, broadening out, rounding to an upward point at the tip.

It had been a long day. We had left Bangkok at eight a.m. and driven our white Volkswagen sedan non-stop for six hours. We were trying to get to Nong Khai and home to Vientiane before the ferry crossing closed at five p.m. It was hot, and the car was not air-conditioned. We were hungry. We kept looking for a shady, secluded place to picnic along the highway. Finally, after thirty minutes searching, we spotted some trees only twenty meters from the road. Some bushes along the shoulder would hide us from curious eyes speeding by. Khounta pulled over and parked on the edge. He took the picnic basket from the trunk, and I carried the cooler, looking for some flat ground under the trees. The dry, cracked earth, the still, hot air, the dusty smell, the noise of leaves under foot, the buzzing cicadas all recalled other pleasantly languid picnics at home in the rice paddies. After walking for about thirty seconds, we chose a level area surrounded by tall, stringy trees with big, shady green leaves. No people or animals were visible in the dusty rice stubble paddies surrounding the trees. We lay the picnic cloth directly on the crinkling, brown leaves, and dried grass. I began to put out the tomatoes and cucumbers, the bread and the cheese.

The first farmer appeared, seemingly from nowhere, for a friendly chat and a cigarette. Khounta asked about how things were going in the area: the weather, the crops. No response. The second penniless farmer rustled in the leaves as he came and joined his friend. My back was to them as I put out the food. Khounta offered them a cigarette. No response. Nothing moved. Khounta's voice, the buzzing cicadas, the drone of cars passing on the highway, and the crackling of leaves under the picnic cloth vibrated in harmony. Funny they don't say anything, I thought, as I glanced up at them from the ground. I smiled. No response.

"Pack up slowly. No quick movements. Keep smiling and talking," Khounta cautioned conversationally.

I felt fear. My body tensed inside my skin. I knew I must not show it. I began to take slow breaths. The hot smell of the leaves and rice stubble intensified. I glanced at the highway. I could hear cars but couldn't see them. I looked up at the men again. They hadn't moved. I became mindful of all my movements. My left arm reached out. I saw my hand pick up a can. My right hand pressed the point of the can opener into the top of the can. I heard a slight hiss as some gas escaped. I smiled at my husband, and asked, "Do you want a Pepsi?" He took it. I opened mine and sipped it. I put the food back in the round, rattan picnic basket. Khounta kept up his monolog in Thai and Lao with the farmers. I stood, casually pulled the picnic cloth over my arm, and holding my drink in one hand and the basket in the other walked towards the car. Khounta followed with the cooler.

Back in the car we looked at each other and wondered grimly if and when our bodies would have ever been found.

An Operation

Khounta and I wanted children. Since I had left the lycée, we were making the right moves, but I was not becoming pregnant. I went to see Dr. Taggert at the American Clinic. He told me I was too old. That I would not accept. I was only 29. He suggested I see a doctor in Bangkok, and he made an appointment for the end of January at the Seventh Day Adventist Hospital. I took the train down, expecting to have a simple procedure of some sort, but found things were more

complicated than that. I was very naïve and had never concerned myself with how the reproductive system worked. I learned it was a big
operation. One could not just drop in and have their tubes cleared or
some other procedure. At Jennifer's, I cried because of the futile trip
and exhaustion and took the train back the same day. In mid-March, I
went back to the Seventh Day Adventist Hospital for lots of tests.

At Pimay in April, Khounta and I went to the beach at Pattaya for
a week. We drove down and had fun, but our pleasure was overshad-
owed by our lack of success in having a baby.

I told my boss, Dick Hughes, that I needed an operation in Bangkok that would take about ten days. The end of July would be the best
time. My administrative assistant John Cornel could keep things running smoothly. I had hired him in the summer of 1968, and he had
stayed with LAA during the time I was at the lycée. He was extremely
competent and familiar with the program.

I flew to Bangkok. Khounta couldn't come because of his work. I
had the operation, which showed I had severe endometriosis. One
complication after another kept me in the hospital. The ten days became
two weeks, and I had to have my Thai visa renewed. My friend Patti
Suggs brought her kids' T.V. and set it up in the room for me to watch,
but I was too tired. When Dick Hughes came down on business, he visited me and treated me with a vanilla milkshake, my favorite. I realized
I didn't particularly miss my husband, but I wished I had my cat Bush-
Bush to cuddle with. When I was better, I went roller-skating on the
badminton court behind the hospital building. Finally, after another ten
days, I was released from the hospital. I was so glad to be free. I could
barely endure the confinement. I stayed with the Suggses for a few days
because I still needed some stitches removed. When that was done, I
flew back to Vientiane. I had been gone exactly one month.

As a welcome home present, Khounta had thoughtfully bought
me a tom turkey and his mate. At first, I thought they were to eat, but
they were for pets. We loved to hear the turkeys gobbling around the
garden. I would gobble back to them, and they seemed to answer.
Khounta would pick them up and put them on a bar to roost at night.

Have you ever wanted something all your life—expected it, waited for it, and then found out, years later, it was not to be? I can remember my dream plans from grammar school: I would have triplet boys, and I would name them Jerry, Larry, and Terry. My thoughts concerned whether to dress the boys in long sleeve or short sleeve T-shirts with multi-colored horizontal stripes. I tended to long sleeves, having no concept of fad or fashion.

Now I was thirty, married and ready, and Khounta and I had learned that, through a combination of circumstances, we would never have children. Khounta had had himself checked in Bangkok, too, and the doctor prescribed pills for him. We even tried artificial insemination. Nothing worked, and the endometriosis returned. I had to go back on estrogen pills. Without them, the monthly pain was too excruciating to bear. Words cannot express our disappointment. I wanted to adopt, but Khounta's uncle had had very unfortunate experiences with the boy and girl he and his wife adopted. Khounta compared adoption to Russian roulette and said he would never do it. Sadly, there would be no children for us.

Invitations and Official Functions

Printed invitations could be put into three categories: 1. Weddings and social events; 2. Embassy national days; 3. Official, from persons of superior rank (ministers and the king).

Khounta was very perceptive and in some ways knew me better that I knew myself. I did things that interested me and didn't question why. We enjoyed being together, not talking. The silence was pleasurable. Our best times were passed at home, reading. Khounta knew that I wouldn't enjoy endless parties where only Lao was spoken. I would be bored and uncomfortable with tens of people I didn't know and couldn't chat with. Khounta never introduced me to his friends, and when I asked him their names, he wouldn't tell me. The few times we had to go to dinner at his minister's house, I came home with terrible migraines and a backache.

At the same time, since I didn't know about all the celebrations and weddings we were invited to, I didn't miss going to them. I know we received invitations because Khounta was very sensitive about being included. Invitations were the mercury in the thermometer of the social scale. Sometimes he would wonder aloud where his, our, invitation to an event might be. He would be irritable until it finally showed up. I ignored how he felt because it meant nothing to me. I never saw the wedding invitations.

Once, however, an invitation slipped through. We had been married almost two years, and this was the first invitation I had seen. I was very excited. Khounta wanted to know what we would give as a wedding present. We had some nice towels, but I didn't want to give them away. I thought we could give money in an envelope, which is the customary Lao gift. People didn't give presents of useful things as in the U.S., where it is considered gauche to give money.

I discussed what to wear with my girlfriend Patti and had my nails and hair done at Queen's Beauty Salon. I told my student who was the brother of the girl who was getting married that I would see him at the reception. It was to be a very grand affair. Khounta and I had given ourselves a tour of the house where it was to be held when it was under construction. It was a marvel. One huge room was devoted to housing the works for the only central air conditioning unit in the country. I was interested in seeing the completed and decorated house. When it was time to get ready, Khounta announced that we weren't going. He never said why. I was very disappointed and, I told myself it was because I hadn't produced a wedding gift.

In Laos, there was and is no mail delivery system. Government offices, businesses, embassies, schools, associations and the like have a post office box. Employees use the post office box of their employer. Someone at the office has the job of picking up the mail every day, after which it is distributed. If you don't work, it is possible to get a personal post office box. Invitations, however, do not come through the mail. They are usually hand delivered by the driver at the originating embassy or business to the destined person's place of work.

The only invitations I ever saw, other than the one I mentioned, were from embassies for their national day, and they never had a stamp. Khounta brought them home from the office. They were invariably addressed: M. Khounta et Madame. I always found this amusing, and sometimes irritating, as if Madame were an afterthought. I supposed the Lao were following French etiquette.

The embassy national day celebrations were the city's society highlights. The Lao ministers, army generals and the foreign ambassadors and heads of missions came with their wives. People a step or two below the chief personage were also invited. That is why we were always included. The Lao women wore beautiful Lao silk tops and traditional *phasinh*, and the foreigners wore long gowns. I felt like I was playing dress-up, and we would stand around at the embassy residence, drink wine, and enjoy beautiful, delicious hors d'oeuvres. The women gravitated to talk to the women and the men to the men. Khounta liked to tease his sister's friends. My friends and I would chat about the price of gold, trips to Hong Kong and Thailand, where to buy what, and tell funny stories. Later, the host ambassador would drink a toast to Laos and Prime Minister Souvanna Phouma if he were there, or Pheng Phongsavanh, the Minister of the Interior, would make a rejoining toast, and everyone would raise his champagne glass. I had never been to a cocktail party in the U.S., but I had heard people say that they were boring. I couldn't understand why they said that. I adored these parties where I could talk with interesting people from many different countries. I could relax and not get tied in knots trying to understand Lao and worrying about what to say in reply.

My favorite receptions were for the Queen's birthday. They were held in the afternoon on the lawn behind the British residence. The sun was always shining, the sky blue, and the garden alive with colorful flowers. The children of the British staff charmingly circulated with savory appetizers and petits fours. The ambassador and minister would smile, say cheerful things, and toast each other's country. Everyone would be fashionable and charming. It was like being a brush stroke or two in a beautiful watercolor in a time warp of pleasantries.

At the French Residence, we had delicious caviar, at the Embassy of the U.S.S.R., cold vodka, and at the Chinese Embassy, Chinese fruit wines. I was usually the only American at the latter two embassies other than the second or third secretary from the U.S. Embassy checking out who was there, or so it seemed. He would see me and his eyes would grow large. He always ignored me. I could see him thinking, what is she doing here? Doesn't she know not to come? I didn't care. It was interesting to see the photo exhibition of Chinese events and progress and talk to Russian diplomats and KGB agents. It was the Cold War Era, before Nixon's visit to China in 1972 and the Berlin Wall came down in 1989.

Official invitations meant command attendance. Every year in November we received invitations from the King to attend the That Luang celebration and palace reception. Pha That Luang is an impressive gold Buddhist stupa in the center of Vientiane purported to date from the 3rd century A.D. It is the national symbol of Laos. Khounta liked this one public event. The military and civil service officers wore white uniforms with their medals, and the women dressed in their finest silks. We would get a chauffeur to drive us to the reviewing stand at the That Luang Fair Grounds. The King and Queen attended, and the King awarded medals. There was always a horse race on which the men would make small, noisy bets. That was fun with lots of shouting and hooting. Khounta often won. Afterwards, was a game of tiki where a huge tiki ball, about eight feet in diameter, was pushed back and forth across the fairgrounds by two teams, one of the local citizens and one composed of government employees. The townspeople usually won.

In the evening, the King and Queen invited the same people to a party at the palace. It was the cool season, and I wore a long gown with long sleeves. We gathered on the large gravel patio next to the palace to watch Lao classical dances depicting stories from the Ramayana. We sat in rows on metal folding chairs. After the beautiful dancing to the classical orchestra was a stand-up buffet dinner on the verandahs and inside the palace. As there was no heating, all the doors would be open. People would stand around eating and talking, and the King and Queen would sit on comfortable stuffed chairs with the Prime Minister and other ministers.

CHAPTER 22

The Fourth Year: 1972

We ended 1971 with a trip to the beach at Pattaya for two weeks. We stayed at the U.S. government bungalows and had a wonderful time relaxing on the beach, people watching, and eating seafood. Our friend Jack Stoops came and stayed nearby for a couple of days. Together we went exploring farther down the coast. We found an empty beach where we picnicked in privacy.

We didn't make any picnic stops on our return to Vientiane.

In January, Khounta told me his sister wanted her house back. It was much too difficult for her to live with her mother and keep five young, energetic boys quiet. While we were living in his sister's house, we had built our dream house on the Mekong River, and I wanted to live there, but Khounta felt we needed to rent it for the time being to repay his mother for the money we borrowed to build it. USAID brought water in a truck for the occupants.

Instead, Khounta showed me a few potential rentals. I said no to all of them. They were impossible. In the end, he found a small house on the banks of the Mekong River near Chinaimo, the RLG Army Camp, about two hundred meters downstream from the house we had built.

The rental house needed a lot of work, but Khounta's hobby was designing and building houses. We were downsizing again, and it would be very cozy. Khounta had it fixed up, and we moved in. The house was only two big square rooms, one upstairs and one downstairs. The one upstairs he split in half. We took the half overlooking the river, and he had shelves and a closet built in. The other half he divided. At the head of the stairs was the study with just enough room for our large desk and the four bookshelves. The other room was for guests.

Downstairs, he had an extension built onto the right-hand side of the building that was an entrance foyer and passageway. It led directly into the living room and the newly constructed indoor kitchen on the right, making an L-shape. He divided the room in half at the center column, but with no walls. The dining room was on the left separated from the living room by a sideboard.

The best part was the garden and the platform built out over the river. We ate all our meals there, other than breakfast, which the maid now prepared and brought upstairs.

There was no running water this distance from Vientiane center. It was possible to have water delivered by truck, but that was expensive. Khounta had a pump house rigged up. In the wet season the pump house floated near the top of the river bank near the house, but when the dry season began, it had to be pushed out and down a little bit every day as the water level fell until it was away from the house about one hundred yards.

Next to the entrance to the kitchen, he had eight oil drums connected with pipes at the bottom, with two oil drums sitting on top of two of the lower drums. The river water was first pumped into them. They had charcoal in them for filtration. Every night, water was pumped up to fill the drums, and Khounta stirred alum in them to settle the dirt. In the morning, the water was pumped to the roof for use in the bathrooms and kitchen. In the kitchen, we had a ceramic water filter with three long cones in it to further filter dirt from the water. Then Khai, our Thai maid, boiled it for drinking. There was no bottled water in Laos. The system worked very well. The biggest problem was thieves. They came in the night at least three times to steal the wiring that went from the house to the pump to sell for its copper content.

It was about this time that I noticed Khounta was taking some pills called Diabinese. I asked what they were for, and he said blood sugar. Khounta said he had high blood pressure too. I asked what it was, and he said 17/11. The numbers meant nothing to me. I asked my assistant at work, Joan Rogers if she knew what it meant, and she said that was how the doctors in Laos referred to blood pressure, to just add zeros, that is 170/110. She said that was high and asked me who Khounta's doctor was. It was his good friend, but he was not treating the blood pressure.

Joan suggested that he see someone in Bangkok for a second opinion. I suggested it to Khounta, and he agreed. Joan told me about a doctor at the British Dispensary on Sukhumvit Road. I had heard of him because he was a friend of Brian Hackman from Thakhek days. Joan called him and made an appointment, and Khounta drove to Bangkok. I didn't hear from him for several days. I became worried and called Patti Suggs. She hadn't heard from him, either. I decided to take the train to Bangkok. Before I left, I learned from the doctor that he had been admitted to the Bangkok Nursing Home.

From the train, I went directly to the hospital. At the door of Khounta's room, I saw that he was packing to leave. He saw me and asked me what I was doing there. I said I was worried that he hadn't called me. He was angry that I had come. We drove directly back to Vientiane. On the way, he told me that after the doctor had examined him, he asked him how he had gotten to his office. Khounta said he had driven from Vientiane. The doctor said he had to go to the hospital for observation, and because his blood pressure was dangerously high, he shouldn't drive. Khounta felt the same as he always had so he drove. The doctor prescribed some pills to control his blood pressure. It was the beginning of a lifetime of medicine adjustment because the high blood pressure pills interfered with the diabetes pills. The blood pressure would be okay, but the diabetes count would be high and vice-versa.

A Son, A Daughter

One night the light awakened me. I turned over in bed and saw Khounta looking at me. He was standing in the middle of the narrow rectangle bordering the bed. I looked at the clock. It was after midnight. Khounta had just returned from an evening at his favorite aunt's wake, and he looked very serious. "Do you want a son?" he asked.

I sat up. I had been asleep for hours and though instantly awake could only mumble, "What?"

"Do you want a son?" he repeated.

My heart screamed, yes, yes. I moved over to the side of the bed to be closer. I looked at him, his white, brown, and yellow, short-sleeve shirt, his brown slacks. His face was shiny. It must still be hot out, I thought. "What do you mean?"

"My uncle has a son about seven years old that he has offered us."

I had hardly met the uncle and could only remember a couple of adult children. "Why would your uncle give us his son?" I asked.

I was overwhelmed because more than anything I wanted children. We both did. "We don't have any children," he said, "and he has ten. He's older now, and he's tired. He says he doesn't have the energy to give another boy the time he needs. He feels he would have more opportunities with us."

Can this be possible? I wondered. "How does the boy feel?" I asked.

"Uncle Noukham asked Toi if he'd like to live with us, his uncle and aunt. Toi said he would."

The light in the room seemed strained through a mosquito screen. There was only one small globe on the wall near the bedroom door and another one over the full-length mirror in the alcove off the bathroom. Minute black dots seemed to vibrate before my eyes. I could hear the drone of the window air conditioner. It came to me that they had been talking about this at the wake.

"Do you want a son?" he asked again.

I was sitting up cross-legged on the bed. "Yes. But, Khounta, I don't want an only child. I think it is too difficult for everyone," I said. I thought but didn't say, I want a daughter, too.

"There are two younger girls. I'll talk to my uncle." It's possible, I thought. "I want the youngest," I said.

"You should look first and then decide."

"I don't need to." The suggestion surprised and revolted me. "I want the youngest."

"We'll look," he said and went to the bathroom to shower.

A son . . .

A daughter . . .

I moved back to my side of the bed thinking . . . He'd said he'd never adopt children, and now we might get two. I slept.

A few days later, Khounta came home to tell me that his uncle agreed that we could have either of his younger daughters. I said I wanted the youngest, who was two and one-half years old. She was the youngest of ten and the last one because, as Peter told me later, his mother had had her tubes tied.

My husband had seen the girls and wanted me to check out the baby. Her eyes looked funny he thought. We went to the house a couple of nights later, and there she was. Absolutely beautiful with black, black eyes! It was almost impossible to distinguish her pupils. Her mother said she didn't think I'd want her. "She cries all the time." I didn't care.

What I didn't understand—and what wasn't said to me until Khemphone, the ninth child, told me about thirty years later—was that her mother didn't want to give up her baby. She wanted me to take Khemphone.

So it was decided. We would take the children to live with us and raise as our own. The legalities were simple in Laos. We would simply have new birth certificates issued with Khounta and me as the natural parents. That was done.

Soon after, one evening after work in late October, we picked up our son with all his worldly possessions: two white school shirts, three pairs of shorts, and a pair of rubber thongs. He had no toys. His name was Bounpeng. He had been named after the temple across the street, Wat Inpeng. His nickname was Toi. We added the first name, Peter, after my father.

I noticed right away that something was missing. In the car, I asked Khounta, "Where's his toothbrush?"

As parents, it was our first purchase for him. We went home and showed him his room and, as it was late, prepared for bed. For Toi it was easy. After brushing his teeth, he just lay down on the bed in his shirt and shorts.

"Where are his pajamas?" I asked Khounta.

"He doesn't have any. He wears his shirt and shorts and changes to clean ones in the morning."

"Oh," I said. I was learning.

The next day I asked, "Where are his underpants?" Khounta explained to me that little boys didn't wear them.

Peter seemed to have trouble chewing his food. He would have to stick his finger in his month to move the food around, and it took him a long time to eat. He had had his four front teeth removed the year before. I was concerned and took him to the dentist. The dentist looked at his teeth and said not to worry; new ones would replace the existing baby teeth.

Peter Visits the USA

Peter came to live with us just before the end of Buddhist Lent and the annual boat races in October 1972. Khounta and I took him to the boat races. It was the first time I had gone with Khounta and the last. There was a viewing stand for the *phu jai*, that is, the officials, to view the races from, but that meant dressing up and being on show. Khounta felt that that was being pretentious. We stood on the dike on top of the riverbank like everyone else. Khounta hated crowds, but for Peter, he went.

During this period, Peter continued in the second grade at a French primary school not far from where he used to live. The school was reached by crossing marshes on a plank next to Khun Boulom Street. They are now filled in and are the site of shops and a night market, constructed in 2009. He was ranked forty-sixth out of fifty students. He couldn't read, write, or speak a word of French, and Lao wasn't taught. The school was under a wooden house, and the floor was hard earth. The children sat four to a long wooden bench behind a single wooden desk, which is still the practice in Lao schools today. At some schools, if there is room, only two students need to share a desk.

Also, at this time, Khounta was getting Peter his new birth certificate and a passport. I was taking him to the USA to meet my family. Peter was a quiet, well-mannered boy, and we loved him very much. We were becoming a family.

On November 30, Peter and I embarked by ferryboat at the Thadeua crossing to Nong Khai. Khounta drove us, and Peter's eldest brother, BounNyok, came along to see us off. We took the train to Bangkok. From Bangkok, we flew to Hong Kong for a few days where we shopped for some appropriate warm weather clothing for both of us, and I met with friends Walter and Jean Lee whose son Andy was a few years older than Peter. Jean and I took them to a playground near Victoria's peak. They played like old friends although they had no mutually comprehensible spoken language.

From Hong Kong, we went to Honolulu. We stayed with my friend from graduate school Janet Calendar from whose apartment we could walk to the zoo and the beach. Peter engaged in a boy's universal pleasures of building sand castles and trying to catch pigeons on the lawns.

On December 8, we arrived at San Francisco Airport. My mother met us and took us home to Piedmont. (We had lived there since 1945. It was my address in the States until 2011 when we sold the house.) It was Christmas time, and the house was colorfully decorated. My mother enthusiastically embraced all holidays with decorations, activities, food, and gifts. I told Peter that he could have three presents, and he decided on "a gun, a train, and a camera." It was all new to him, and he readily adapted to the tradition.

My mother treated us to two nights at the Ahwahnee Hotel in Yosemite. It is a beautiful old hotel. My father had helped with the interior art deco painting in the 1920s. Peter taught me two rules in handling children while we were there. The first one was not to change my mind. He had asked me which color socks to wear, and I told him the blue ones. Then I said it didn't matter, and he could choose. That was very frustrating to him, and he told me angrily not to change my mind. The second lesson was with teasing. We had a delicious dinner, and Peter ate and ate and took more than he could finish. I teased him about being a little piggy. That incensed him and made me realize it was unkind and unnecessary talk, especially the comparison with a pig. My Lao was at the level of a seven-year-old so communication was not a problem with him.

The next day was beautiful. Peter watched people skiing and wanted to ski himself. We rented the necessary equipment and off he went. It didn't occur to him to be scared or to need lessons. He watched and imitated what he saw. My mother and I watched him from a nearby slope being used by kids with sleds. The air was brisk, and the sun was shining. We enjoyed just standing there, talking and admiring Peter side step up a slope and ski down. He did very well.

We drove to Carson City for Christmas where he met his Aunt Melissa and Uncle Dave and his cousins Jeffery, 10, and Teresa, who was the same age. We went to a tree farm and cut down a tree. On Christmas morning, Peter was delighted to receive the gifts he had asked for.

My father was enchanted by Peter and could not take his eyes off him. My father and I had been alienated for about seven years through a misconception about the ownership of the Piedmont house, but Peter brought about tacit forgiveness and reconciliation. The misconception was not clarified for another nineteen years.

My mother, seeing Peter trying to eat, insisted that I take him to see Dr. Bent, her dentist. I told her that I had taken Peter to the dentist in Vientiane just before I left, and was told not to worry. She insisted. We went. The dentist said he had to have all his remaining teeth pulled immediately. I said okay I would have it done when we returned to Vientiane. He said, "No, today." He had me look at Peter's gums. Above each tooth was a white spot. He said, "Those are abscesses." I was horrified. He scheduled an appointment with an oral surgeon for that afternoon.

I told my father, and he took Peter fishing off the Berkeley pier until it was time for the appointment. The weather was cold, and the wind was blowing. I waited in the car while they fished. When it was time, we took him to the surgeon. We didn't tell him what was going to happen. He had a general anesthetic, and the teeth were removed as completely as possible. Afterwards, I took him in my arms and carried him to the car. We put him to bed in Piedmont. Another thirty minutes passed, and he came to, crying in pain. It was very frustrating and distressing to me not to be able to talk to him and explain. He had trusted us, and we were responsible for hurting him. I gave him a silver dollar. The pain went away, and he ate well-cut up and soft foods until the second teeth grew in.

After the New Year, Peter and I drove to Carmel to visit my brother and his wife, Sherrie. They had a horse, and Peter had his first ride with his Uncle Wade. Later he patiently fished in the surf for hours.

We retraced our steps to Vientiane by plane, train, and ferryboat, arriving on January 20.

Now that my family had met Peter, only Khounta was an unknown entity, except to my mother from her brief visit six years before, but Khounta expressed no interest in meeting the rest of my family. Perhaps that was because he felt I didn't get along with his family. At the same time, he made no effort for us to get along with his mother and sister and her family. Although I would have liked to participate in family activities with them, I pushed the idea out of my mind. I believe he was angry that I didn't know correct cultural dos and don'ts. I felt if it was not important enough to him to teach me, and if he didn't want to bother to make an effort, I wasn't going to either. I felt this was Khounta's character, and I accepted it.

Then again, perhaps he was just shy. I knew he didn't like to be in crowds or to meet new people. We were alike in that we didn't talk much until we knew someone fairly well, but after he felt comfortable with someone he would talk, laugh, and tell stories without end.

I thought it strange, however, that he didn't want to at least meet my father. Lao marriage customs are different from those in the U.S. where it is customary for the boy to ask the girl's father for her hand (though not so much these years), and dowries are not a requirement.

In Laos in the 1960s and '70s, when a boy wanted to get married, his father talked with the girl's father. Often, though, at that time, a couple had no say in the matter of the marriage. The parents did all the arranging. An agreement was reached on what the boy's family must provide regarding a tribute to the guardian spirits (*kha khun phi*). It was figured at a fixed rate, depending on the financial and social status of the bride and her family. There was also a kind of bridal gift (*kha dong*) that was paid to the bride's parents. This last gift, while optional under law, was compulsory in practice. It wasn't fixed but was negotiated between the families. It was usual, however, for the girl to be given gold jewelry and some land. Also, the boy's family paid for the wedding and reception. That is still the practice today. After the marriage, the boy moved in with the girl's parents until he had saved enough money to buy some land and build a house for his family. This custom, too, is still followed. The traditional system of arranged marriage, however, is pretty much in the past. Young couples meet and marry for love, but the *kha dong* is still negotiated.

Our situation was very different. First, I was an American, and I was going to live in Laos. Second, Khounta was older, and he already had many houses and property of his own. Third, Khounta's father had passed away some years before. We couldn't have followed the marriage traditions of our cultures.

CHAPTER 23

The Fifth Year: 1973

Alice Comes

While Peter and I were away, Khounta had made some more house renovations and improvements. He had black tiles laid in the entrance and downstairs. In the children's bedroom he had bunk beds built. Khounta had waited for Peter and my return to get Alice.

Alice was 2 ½ years old and chattered non-stop in Lao. Fortunately, Khounta and Khai could understand her. Her Lao was too fast and not developed enough for me. In the beginning, she cried a lot for an older sister Khemphone, but that stopped after a few months. Peter never asked about his siblings. She wet the bed every night and at naptime. That ended abruptly on her fourth birthday when she decided to be a "big girl." Peter was a superb big brother and dressed her every morning. We enjoyed breakfast outside on the platform overlooking the Mekong River until the river took it away.

I talked to my friend Dee Dick, now Dee Quill, who had returned to Vientiane with her husband and two sons in October 1972. She suggested that Alice attend the same pre-school her sons were going to, so that was arranged. Alice enjoyed riding a tricycle and playing with the other children. Learning English was slow. Her first words were "kitty cat," uttered in the back seat of the car as I was driving to the market one day. The only English sentence we insisted on was, "May I have a banana please."

My friend in Bangkok, Patti Suggs, gave me many dresses that her three daughters had outgrown. Alice loved them. She wanted to wear them every day. On the weekends, Peter had to hide them because she wanted to wear them instead of her play shirts and shorts. Her ears had already been pierced, and she wore tiny gold rings in them. Whenever I went to the beauty salon, she wanted to have her nails painted, too. She was very much a little lady, very unlike me, who had been a tomboy. Experiencing the contrast between my childhood priorities and hers was delightful. She loved to play with dolls whereas I had preferred a can of earthworms and frogs.

Our good friend John McClean was the director of the International School. With him, we arranged for Peter's enrollment in the first grade. His ESL teacher was Christine Segalini, and soon he was speaking English. On school days, because of where our offices were located, I drove Peter to school, and Khounta took Alice.

John and his wife Valerie returned to England at the end of the school year in 1973 and Peter began second grade at the American School of Vientiane, located in the American housing compound at KM-6. It was very convenient for me because the school bus picked him up at my office at the Lao American Association. Alice changed to a French pre-school on the way to Khounta's office, so he took her. She learned French songs and had a good ear for the words and melody. That impressed me because I cannot sing a note nor remember words.

On Saturdays, we went to the American Community Association swimming pool in the USAID compound in Ban Nahaidio. The first time we went, I asked Peter if he could swim. He said yes, so I stood in the water and watched him come down the ladder in the shallow end and sink when he stepped off. Then it was all arms and splashing as I gathered him up. He couldn't swim. After that, he always moved around the pool holding on to the edge.

On Sundays, a bus came to pick them up at the end of our street on Thadeua Road and took them to Sunday school. Khounta and I enjoyed this luxury of a morning alone together.

Khounta put Alice in his passport and that summer, we drove to the beach near Hua Hin in Thailand. We stayed in a bungalow on a beautiful bay, but even back then there were signs of an oil spill on the beach.

The Bomb: August 20, 1973

Boom, a low, solid resonating thud. I was instantly awake. I turned to Khounta and instinctively, incredulously, said, "That was a bomb." We lay there a moment and then we heard a plane fly by shooting rat-a-tat-tat-tat-tat-tat. He immediately told me to get the kids, go downstairs, and get under the table. He was already out of bed and getting dressed. It was early morning. Cracks in the shutters allowed light to permeate the room. I got Peter and Alice, whose room was through a connecting door, and hurried them to the semi-darkness downstairs. I pulled a few chairs back from the dining room table, and we ducked underneath. The children didn't say anything, not a question, not a word. They did not speak or understand English, and even if I had known what was going on, I couldn't have told them in my limited Lao. What did they think?

We could hear excited talking outside. I couldn't see, but I imagined a crowd gathering to see what was happening from the riverbank at the end of the road next to our house. Our place fronted on the Mekong River and was only accessible from this road. Khounta passed us on his way out the front door. He told the villagers to take cover in their houses.

It was just after seven a.m. so I knew LAA in central Vientiane would be open. I crawled out from under the table, got the telephone and called Joan Rogers, my assistant, to see if she knew anything. I told her we had heard a bomb explode, and a plane was flying up and down the river strafing the houses. I held the phone up for her to hear. "What's happening in Vientiane?" I asked.

"Nothing," she said. "It's quiet. We are having classes as usual." It seemed unreal. We were being shot at while fifteen minutes away all was normal.

I could hear the plane flying back and the machine gun going rat-a-tat-tat-tat-tat-tat; then silence. Khounta must have persuaded the people to go home. A little later the plane came again, rat-a-tat-tat-tat-tat. We lived next to Chinaimo Army Camp. Khounta figured that if the Communists invaded, by living next to the army camp we would have early warning and could escape to Thailand across the Mekong River. We didn't have a boat, however. So much for living in a safe place!

After fifteen minutes, during which time we didn't hear any more shooting, Khounta told us to get dressed. We were going to evacuate. The children and I got ready and came back downstairs. There we found Keith from England and his American girlfriend, Marjorie. I was surprised to see them. They both worked for me at LAA, and I wondered what they were doing there. Apparently, Khounta had rented our little house across the road to them and had never mentioned it to me.

The children, the teachers, and I got in my VW 311 sedan and took off for town. It was a lovely, sunny day and the sky was blue. On the way I stopped for gas, thinking I should top up, just in case. In case of what? I didn't think that far. Khounta drove by a few minutes later and gave me a ferocious glare. He didn't stop but scolded me later for being so stupid as to stop so close to the shooting. I filled up and continued to town. I hadn't thought we were in danger anymore, especially since we were on the main street away from the river. I never felt frightened, only curious. It was as if I were viewing a movie rather than experiencing the action. I learned later that the gas station had been struck earlier that morning and Khounta's masseur had been hit in the arm by a bullet . . . Or maybe Khounta only said that to scare me.

It felt strange to be in the office where everything was so calm and normal, in contrast to the noise and confusion in our neighborhood. The children were with me, but it didn't seem necessary, so I sent them to school. The day proceeded as usual. We went home in the evening as if nothing had happened, and, in fact, nothing had changed in our lives.

I learned later what had happened. Brigadier General Thao Ma, the Commander of the Royal Lao Air Force in Savannakhet when I lived there in 1965, was a fierce anti-communist and patriotic Lao. He had gone into exile in Thailand in October 1966 after he had unsuccessfully tried to lead a coup against what he felt was a corrupt government that was sharing more and more with the Communist Pathet Lao.

That morning, he was trying again to take over the government. Very early, he had slipped into Vientiane and stolen a T-28 fighter-bomber from Wattay Airport and had deliberately bombed the Army Camp at Chinaimo. While he was stealing the plane, some of his men captured the national bank, and some others seized the radio station, so no news of the takeover was being broadcast. To this day, more than forty years later, short, red and white, easily movable barriers are placed across the streets leading to this very radio station and bank every night just before sunset. A soldier lurks near each barrier to wave back anyone who has turned into the street not knowing that it is blocked halfway down. One can surmise that the pathetic ease of capturing these two key institutions has carried over into the psyche of the present government that does not want to experience a similar embarrassment. Still, all these years later, it seems an unusual way to protect the buildings. The other radio stations, and now TV stations, do not receive any protection.

General Ma's plane was severely damaged, and he crashed landed just short of the runway at Wattay Airport. He was captured and taken to Chinaimo. When the bomb dropped there, the soldiers had run outside, like the villagers, to see what was happening. Unfortunately, when General Ma came back strafing the camp and dropping a second bomb, he had killed several soldiers, including General Kouprasith's nephew.

Somchanh, an assistant in our office whose army colonel uncle lived on our street, came in with secret, glossy 5 x 7 photos the next week. Even today, General Ma's beaten and swollen face and the clean, wide, vertical 7" knife gash in his abdomen vividly appear when I turn back the pages in my mind.

Changes

My brother, Wade, came to live with us in October of 1973. We partitioned off a fourth of the downstairs area for his bedroom. As a family, we had fun together carving pumpkins at Halloween, lighting candles on the back fence at the end of Buddhist Lent, and celebrating Christmas.

Wade taught English at the Lao American Association, and we helped him move into his own place in early 1974. The move was good for him because now he was in town, and he could walk everywhere. Our house was a considerable distance out of the city, which required taking a taxi. He never complained to us, but I had heard he felt trapped in the evenings. Because he didn't have a Lao driver's license, he couldn't use our cars. A taxi was expensive for someone on an LAA teacher's income.

Lao politics were changing, too. A coalition government was formed in early 1973 with the Neutralists, the Rightists and the Pathet Lao (PL). The ministries were divided among the three groups. Khounta's new Minister General Singkapo, whom he liked personally, was with the Pathet Lao. However, Khounta would complain to me about the Vietnamese advisors whom he believed were the real authority behind the PL ministers and were dictating to them. Therefore, although he liked General Singkapo, he couldn't trust that his work decisions were necessarily being made in the best interests of Laos. But the general, like Khounta, did what he was told.

The streets, which had always had soldiers carrying AK-47s in them, had even more soldiers now. The Pathet Lao soldiers always walked in pairs. They looked extremely young and not like the Lao we were used to. They didn't appear to speak Lao. In the yard and house next to the LAA, a large contingent of PL soldiers moved in. They set up a large tent in the garden and began digging a well. They never did find water. That house is now the Khop Chai Deu restaurant and the front garden the site of the Lao Journalists' Association building, many ATMs, and little cafes.

CHAPTER 24

The Sixth Year: 1974

In the spring and summer of 1974, because of the change in the Lao government, the American government transferred out most of its CIA agents. That was a sad time for me because my close women friends were married to these men. I felt bereft. Khounta and I talked about the end of the Kingdom coming. I believed it was going to happen and I thought Khounta did too, but he, in fact, didn't. Khounta was fencing in some farm property he had bought for growing fruit trees, while I, unable to sleep, was getting up in the night, typing packing lists, and packing my books for shipping out.

I didn't tell Khounta, but I had begun to get a little bored with Vientiane and was actively looking for jobs abroad. Some of my friends had found good paying employment in Iran, and I was looking into that possibility.

Khounta had a small gun in a holster that he kept in the safe. When he went out at night, he tucked it into the small of his back, under his belt. I am confident he would never have used it, but it gave him a sense of security. He also acquired an automatic that didn't have any wood in the stock. He hung it on the side of the closet for me to use, if necessary. It was ugly. I hated it, and I never touched it.

One evening over dinner, Khounta announced he had some tickets for a formal fundraiser at the Malaysian Embassy that night. I was happily surprised because he had never bought tickets to a charity function before, and I began to think about what I would wear. Then Zorro and Victoria began to bark. Khounta went out front to see what was disturbing them; he saw that the copper wires going to our electric water pump down on the Mekong River had been cut. The river was down, so there was about 150 feet of wire. Twice before the wires had been stolen for their copper content. This was the third time. Khounta got his gun, went outside and sat in a chair in the dark in the cover of a tree to wait for the thief to come and take the wires. He waited for hours and then, at eleven o'clock, a small boy came and dragged the cables away. Khounta didn't shoot because it was a child, but I don't think he would have shot no matter who it was. By then, of course, it was too late for us to go out.

CHAPTER 25

The Seventh Year: 1975

Fleeing Laos

Beginning in 1973, Khounta spent many days in negotiations with the Chinese. That led to his coming home late from work. He didn't tell me what was being discussed. I only knew it was with the Chinese because I had supplied him with his interpreter, one of the LAA teachers.

On February 28, 1975, Khounta went on the Royal Air Lao inaugural flight to Canton (Guangzhou) and Beijing. I wanted to go to the airport to see him off, especially since I would leave for the States before he came back. As usual, he said no. We had lunch at a little restaurant on Luang Prabang Road, now Soupanouvong Street, and he was gone.

I left for the States on March 3 to attend the Teachers of English to Speakers of Other Languages (TESOL) Convention in Anaheim, California, and to visit my family. Peter and Alice stayed home with Khai. When I returned on April 10, Khounta complained a lot about his trip. He said he hadn't known that he would be the head of the delegation and therefore expected to make the dinner speeches. He wasn't prepared, and when the Chinese didn't like what he was saying, they became very noisy and ignored him.

One day later in April, standing near the secretary's office at LAA, Jane Kenny asked, "Do your kids have passports?"

"No. What for?" I gave her a puzzled look. She knew Khounta and I were leaving for Bangkok in a couple of days.

"You never know," she replied. But she did. Her husband, Ed, worked for the CIA, I learned afterwards. I had thought all the CIA agents had left Laos in the summer of 1974 after the coalition government was formed.

I laughed, "We're only going for a week or so."

An Operation

I had been in constant pain for a few months, sometimes ameliorated with a hot water bottle and a bit of Scotch. While I was visiting my sister in Nevada, I went to see the gynecologist my sister worked for. He advised me to have a hysterectomy as soon as possible. My mother wanted me to go to the hospital in San Francisco, but I didn't have any medical insurance, and I knew that an operation would cost thousands of dollars. I explained to her that the doctors in Thailand were excellent, many of them trained in the United States, and that I could afford to pay for an operation there.

When I passed through Bangkok on my return to Vientiane, I went to the Bangkok Nursing Home on Convent Road and scheduled the needed surgery with Dr. Sermsakdi. He had delivered my friend Patti's twins. I planned the operation for right after *Pimay*, the Lao New Year celebrated at the time of the full moon, but Khounta wanted me to wait for the waxing moon. He asked me to change the date to the end of the month because he had read in *Paris Match* magazine that, statistically, more people die in the hospital during the waning moon. The source of his information did not impress me as much as his sincere belief in the definitiveness of this information and his concern for me. I changed the date.

We drove down to Bangkok in the big American car Khounta had recently bought from some departing American, leaving the children in Khai's care. That is, I assume the seller was an American—the car just appeared one day. I was surprised, but I never asked about it. I admired it, and he was happy to have it. That was enough.

I checked into the hospital for some tests, and then we went out to dinner and the movies. The operation was the next morning, April 30, 1975. On that day, besides my undergoing major surgery, helicopters evacuated the last Americans from the roof of the American Embassy in Saigon, and three alert ministers in the Lao government fled Laos.

For a week, tubes protruded from my body. My insides wouldn't work. Gas blew up my midsection, stretching the skin taut like an over-inflated inner tube. The pain was constant. I moaned so much that the second bed in the room was rarely occupied. I thought if only I could pierce my stomach somehow and let the gas out before I exploded. I insisted on a 24-hour stomach pump, but it didn't help. After a week, my surgeon called in another surgeon. They decided an exploratory operation was necessary, but they didn't tell me. When they came to take me to surgery the next morning, however, they found my body had begun to do its job. I was going to be okay. After Khounta had found out I was in no danger, he informed me there were difficulties in Vientiane, and he had to go back. He had told me about the fall of Vietnam, and I had read about the Lao ministers in the newspaper.

Khounta Returns to Laos

Khounta's position as the Inspector General of the Ministry of Public Works and Transportation translated into "influential and probably dangerous" to the new Communist Pathet Lao leaders. Khounta knew this, and so did General Singkapo, his Pathet Lao Minister. Eventually, everyone in his ministry at the level of director and above who had not fled the country was sent to Viengxay, the re-education camps in the northeast of Laos. There they remained for a minimum of seven years if they were not shot or did not die of sickness and lack of medical care first. As a severe diabetic, Khounta would never have survived the cold season and lack of proper food and medication in the camps. Khounta learned eighteen years later that he had been placed on the so-called black list.

On Khounta's return, he went to see General Singkapo and asked to have his leave extended because I was still in the hospital in Bangkok. The minister gave him leave and permission to return to Thailand. This authorization was crucial because he would not be able to get an exit visa without it, and it would appear that he was fleeing the country.

Nevertheless, he didn't go right away. Afterwards, friends told me that they had seen him driving, seemingly aimlessly, around Vientiane, and exclaimed, "What are you still doing here? Leave!" Khounta told me that even General Singkapo saw him a week after he had given him permission to leave and told him to get the hell out, immediately.

However, Khounta had a problem. He didn't have passports for the children. Years later, Margie Manley told me of how he had come to her house one evening after dark. Her kids were already tucked in bed for the night. Looking desperate, he said, "I don't know how to get myself and the children out of Laos."

She immediately got on the phone and called the Kennys. Jane answered the phone, and Margie asked, "May I please speak to Ed." She and Jane were close friends, so such an abrupt greeting was not usual. When Ed came to the phone, she said Khounta was at her house and needed help.

He said, 'I'll be right there." The Kennys lived in Silver City, an American Embassy compound in Phone Sa'at in the same village as the Manley's house. Ed was there in five minutes. He said to Khounta, "Come with me," and they drove off.

When Khounta went to Bangkok with me, he had used his official passport, but he couldn't put the children in it, and the government was not issuing new passports. At home, he had a passport that had expired on March 30. With Ed's help and his personal contact with a Lao immigration officer, he was able to put the children in the expired passport and obtain an exit visa from Laos on May 16. Then on May 19, he got the passport extended for two years until March 29, 1977, and a Thai visa for two journeys.

When Khounta returned to Vientiane, he asked Joan Rodgers to come and pack the children's suitcases to go to the beach. The beach was his cover story, and Joan was his diversion. Besides, he didn't know what to pack, and, as it turned out, their bathing suits stayed behind. That night after Khai had gone to bed, he packed the back of the car with items one does not ordinarily take to the beach, such as a friend's pair of lamps. He didn't want Khai to know that he was leaving, never to return. They left the next day May 20.

At the Border
He drove to Thadeua, the immigration office on the Mekong River, where he had his passport stamped. Khounta told me that when he couldn't get Lao passports and exit visas for the children he had to put them both in his passport, but only with their Lao names. The immigration official would not accept the names Peter and Alice, only their initials and Lao names. However, he didn't tell me about his visits to Margie and Ed, nor that his passport had expired. I only learned that from looking at the dates in his old passport. From Thadeua, he backtracked to Thanalang, the car crossing, and drove onto the ferryboat. The ferry had just started across the river when a soldier ran down the ramp pointing his gun and shouting for them to return. The ferryman said he had to go back. Khounta told him, "No, keep going." He did. They both held their breath. Thankfully, the soldier didn't shoot. Later, many others were not so lucky. He probably drove the last car out of Laos into Thailand. After him, no one got permission to take his or her things out, or even to leave the country. The border was sealed to Lao citizens.

In the meantime, I was glad to be able to feel and think beyond my physical being. I started to read the *Bangkok Post*, and friends began to talk to me about what was happening in Indochina. While I had been lying in hospital, the end had come! Vietnam had fallen. The Kingdom of Laos was falling. There was no going back. All I had was what I'd put in my suitcase for the trip to and from the hospital. I had an eerie sense of release. I didn't have to deal with the contents of a house. I was free to go anywhere, weightless. At the same time, I regretted not having our photo albums or my jewelry, but over the next several weeks, friends smuggled them out. My brother even surprised us with a trunk load of Khounta's treasures: a pair of Lao elephant tusks and twelve Chinese soapstone figures.

B. Ellen's Problem

While Khounta was trying to get out of Laos, I had been recuperating, first for a few more days in the hospital and then at my friend B. Ellen's apartment. Khounta had stayed with her during my surgery. It had made him very uncomfortable staying with a single woman. Wouldn't her reputation be ruined? B. Ellen Mathews was my counterpart in Bangkok. She was the USIS Director of Courses at AUA, the bi-national center. We each ran English language programs for thousands of students daily with a staff of about fifty teachers and had branches in the main cities.

Then one morning two weeks after Khounta had returned to Vientiane, I got a phone call from Nakhon Ratchasima, which is about 157 miles northeast of Bangkok. "I've got the kids," he shouted joyously. In a few more hours, they were in Bangkok. He also brought his sister's two oldest sons to send to a cousin in Paris. The brothers Hum and Me left to stay with friends in Bangkok, and the four of us camped out on the floor in B. Ellen's guestroom.

About this time, B. Ellen swore me to secrecy and told me she had received a death threat. She had given the letter to the embassy. They had no idea who had sent it, but they were taking the matter very seriously. She was to prepare to leave immediately. Within a couple of days, the embassy had made the necessary travel arrangements. B. Ellen wanted to do some last minute shopping and go for a final trip to the beauty salon. Beauty parlors were a ritual in those days, and everyone went at least once or twice a week for a shampoo, set, manicure and pedicure. Khounta went along with B. Ellen on this last excursion as her bodyguard. He sat for hours while she had her long hair wrapped in rollers and dried to remove its slight frizz. Of course, the humidity and rain in May would destroy the effect within hours, but by then, she would be gone.

Embassy personnel took over from Khounta and escorted her to the airport. She had worked at AUA for seven years. Her friends and colleagues didn't know about the death threat. For them, she just mysteriously disappeared one day, with no explanation, and nobody in Thailand ever heard from her again.

We stayed in B. Ellen's apartment another two weeks. We oversaw the packers when they came for B. Ellen's belongings. Khounta began filling out U.S. immigration forms.

Everyone was very kind to us. We moved to the home of a USIS family that was going on home leave. It was a large two-story house on Asoke Road. They had children, so there were toys to play with and a tricycle for Alice to ride. Some friends of B. Ellen took the kids to the beach at Pattaya and to the Siam Intercontinental pool to swim.

At this time, hundreds of USAID and American Embassy personnel and their families were being evacuated from Vientiane. Student protestors surrounded the USAID compound at Km-6 on May 17, and the residents were virtual prisoners for a while before they were allowed to be bused to the airport. I had the opportunity to say goodbye to many friends at the Ambassador Hotel on Sukhumvit Road, where they were put up while waiting for their flights out of Bangkok. They had been limited to two suitcases each when they left. Most people had been able to send things out through the APO and to pack their belongings for later shipment, but some lost their household effects and mementos of a lifetime with no possibility of ever getting them back.

Back to Vientiane

However, I was not Lao or an official American. I had a valid Lao visa. On June 12, after the requisite six-week recovery period, I returned to Vientiane. I had to. I was the one with a job and, after my operation, we only had enough money for living expenses in Bangkok and air tickets to the United States. I went by my preferred modes of travel— train, pedicab, ferryboat, and taxi—which are less expensive than flying. But, more important, it is more interesting, and the trip is more relaxing than being herded onto a plane and being belted into a seat. On the train, one can walk around, meet people, and eat and drink at one's seat or in the dining car. I liked watching the porter make up the berths, all forty of them, with clean sheets, then ducking in under my upper berth, closing the curtains, and watching the landscape pass by. At night, the countryside is black, lit only by starlight and the moon. The towns are infrequent in the vast plains and mountains and the stations dimly lit with yellow light. The train clickety-clacks over bumpy wooden cross-ties and the coaches sway from side to side, lulling me to sleep. Sometimes, just the thought of the ride puts me to sleep sitting upright in my seat before the train even leaves the station. On the boat, there is always a little smuggling of soap powder and other items by the local market women. People smile and squeeze together on the benches running down the sides of the ferry, and luggage is jammed in at people's knees. It is enjoyable to ride across the Mekong River and meet the Lao riverside. In the dry season, when the Mekong drops by fifty meters, it is a long haul down the steps to the boat on one side and up on the other, but this was the rainy season, and the river was up and running fast. At Thadeua, the immigration and customs scrutiny is not as formal as at the airport, and a blind eye is turned to the smiling women and their contraband.

On arrival on the Lao side, I went immediately to our rented house. Khai and some relatives were busy packing up our belongings and moving them to one of our houses for us to live in Wat Nak village, which was much closer to the city center. The Holdens, who had rented our house and been evacuated, lived there for many years. Bill was the airport fire chief for Air America, and Irene taught ballet to young girls from the American and other schools. The house wasn't ready for me to move in, but Khai moved in with our three dogs and the cat. I went to stay at the Manley's house in Phone Sa'at village. Margie was in the States on early home leave with their five kids. They had left because the American School had closed and the children's friends had been evacuated. There was no one for them to play with. But Frank was in town. Margie told me later that her Vietnamese nanny, Madame Hai, and her husband would sleep outside Frank's door at night to ensure that no hanky-panky was going on. We were both very amused. Such behavior never occurred to me. Before Margie came back in September with the kids, I would need a new place to stay. Margaret Converse of USIS invited me to stay at her house, which was very familiar to me. It had been Laurent and Polly's house, where Khounta and I had spent many happy hours playing cards with them and other friends. It would be more comfortable than at the Wat Nak house, and, perhaps, safer because an official American lived there. I felt no threat from the government. There was no rule of law. The government was in limbo. Later this house was the residence of the Swedish Representative for many years.

The city was deserted of foreigners and under a nine p.m. curfew. The Lao American Association continued to hold classes. My brother, my Admin Assistant, and a few other non-official foreigners stayed on to teach. There were only a few of us, but there were not as many students as before, either. The American Consul would come to my office every few weeks and ask the other Americans and me to leave because the Embassy could not guarantee our safety. In fact, no one from the government bothered us.

Lao citizens were obligated to go to re-education seminars in the city for days on end. They hated having to sit for hours and listen to lectures. Women and girls could no longer wear long slacks or jeans, but had to dress in the Lao national costume, a *phasinh*, and wear their hair in the traditional bun on the left backside of their head. The boys had to cut off their long hair, which was the modern style of the time; otherwise, they would be grabbed and administered a butchered haircut on the spot.

In the evenings, I went to the Wat Nak house and packed as many of our belongings as I could in the empty Pepsi syrup shipping boxes my brother Wade got for me from the Lao Bottling Company (now the Lao Soft Drink Co. Ltd.). I mailed them to my mother in California through the APO, which had moved to the U.S. Embassy because the USAID compound had been occupied. I sent sixty boxes of dishes, clothes, linens, toys, and daily paraphernalia, including the five boxes of books I had packed earlier during my sleepless nights. The heavy shackles of possessions were back in place.

On June 20, I went to Bangkok to help Khounta with the U.S. immigration forms and interviews at the embassy. Khai, who was Thai, went with me on the train from Nong Khai. In her berth, she also took Jin-Jin, our Siamese cat. I got Khai a job with Millie Sojak in Bangkok. Millie had worked at USIS in Laos and had been reassigned. Jin-Jin stayed with Khounta and the children. Eventually, Jin-Jin flew to the States, unaccompanied, in a big plywood box, which still comes in handy today. My mother didn't meet the plane because I hadn't had time to notify her. Remember, this was before faxes, the Internet, and mobile phones. No matter. The airlines put the cat up in a hotel, and my mother picked her up two days later.

One of the saddest effects of the hasty departure of official government personnel was that people had to leave their pets, their beloved dogs and cats, to fend for themselves. One can see the result of this in the mixed breeds of dogs walking the streets of Vientiane today. The typical Lao dog has changed from a medium-sized, well-proportioned dog with short, straight hair and a question-mark tail curving over its back, to a dog with a medium body, very short legs, sometimes curly hair, and a straight tail hanging down behind.

Rama, our Pekinese, found a home with a family in Si Hom, but Zorro and Victoria, our German Shepherds, were a problem. Khounta and I got Zorro as a puppy when we were first married. He had moved with us from house to house and protected us for seven years, scaring off attempted burglars more than once. Khounta had even tried to return them to the French man from whom we had gotten them, but he was in the same situation we were. I didn't want to desert them to a terrible street fate, so I bought strychnine and syringes in Bangkok. I told Khai that we would have to put the dogs down. She cried and cried and begged me not to do it. Luckily, I was able to find a French Canadian couple that had just arrived in Vientiane to take them. It was a happy match, and they said they would take the dogs back to Canada when they left. Zorro especially took to the couple, and he attacked me once when I went to visit him. Poor Rama was not so lucky, the man who took him kept him tied up all day so that he would not run away. He would recognize my steps from a block away, and would jump and yelp with pleasure when I was still out of sight. When I was close enough, he would wiggle with joy, jump up, and lick me. I hated to leave them and was glad they had good homes.

After two weeks, I returned to Vientiane. When I was in Bangkok, Khounta had persuaded me to visit General Singkapo to see if there was any way he could intercede with the Thai authorities so that he could stay longer in Thailand. I wrote out my lines in English and had them translated into Lao, which I then transcribed into phonetics. I was extremely shy and nervous, but I went to see him. He graciously agreed to meet with me. He was small of stature, had a lovely smile, and almost put me at my ease, but I was too anxious about making myself understood that I couldn't think of anything else. I perspired, felt hot, and fumbled through the request; Lao is very hard to pronounce. And no, he couldn't do any more to help Khounta.

Children Depart for America

I went to Bangkok again on July 19 to see the children off to America. They had their American visas, and the Red Cross issued them laissez-passer travel documents. On July 27, we took them to Don Muang Airport. We checked them in and took them to Immigration. It was an open counter and not in a separate room as it is now. A flight attendant with China Airlines was waiting for them behind the immigration desk. He cautioned, "Hurry up. The plane is ready to take off." However, the Thai authorities were not going to let them leave. We did not understand. We had the necessary documents and boarding passes. I began to feel flustered, what was wrong? The officials were demanding entry stamps in their new laissez-passer documents. They suspected the children of being illegal immigrants. They wanted to know how the children had come to be in the country. Fortunately, Khounta had thought to bring his passport, and he took it out of his shirt pocket and showed the immigration officials the children's Thai entry stamp. They flew to San Francisco on China Airlines.

I had informed China Airlines of the children's ages and their service was fantastic. The attendant who met them after they had gone through Immigration stayed with them overnight in a hotel in Taipei, where they had to change planes. Alice spoke no English and Peter's was limited. I had arranged with my sister Melissa and her family in Carson City, Nevada to take care of them until we could. She agreed to do this with the caveat that they stay with her for one year. She felt that only a few months would be too much of an emotional upheaval for Peter, Alice and her two children. We were sad and apprehensive to see them go.

On the way back to town, Khounta remarked that the kids didn't seem sad to leave us. Which is true, they hadn't. They were so excited to go to the USA. It was Alice's fifth birthday, which we had celebrated that morning, and Peter was nine. We had had his birthday party around B. Ellen's pool in May. My mother and I had bought special party favors and decorations for him when I was in California, and Peter had brought them from Vientiane to Bangkok.

My mother met them in San Francisco. Because they had crossed the International Date Line going east it was still July 27, so Mama gave Alice another birthday party. After a week with my mother, my sister picked up the children and took them to Nevada, where she gave Alice a third birthday party.

I caught the train back to Vientiane on August 2. A few days later, I received a note from Khounta that said, "On 5 August Khounta drove to Nong Khai." His Thai visa and extension period had expired. Therefore, he had to leave Thailand. When he first requested his Thai visa in Laos, he had asked for one good for two journeys. He had used one. He took the ferryboat to Laos, checked in at Immigration, checked out immediately and returned to Thailand. That meant he could stay in Bangkok another month. He had a friend at Lao Immigration deliver the note so I would know.

I flew down to Bangkok three weeks later to spend some time with him before his Thai visa expired and he would have to leave the country. He had obtained a five-day extension, but he couldn't get it extended for a longer period. I took the train back to Vientiane on September 10, and Khounta flew to Paris the next day.

Life in Vientiane

For the next two months, I went to work as usual. I taught a couple of classes. In the evenings, I usually went to Margie Manley's house. There was not much to do, but we drank a lot of gin and tonic, told stories, and laughed a lot. Because of the curfew, I would drive home a little before nine through the empty, silent streets. On the weekends, I would get our push lawnmower and cut the grass at our two unoccupied rentals. French families rented three of our houses. A Lao cousin, one of Alice and Peter's sisters, and her husband moved into the Wat Nak house, to which Khai and cousin BounNyok had moved all our furniture. I continued to pack and ship boxes with my brother's assistance. It was a very peaceful existence. There were no phone calls or letters, so I didn't know where Khounta was, what he was doing, or how Peter and Alice were getting along. Admittedly, I enjoyed the peacefulness of no family responsibilities.

The new players in town were the Russians. Instead of Americans, hundreds of USSR personnel and their families settled in to do aid work and support the new government.

Now they were the spenders of U.S. dollars in the markets and shops. As far as foreign support was concerned, the average person would not have noticed. There was a big difference, however, at the restaurants. The Russians demanded bread instead of rice. Fortunately for them, Laos has always had excellent French bread, a legacy of colonial France.

One day when I was sitting at my desk at LAA, my brother-in-law Phanh came to see me. He said that he was going to Viengxay in a few days. I looked at him, astonished. "But you promised Khounta you would leave if you knew you were going to be sent away for *semina*."

Semina is the Lao word for re-education. It sounds like seminar, a nice soothing chain of syllables, and, calling up to the Western mind, visions of sitting around in a comfortable, relaxing atmosphere of study and exchange of ideas. In Lao, it is pronounced flatly with no accent and the final *"ah"* drawn out. It means sitting on wooden benches for hours listening to endlessly repeated communist rhetoric and publicly criticizing yourself for what you have done, which under the new politics was bad. Phanh explained that Nang Kellie didn't want to leave Laos. "But you promised," I pleaded. He said he would be all right. As a colonel in charge of veteran affairs, he was due to retire in six months in any case. They would return him to Vientiane then. I continued to try to persuade him to leave, but he didn't want to go without his wife and remaining three sons. Phanh went a few days later and didn't return to Vientiane for almost nine years.

When the communists took control in May, they began to divide each village into cells of ten houses, in one of which they quartered a soldier. Next, they divided the men, women, and children in each cell by sex. After that, they divided the people into three to four age groups, each with a leader. It was the leaders' duty to report on the others in their group; what they said, what they did, children against parents, siblings against siblings and neighbor against neighbor, under threat of being sent to Done Chan Island in the Mekong River or an island in Nam Ngum Lake. The leader was responsible for his/her group, and if he/she did not report an infraction of the rules, then the leader was sent to an island. The communists were skillful at cultivating fear and mistrust. Even I trusted no one.

In November, I received a job offer from Bell Helicopter International in Iran. In the months before the fall of Laos, I had been inquiring into employment overseas. Some of my friends had gone to work at BHI and had been supporting my application. It had come through. I told Margie I had a job in Iran. She decided to come to Bangkok with her five children to see me off and to do annual doctors' visits with the kids. We planned to take the train as usual. We arranged to leave on November 14 after the That Luang Fair.

"That Luang" as foreigners refer to it, is the biggest celebration in the country. It falls on the evening of the first full moon after the end of Buddhist Lent, and it is preceded by a fair of one or two weeks. Embassies would have a stall telling about their country, businesses would exhibit their products, and ministries would explain what they did, and, of course, there were people selling food and drinks, clothes and local products, and games of chance, and rides for children. One year I took Alice for a merry-go-round ride. The wooden horse bumped her so hard that she became frightened and cried so loudly that I had to rescue her. It was at That Luang at the USA booth that I first saw moon rocks, astronaut suits, and pieces of the spaceship. Hundreds of people from all over the country attend the celebration.

In 1975, there were only a few embassies with exhibitions. The newest embassy was the Cuban Embassy. At their stall, they played typical Caribbean music, and embassy personnel danced salsa and other West Indian dances. They laughed and obviously enjoyed themselves. The story was that the new Lao government interpreted the rhythm and dancing as representative of Western decadence, and asked the Cubans to stop. That led to a bit of a showdown. The Cubans said that if their cultural heritage were to be denied, they would close their embassy. The music stopped for one night. The Lao backed off, and the music started again. After so many months of very long faces around town, it was lovely to hear vibrant music and see happy faces, if only for a few evenings. On the night of the full moon, the government sponsored the most spectacular fireworks display I have ever seen. I watched from the Manley's driveway, less than a kilometer from the fairgrounds and the fireworks appeared to be almost overhead. They boomed and dazzled onlookers for a long time.

The night before I was to leave Vientiane, the Chom Chang village cell requested that I come to a meeting at the village chief's house near Chinaimo, ostensibly over the ownership of one of our properties. We were renting our house in that village to some French teachers at Dong Dok. I went with Khounta's Uncle Noukham. We arrived and added our shoes to the pile of footwear at the door. It was evening, and the typically unpainted wooden house was dim inside with dull light coming from a few naked light bulbs hanging down from the ceiling. When you step into a Lao house, you enter into one large room. At night, the owners string this room with mosquito nets and put mats and thin mattresses on the floor for sleeping. Everyone in the household sleeps together. When I entered, I faced eleven men sitting in straight-backed wooden chairs placed against the walls around the room, six officials and five soldiers in green uniforms with their AK-47s at their sides. They had not left them at the door. They all looked very grim. We sat down. They interrogated me for an hour, "Where was Khounta? Why hadn't he come back with me? When was he coming? Where were the children? What were they doing? What were my plans?" One man would ask, and then another would ask the same questions. There was no interpreter, and my Lao was limited. I simply said the children were going to school and that Khounta would be back soon. They also wanted to know about our property on the river where the French teachers were living. The meeting was eerie, but not frightening. I knew they would never hurt me, but I worried, groundlessly, that they might hold me hostage until Khounta returned.

On the morning of the 14th, we went to work at LAA as usual. Later, Joan Rogers came to my office with some startling news. The train was on strike! I couldn't believe it. It had never happened before, and I had been taking the train for twelve years. Shocked, I went to Margie's classroom, which I never did, and stood in the doorway. She looked up and knew something was wrong. I explained. We decided to go anyway.

I didn't tell any of my Lao family or friends. Whom could I trust? I simply assured them that I was going to Bangkok for a short visit as I had done many times before. I felt bad that I left like that, but I was afraid for them.

At Thadeua, we took the ferryboat to Nong Khai and from there an overnight express bus to Bangkok. The kids settled down all right, but Margie and I spent a sleepless night in semi-reclined seats, sharing one blanket in the cold air conditioning. When we arrived, Bangkok was flooded due to heavy rains and high tides and looked very bleak under a gray sky. We went to Millie Sojak's apartment, and the seven of us camped on her floor.

I got a visa for Iran and flew out on November 20, arriving at Mehrabad Airport, Tehran the same day.

Iran

November 1975

Iran! What did I know about the country? I knew it had high mountains. Airfare was high because of them. I knew the country was mostly a desert. I knew the Shah and his beautiful wife Princess Soraya had divorced because of fertility issues when I was a teenager. It had shocked and saddened me that such a thing could happen. I knew that the Shah had a fabulous 2,500-year anniversary party in 1971, celebrating the foundation of the Persian Empire. He invited all the foreign royals and the heads of state from around the world to Persepolis, the ancient capital near Shiraz. I saw photos of the celebration in National Geographic. I thought that the Shah was the richest and most powerful man in the world. The riches came from the oil under the sands in the south of the country. I knew the Shah had an Internal Security Service: SAVAK. I had heard rumors that it was the strongest and most brutal security force in the world.

And BHI! What did I know about it? I knew that many of my friends from IVS in Laos who had been teaching English had obtained a job with them and that Bell was the name of a helicopter.

Why did I decide to go there? Why didn't we fly as a family to the States? Why didn't Khounta go with Peter and Alice? There were many reasons. The primary one was money. We didn't have any. Job outlooks in the States weren't good. Khounta was 48. Though that isn't old, some people consider it old regarding hiring in the United States. My perception was that companies liked to hire young people just out of college with the latest engineering knowledge. I didn't say anything about this to Khounta, and I don't think it occurred to him. Also, Khounta's English was poor. His accent was hard to understand, and he couldn't write in English. His language of choice was French, but the rest of us didn't know French. Additionally, my job prospects in the USA were negligible. I had never held a full-time position doing anything in the States. I didn't know what kind of a job I could get. I was a teacher, but I didn't have a California teaching credential. All of these things made me afraid to risk going to the States. Then there was the condominium we had bought in Honolulu. The mortgage and maintenance fees were due each month. I was following the rule of a bird in the hand is worth two in the bush.

When I arrived at the airport in Iran, BHI Human Resources met me and took me to the Commodore Hotel on Takte Jamshid Boulevard in downtown Tehran. BHI had contracted with this hotel to house all incoming personnel. New hires could stay there for up to six weeks while they looked for a place to live. BHI had a housing service, and someone helped new employees search for and visit available housing after work.

The day after I arrived, someone from BHI took me to Amirabad, the name used for the training facility for depot-level helicopter maintenance on Amirabad Street. At this facility, I met my future boss and caught up with many of my friends from Laos: Doran Butts, Jim Gershin, Tommy Tufts and others. Doran and Tommy invited me to dinner at their homes to meet their Lao wives and to see their accommodations. It was very comforting to have friends in this new and unfamiliar environment, and I appreciated their hospitality very much.

After that, I went to Corporate Headquarters to discuss my contract. I didn't sign it but took it with me to compare it with those of my friends. They looked at it and said it was the standard contract. Besides a salary, there was a monthly cost-of-living allowance, a housing allowance, a moving-in stipend and a travel allowance, although BHI bused us to and from work every day. Also, I received BHI clothing: four blue shirts (two with long sleeves and two with short sleeves), two pairs of gray slacks, a matching vest, a dark blue jacket with the BHI logo on the breast pocket, all made of synthetic material. Instead of slacks, I could have chosen two gray skirts with elastic waistbands.

The next day I signed my contract and went to the office. There was not much to do but talk to my friends and learn about the company. BHI was a paramilitary venture contracted by the Iranian government. It was supplying Cobra Attack helicopters and training Iranians to fly and maintain them. It had two divisions. One division was in Esfahan, where the pilot training took place. The second division was the Training Division in Tehran, located at Amirabad and Mehrabad Airport Depot. The Training Division employed about 700 American men, the majority of whom were Vietnam War veterans or had acquired experience somewhere else with the armed forces. The heads of the different departments were retired majors, colonels and lieutenant colonels. The director, whose office was at Mehrabad, was a retired army general. There were only two American female employees not in secretarial positions and wives of other personnel: Betty F, who had worked with IVS in Laos, and me.

Another important thing to learn about was the Iranians. BHI policy was that we were not permitted to fraternize with our Iranian colleagues or our students outside of the office. That made it almost impossible to meet people. What I learned about our colleagues was that many of the Iranian women who worked for BHI were Jewish. Jewish women didn't wear chadors. The Shah didn't allow women to wear the chador, a head-to-toe black cover-up cloth, in the workplace of any of his undertakings. Consequently, there weren't as many Muslim as Jewish women at BHI because they didn't want to go without the chador.

The next thing I learned was that the Shah had promised BHI that the men to be trained as pilots and maintenance workers would speak English. However, BHI was receiving trainees who didn't speak English. Therefore, it had to arrange for the men to receive instruction in English. It contracted Telemedia, Inc., an English-teaching organization based in Chicago, to provide this English teaching.

That is where I came in. Because of my background in teaching and directing programs in English as a second language, the Director of Amirabad moved me from the Learning Center to Quality Assurance. I became BHI's English language expert, working with BHI Headquarters' contract personnel. It was my job to write the Statement of Work (SOW) for the contract with Telemedia and to monitor its activities in fulfilling the terms of the contract. I had never heard of or seen a SOW. It was all military jargon to me, but I set about doing the job with help from the contract personnel. It was an ironic turn of fate. I had interviewed for a position with Telemedia in April 1975 at the TESOL Convention, but they had turned me down.

Outside of work, I was making friends with other new employees staying at the Commodore Hotel and looking for an apartment. One thing my new friends at the Commodore interested me in was skiing. I didn't know how to ski, but it was a very inexpensive pastime in Iran. I bought skis, and all the other paraphernalia one needs and joined the BHI ski bus on Thursdays. (In Iran, our weekend was Thursday and Friday. Friday is the Muslim holy day. The workweek was Saturday to Wednesday.) It took us to Dizin in the Alborz mountain range, fifty miles north of Tehran. There were no trees, and the highest ski lift went to about 11,500 feet. One could start at the top and ski for thousands of feet to the bottom. It easily took me an hour because I was afraid to go fast. The Shah had the ski area built in 1969 with T-bars, chair lifts, and gondolas. It was where Crown Prince Reza Shah and other family members came, but I never saw any of them.

In the mornings, the bus let us off at a parking lot, and we had to ski down to an ugly cement building where there were toilets, and it was possible to warm up and get something to eat. The way to this building was down a narrow, icy ski slope with a high embankment on one side and a steep drop on the other. It was very frightening, and I always took a long time traversing back and forth on the way down.

By the time I was down, the sun had melted many of the icy patches. And the skiing was easier. My friends taught me how to walk uphill, slow down, and stop on skis. It wasn't easy, but it was very exhilarating. The bus trip back was always lots of fun.

In the evenings, I looked for an apartment. I finally found one near Niavaran, down the hill from the Shah's palace. I chose it for many reasons. Tehran is on the slope of a high, bare desert plateau, and it is about 10F degrees cooler in the north of the city than in the southern part where the bazaar is located. Also, it would be a short bus ride for the children to go to school. It was one block from Medone Ektiarieh, the neighborhood plaza, and surrounded with shops, a bus stop, and a blue taxi stop. My new home was the bottom apartment in a four-story building. The front rooms on the street side, the kitchen, and living room were four feet below ground level, but in back the two bedrooms had glass walls and doors looking onto a small hard plot of ground with a couple of trees. An eight-foot high wall enclosed the garden, just as walls hemmed in all houses and gardens in Tehran. That was for privacy. Our landlord was the chief of the fire department for Tehran. That was a tremendous job as more than ten million people lived in the city. His name was Mr. Jenabzedah, and our street had the same name. Every month I would walk up the hill about five blocks to their palatial villa to pay the rent. I looked forward to this visit because Mrs. Jenabzedah was a beautiful and charming woman and I didn't know any other Iranian women. She spoke a little English and was sympathetic to Khounta and our position in having to flee Laos.

I bought all our furniture and appliances in one fell swoop from a family that was leaving. I had never furnished an apartment or house before, and it wasn't something I felt comfortable doing. I had always left it to Khounta. In Iran, there is almost no wood. There are no big, old trees for lumber. Trees are planted close together, so they grow straight, and cut young to make ladders. The kitchen cabinets were metal. The dining room table reminded me of garden furniture. It was wrought iron and painted white with a glass top. The washing machine had a wringer on it. Before moving the furniture in, I had beige carpeting laid on the cement floor. Later we purchased carpets to put on it.

I joined the Pars-American Club, which was a short bus ride down Saltanintabad, one of the main north-south streets in Tehran. The Pars Club was a paradise of coolness and relaxation. It had a huge swimming pool, tennis courts, and a restaurant. In autumn and winter, work ended at BHI at 4:30 and in spring and summer at three o'clock. It took about thirty minutes to get home on the bus. One couldn't work late because it would mean missing one's transportation home. Therefore, in summer, I could always be relaxing by the pool before four p.m.

Another thing I thought I should do before my family arrived was to learn to speak and understand some basic Farsi. Classes were in the evening, and I had time to attend, which I wouldn't have after they arrived. I signed up for classes at the Iran-American Association, the USIS binational center in Tehran. It was easy to get to the school in the afternoon, but at night it was a challenge to get home. That was when I learned about the blue taxis. I learned they had a set route. The way to catch one was to stand in the street and shout at the taxi where you wanted to go. I always shouted, "Saltanintabad." If it was going there, it stopped, and you jumped in. One shared the taxi with three or four other people. When you arrived where you wanted to get out, you said, "Stop" in Farsi. The cab driver remembered where he had picked you up and charged you the number of rials you owed him. There was a blue taxi terminal for one of the routes near Medone Ektiarieh, which was very convenient for me. A taxi from there went to the south of Tehran, a very long distance. At the end of its route, I would later learn, was the only place possible to buy pork.

Getting around in Tehran was confusing and exasperating. Some streets run almost straight from north to south in the city, but there are no straight east-west streets. The BHI bus that took us to work varied its route frequently to confuse potential terrorists. While I was there, murderers attacked an American Embassy car and killed the occupants. I lived in the northeast of the city and Amirabad was in the west. Consequently, for more than a year, I couldn't recognize where I was at any given moment, and I would never have been able to direct a taxi to my house. That was very disorienting and made me feel directionally dim-witted.

I wanted to learn the bus routes, so I wouldn't have to depend on shouting at blue taxis. So one Thursday I caught a bus at the bus terminal and rode it to the end of the line. The driver got out and went to have some tea with his friends. I thought I would walk around the dusty little plaza where the bus stopped to see what was there. Soon, three children started following me. I said hello in Farsi, but they weren't friendly. I felt threatened, but I continued walking around the plaza, but also in the direction of the bus, as quickly and unconcernedly as I could. I felt something hit my back, then again. I realized the children were throwing rocks at me. I was surprised, but I got on the bus quickly and sat down. Then the kids started throwing dirt clumps and stones in the door at me. So many came in that I had to move to the back of the bus and put the windows up. I'm sure the bus driver wasn't very pleased with the mess the children made, but I was fair game. The kids were probably bored, and I was a woman not wearing a chador in a small, traditional village. So much for a fun-filled day of exploration! I never did it again.

Family Arrives

One morning in April 1976 while I was standing on the corner waiting for my bus to work, another man in a BHI uniform showed up. It was Ron Orbas. We introduced ourselves, and I learned that he worked at Corporate Headquarters and had just returned from home leave with his family. Although we had been neighbors for more than a year, our paths had never crossed. High walls enclose houses in Tehran. Therefore, although the Orbases lived across the street, all I had seen was a high wall. The entrance to their house was on the road parallel to ours. To get to it, one walked up the alley along the wall on the side of their property. The house entrance was around the corner.

In July 1976, BHI informed me that Peter and Alice would be arriving on the 26th. With great excitement, I went to the airport to meet them. We had been apart for one year. When they arrived, we hugged and kissed and talked all at the same time. I took them to the apartment and showed them their room. The next day we went to the Pars-American Club to swim and eat. They told me about Carson City, and I told them about what I had been doing. On Saturday, I had to go to work. I had to leave the children in the apartment. Alice was six and Peter was ten, but they were very mature children, and I had no qualms about leaving Alice in Peter's care. I knew he could take care of her. After a year in the States of hearing and speaking only English, they both were fluent. In fact, they had forgotten most of their Lao.

Every day I would go to the toy store down the street from Amirabad and get them a new game or craft activity to do while I was at work. When I got home, and Peter heard my key in the lock, he would shout, "Mommy's home, Mommy's home." They would come running. It was music to my ears, and I can still call up his soprano voice and experience the joy he gave me. They would throw their arms around me in great hugs and show me what they had made that day, and I would present them with the activity for the next day. Then we would grab our swim gear and catch the bus down Saltanintabad to the Pars-American Club. On the way home, it was late enough that the evening taftun bread was just coming out of the tandoor oven in the sidewalk at the bread shop. We would get a piece and tear into it as we walked to the bus stop. It was hot and delicious.

Before the children came, I consulted my sister about getting a TV. I had never owned one. Today I don't own one. She said it was a good babysitter, so I got them one. TV broadcasting began at noon, and the two or three stations that came on were in Farsi. However, there were four evening programs a week in English, and we never missed them: *Charlie's Angels*, *The Million Dollar Man*, *Rhoda*, and *The Donny and Marie Osmond Show*. They were all reruns, but since I had never watched TV before, they were new to me.

Peter had brought his skateboard with him, so on the weekends, we went to Shahenshah Park, the biggest park in central Tehran. He would skate and Alice, now six, would run. She always wanted me to time her. "Time me, time me," she would demand and race to some predetermined point and back. Then she would do it again, and again, each time asking, "Was I faster that time?"

The Tehran American School (TAS) started in September. It was immense. Alice began the first grade, which was divided into four classes. Most girls wore T-shirts and pants or shorts to school, but not Alice. She preferred to wear the long dresses that her cousin Teresa had given her. Peter went into the fifth grade.

The school had four baseball fields, and formal T-ball and Little League for the elementary students. Peter joined Little League. Peter was a skillful player and was usually his team's pitcher or catcher. He had played Little League for the Pirates at American School Vientiane. I signed Alice up for T-ball. That was a challenge. She loved to run, but she was afraid of the softball and couldn't catch or throw it. In the evenings, I would take her up on the flat rooftop of our apartment building and roll the ball to her, and she would roll it back. She cried and shied from the ball in the beginning, but eventually, we got it into the air. Ultimately, she overcame her fear and became an enthusiastic player.

Slow pitch softball and baseball teams for men and women were the rage. I belonged to the women's slow pitch BHI team. I was a good ten years older than the other women on the team. I couldn't control the direction I wanted to throw the ball, nor throw it very far, so I played right field as the ball rarely came there. At bat, I could get to first base sometimes and then get as far as third before the inning was over. In spite of me, the team usually won, and I shared in the glory.

It was not until after school started that I met the rest of the Orbas family who lived across the street. Sallie Ann, Ron's wife, taught math at TAS, and they had three children. Jim was Peter's age, Sallie Carol was a couple of years younger, and Christy was Alice's age. One

Thursday afternoon in mid-September, a national day of mourning for the death of Ali, Muhammad's grandson, Christy came over to play with Alice and Peter went over to the Orbas' house. When he arrived, their dog Abejo jumped up and sunk his teeth in Peter's upper arm. Sallie Ann doctored Peter up but didn't think it was necessary to telephone me. She realized Peter had had a terrible scare but decided not to overreact and scare him further. Furthermore, she was worried about what to do with the dog. The Iranian kids teased him from behind the gate, so Abejo didn't like children. The Orbases had a place to lock him up but had forgotten to do so before Peter arrived. Peter never complained about the bite. He spent the afternoon teaching Sallie Carol how to skateboard, and together they tried to learn their five-times tables.

Around five o'clock, I escorted Christy home with Alice and was shocked to see Peter's puncture wound. It had been bleeding all day long. I had never met Sallie Ann before, and I thought it strange she hadn't called me. Peter plainly needed stitches. I immediately got Peter and Alice into a blue taxi and went to the nearest hospital about fifteen minutes away. At the hospital, they said that dog bites had to be treated at the Pasteur Institute, and the hospital wasn't allowed to dress his wound.

We caught another taxi. The Institute was fifteen minutes farther south in the city. When we arrived, the doctor asked where the dog was. He explained that he couldn't treat Peter without having the dog. I felt confident that Abejo didn't have rabies and wasn't going to bother Sallie, whom I had just met. He said, "No dog, no treatment."

I bought some bandages and iodine. For a week I made butterfly bandages for Peter's wound before it closed and stopped bleeding. To this day, Peter keeps his distance from dogs. Cats, too for that matter. That was a dramatic introduction to Sallie, but our families became wonderful friends over the next two years, playing baseball, skiing, taking hikes, and cooking and eating together.

By November, I had completed the Statement of Work. It was time to leave for contract negotiations between BHI and Telemedia at BHI Corporate Headquarters in Bedford, Texas. BHI was a subsidiary of

Textron, which is listed on the New York Stock Exchange. BHI asked me to go as part of the corporate contract team. I felt excited and mystified. How had I had gone from mowing lawns in Vientiane to flying half way around the world to help negotiate for a multi-million dollar corporation?

Khounta arrived at the end of November, about five days before I had to go to Texas. It was wonderful to be a family again but terrible to have to leave so soon. Tehran is a foreign and challenging place to move around in if you have no one to help you. I was glad that the children were going to be with Khounta and not a babysitter, but it was unfair to leave him so soon after his arrival. Besides, we had been apart for fourteen months. It was a strain to have to go.

In Bedford, the two men from BHI contracts and I stayed in a motel, conveniently across the street from a bank. On the advice of Ed Stewart, one of the retired army officers with whom I rode the bus to work, I began my Individual Retirement Account (IRA). It was the first year it was available, and it was possible to make a tax-deferred contribution of $1,500. It may seem funny information to include here, but by yearly saving for my eventual retirement, I am now happily independent of support from my children and free to live and travel wherever I like. It was a life empowering decision for which I am very grateful to Ed.

It was around the same time that my mother and father also gave me some excellent financial advice. Pa sent me a newspaper clipping with a grid showing how much a family would have to save each year to send their child to a home state, out-of-state or private university, depending on the child's current age. I followed the advice, set up custodial bank accounts for Peter and Alice and funded them each year so that they would have the necessary funds to go to a California university when the time came. My mother put me in contact with her stockbroker, John Tucker, Sr., at Sutro and Company, and he made wise investments for me for many years. For our family, BHI proved to be the pot of gold at the end of the rainbow.

From Bedford, I flew to California to see my mother. She would leave in a few days to visit us in Iran. I always gave Mama a round-the-world ticket to visit me wherever I was living. We consulted on Christmas presents and clothes to bring, and then I departed. We would fly around the world in opposite directions.

Back in Tehran, we met up. As a family, we had a wonderful time showing her the sights in Tehran. My mother especially liked the visit to the crown jewels. She and I left Khounta with the children and visited Isfahan, Shiraz and the ruins of Persepolis. Her visit was over all too soon, and she continued her tour of the Middle East then home to Piedmont.

One change in the family routine that Khounta initiated while I was away was dish washing. Alice was assigned the lunch dishes and Peter the dinner dishes. Peter understood that when Papa said to do something, you did it. Alice rebelled. She was not tall enough to reach the sink, so she had to stand on a chair with an apron tied around her waist. She cried a lot and said, "I can't do this. I can't get the dishes clean." We assured her we would accept the best she could do. At night, when I tucked her in, she told me, "I'm not your servant."

Khounta looked for a job in Tehran, but had no success and was terribly depressed. After six months, his Iranian visa expired, and he had to leave the country. BHI sent him to Kuwait to get a new visa. It was a horrible experience. Khounta said the room in the hotel was like a broom closet and that the Kuwaitis were rude to him.

Khounta could not get a dependent spousal visa because in Iran, a Muslim country, a woman isn't accepted as the head of the family. It has to be a man. Women could get a dependent spousal visa, but not vice-versa. It was and is the same in Laos with some exceptions. Unless one is employed by a government-recognized organization, there are no spousal visas, only business visas. If I hadn't had a job when I lived there, Khounta couldn't have obtained a visa for me. Rather than taking on the expense and inconvenience of sending Khounta abroad for a visa every six months, BHI decided to give him a job. However, BHI was not interested in his education and experience as an engineer or an administrator. The first job it considered was in the warehouse at Mehrabad depot. I was totally against it. It was a demeaning job, and the trip to the airport would take an hour. Furthermore, the supply room was hot in summer and freezing in winter. It would be a miserable place to work. Finally, they gave him a job at corporate headquarters. It was closer to home, it was warm, the people were friendly, and he would have his own space. His job was to sort and assemble the dead files, that is, the records of people who no longer worked for BHI. He liked reading them. He found the stories of the former employees' behavior fascinating, amusing, and almost unbelievable. His boss wanted him to hurry up and not read the files, but Khounta told him that he had to be sure the information was going into the correct file and not into a file of someone with the same name. This job didn't value his potential to BHI, but the working conditions couldn't have been better. I worried about his state of mind after having been a high-ranking government official, but he never complained or said anything.

New Friends and Life in Tehran

Christy, and sometimes Sallie Carol, came over to play with Alice, and often Peter and Alice would walk over to the Orbases to play. The girls loved Barbie dolls and could play with them for hours. Khounta would play Monopoly and other board games with them. He was good that way and enjoyed spending time with them. That was a change from Laos where he had spent little time with the children other than to go swimming. I was more interested in outdoor activities.

The Orbases sometimes came over to watch *The Million Dollar Man* and *Charlie's Angels*. Khounta would cook up Vietnamese rice noodle soup, which we loved. He nicknamed it bone soup. An essential seasoning of the soup was fish sauce. On our return from a trip to Bangkok in November 1978, Peter, Alice and I each tried to smuggle two-liter bottles of fish sauce onto the plane to improve the flavor of our food. It was against regulations to take such strong smelling items in the cabin as hand luggage. We spent several days looking for big, plastic bottles into which we could consolidate the fish sauce. Peter and Alice went ahead of me through the hand luggage checking line. Fortunately, the authorities didn't look carefully at what they were carrying, but they caught me, and I had to forfeit my bottle. Alice helpfully tried to tell the officials that she had fish sauce, too, but I shushed her and pushed her and Peter ahead of me with their bottles. Airport personnel called Margie Manley, and she came all the way from central Bangkok to pick up my contraband fish sauce. A letter telling her not to bother wouldn't have reached her in time.

Reza, a Telemedia student, invited us to visit his sister and her family in Qom, a holy city for Shi'a Islam in Iran. I guess no one had told him that he couldn't fraternize with BHI personnel. It would have been impolite to refuse, so I accepted. We set the date, and Khounta, Peter, Alice and I took a blue taxi to the meeting spot in the south of Tehran. Reza was waiting for us. His brother was supposed to pick us up, and we were to continue the journey to Qom, but after an hour he hadn't come. Reza was embarrassed. After a few phone calls, he invited us to wait at his house, which was nearby. We took a taxi. Upon arrival, Reza asked Khounta if he would like to take off his pants. We were dumbstruck. Khounta looked to me for a sign of what to do. I discreetly nodded. Khounta said, "Yes." Reza went away, came back with a pair of pajama bottoms, and showed Khounta the bathroom where he could change. The custom was for men to lounge in comfortable pants so that their street trousers would stay neat. We had passed the cultural test without a flutter. We gathered on the carpet to wait for his brother. It was getting toward lunchtime, so Reza produced some *ghormeh sabzi* (Iranian spinach and lamb stew) and lovely Persian rice. Eventually, his brother came and drove us to their sister's place in Qom.

In Qom, the women covered themselves with a black chador whenever they went into the street, but at home with only their family in the house, they didn't wear a chador. However, because Khounta was not a relative, Reza's sister wore a white chador inside the house while we were there. We gathered with the family in the front room on a beautiful, $10,000 carpet. It was the only furnishing. When we ate, they put a cloth on the carpet to protect it from spills. At night, they put down bedding, and the four of us lined up in a row to sleep. It reminded me of the Lao custom, but they use woven mats rather than carpets. The family members had their rooms.

In the morning, we went to see the sights. I was very nervous because I had heard inappropriately dressed foreign women had been stoned to death in this center of Islam. I was well-covered, but we were very obviously not Iranian. Reza wanted me to put on a chador and go in the Holy Shrine of Hazrat Ma'sumeh, but I was too scared. Khounta went, however. He said it was very like the other mosques we had been in.

In the afternoon, we took the bus back to Tehran. We loved having this one opportunity to be in the home of an Iranian family and experience how they lived.

When it snowed, we rode the BHI ski bus with the Orbases. I got Alice ski gear, but she was too afraid to ski. The rope tow scared her silly. Peter flew down the slopes all day. Khounta and I struggled at our ability levels.

One of our favorite winter foods was hot beets. A man on the Medone had a pushcart of steaming beets, much like the carts you see on the streets of Vientiane with fruit sellers or in Hong Kong with hot chestnuts. We would choose a large red beet. The vendor would peel it and cut it up into pieces to eat with little sticks. It was delicious in the cold weather.

An unusual spring delicacy was green walnuts. We would find them on our walks in the hills and peel them, but the green walnut hull stained ones' fingers black. It was easier to buy them from the men sitting along Saltanintabad who sold them from tall glass jars filled with water. The walnuts were white and soft and reminded me of laboratory specimens. I never bought any.

In football season, we went to Peter's games. Alice became enamored with the pom-pom girls and decided to be one when she was old enough. The kids took swimming lessons at the Pars-American Club, and Peter took tennis lessons. He had his teeth straightened. I taught Alice to roller skate. Peter joined the Boy Scouts. They camped in the snow, and the eggs froze. It was too cold for me, but they loved it. Alice joined Brownies.

One day, as I was sitting at the kitchen table, Alice, who was now in the second grade, came up to my side and declared, "I know where I come from." That caught my attention. "Oh, I said, where is that?" She pointed to my belly and said, "I come from your stomach."

I smiled and thought quickly. I said, "You're right. You come from a stomach, but not my stomach. You came from your mother's stomach." She looked puzzled, and I explained, "You and Peter have another mother. You came from her stomach. You are very lucky. You have two mothers." She accepted that, and there were no more questions.

Peter had not forgotten his birth parents in Laos or his eight brothers and sisters, but Alice had no memory of them. We never talked about them. By this time, three of them were in the Lao Refugee Camp in northeast Thailand near Nong Khai, waiting to be relocated to another country. Khounta and I couldn't sponsor them to go to the States because we weren't living there.

In good weather, if we had no baseball or football game to go to, we would walk with the Orbases in the hills farther north. That was particularly pleasant in the warm spring and autumn. The children would run around exploring, and Sallie, Ron, Khounta and I could talk at leisure.

On September 8, we joined the Orbases for an exhilarating day of inner tubing down the Karaj River north of Tehran. Christy and Alice played along the riverbank, and Khounta watched. The river snatched Ronald, Sallie, Jim, Peter, Sallie Carol and me, and rapidly carried us through its rough and winding course with us spinning and shouting through the rapids and cheering each other on. The water was quite cold, but the danger of what we were doing kept our adrenaline high and we didn't feel it. After a mile or two, we got to the shore, and our friend T.J. drove us back to the start so we could go again. We had time for four trips that day.

It was late when we returned, and police stopped us at a roadblock on the outskirts of Tehran. That was new. We learned that many people had been killed in a demonstration in the south of the city. A military curfew had been declared at six a.m. that morning, and martial law the night before, but we hadn't known. The announcements had been in Farsi. September 8, 1978, is known as Black Friday in Iran. On that day, thousands of demonstrators marched peacefully toward Jeleh Square. The people were asked to disperse following the ban on gatherings of more than three people, and when they didn't, the military opened fire killing about sixty-five. The newspapers reported the killings to have been in the hundreds. The event turned foreign governments and more Iranians against the Shah's political authority and marked a turning point in the anti-government activities around the country.

A month earlier on August 19, the Rex Cinema in Abadan had burned to the ground with 700 people locked inside. More than half of them were burned alive with the rest escaping through the roof. Accusations went in all directions. Was it SAVAK or Islamic terrorists? That disaster, along with banks being burned down and massive demonstrations in outlying cities showed that the Pahlavi regime was ineffective in controlling the public. The horror of the fire showed me, as none of the reported protests and bank burnings had, that the Shah's government could not survive. The people's exuberance for change reminded me of Laos and made me sad. The Shah had modernized the country. He had granted women many rights in education, dress, and the workplace. I believed the loss of the Shah would change everything, and not for the better.

Getting Citizenship

When Peter and Alice came to Iran in 1976, they traveled on a white booklet called a "Permit to Reenter the United States," not U.S. passports. I was annoyed that my sister and mother had not gotten them passports.

The children were in the U.S. for a year. It would have been very easy for them to get them naturalized, or so I thought. I had no idea how difficult it would be. Because I was working for a U.S. paramilitary organization, my family was entitled to expeditious naturalization, that is, they didn't have to live in the United States the obligatory five years. They didn't have to live there at all. I understood that I just needed to send in the application forms, birth certificates, and a letter from BHI.

Now I had to get the children naturalized from half way around the world. Doran Butts, my friend from Laos who had married one of his Lao students, told me that the Immigration and Naturalization Service (INS) workload in San Francisco was so great that it would take a year to process their citizenship through that office. Because not many people applied through Hawaii, the paperwork would move much faster there. I, therefore, decided a trip to Hawaii would be much more pleasant. In May 1977 I wrote the INS and applied for an interview. They wrote back that Peter and Alice were not my children!

I remember reading the letter in the muted flickering of the fluorescent lighting in the sterile, impersonal, windowless, gray-walled Quality Assurance office at Amirabad. What did they mean? Of course, they were my children! I was incensed. How could they say that? I couldn't believe it. What was I going to do? The problem centered on the fact that we didn't have any adoption papers. When we got Peter and Alice, we simply had new birth certificates made naming Khounta and me as the father and mother. All the required officials witnessed and stamped the new birth certificates. I supposed we could have lied on the INS forms and said that the children were our natural children, but that could have raised many questions. Why had their births not been registered at the U.S. Embassy when they were born? In fact, I didn't know Khounta when Peter was born. We were married several years later. What if they took blood tests? Khounta, Peter, and I were B+, or so I thought, but not Alice. We didn't know. DNA testing didn't exist. What were we going to do?

In December 1977, we all traveled around the world on vacation. First, we spent Christmas in California with my parents and sister and her family. Then we went to Thailand, stopping in South Korea on the way. The children, Peter now eleven years old and Alice seven, had visas, but Korean Immigration did not want to let them in the country because they were from a communist country. After many consultations at different levels, they were permitted in. The departure was somewhat bizarre, too. The children had been allowed entry, but now there was a question of whether or not to let them leave. After some delay, they were authorized to go. To enter Thailand, the children had to have a Thai sponsor who put up a bond ensuring their departure. I am very grateful to my friend Khun Oie at AUA who sponsored them and ran the paperwork.

When we arrived in Thailand, we went to the Lao Refugee Camp near Nong Khai. After two years, Nang Kellie had finally found the conditions in Vientiane unbearable, and Phanh was still not back from re-education camp. Their middle son had escaped Laos on his own a year after his father went to *semina*, and, as an unaccompanied minor, was sent to join his two older brothers in France. In Laos, the remaining two sons had not been receiving a proper education because their father was in a re-education camp. There was no medicine in the country, and nutritious food was insufficient. Nang Kellie had escaped across the Mekong River with her cousin Oudone, a close friend, and some of their children. The three women, whose husbands were all army officers in re-education camps, had enough money to build a small house of bamboo. It was a cooler, more comfortable and private place to live compared to the refugee housing provided.

Peter and Alice's brother Deng, and sisters Vongphet and Vongkeo, and Vongphet's son Joe were also in the camp. They wanted to go to the USA, but Khounta and I couldn't sponsor them because we weren't living there. Their brother Van and sisters Air and Khemphone joined them in May 1979 by escaping across the Mekong River, holding onto banana trees and kicking with all their might. They all finally got to the United States in September 1979, settling in Anaheim, California. The four in the camp lived in two small, bare cement rooms in a row of long buildings built for the refugees. They had come with nothing and slept on mats on the cement floor. They threw their arms around Peter and Alice and were delighted to see them, but Alice didn't make the connection that they were her siblings. There was nothing to do in the camp, but walk around and chat with friends. Some Hmong women were making beautiful appliqué cloths, and I bought several.

In the afternoon, Khounta, his mother, his sister, his cousin, the close friend, our children and I gathered on the bamboo slats of the front porch of the bamboo house. It seemed quite grand and comfortable after seeing the cement buildings. Khounta's mother had come over from Vientiane. She had diabetes and high blood pressure. The Lao government allowed her to go to the hospital in Nong Khai, but she had to return after her treatment, which she did. The government did not consider older people a risk of becoming refugees and Nang Im was about sixty-seven years old. Khounta was grateful for this opportunity to see his mother. We had a *baci* ceremony and spent the night in the bamboo house. I was gratified at last to have a Lao traditional ceremony with my loved ones, even though it was in these unfortunate circumstances. We didn't know if we would ever see his mother again.

We spent New Year's in Chiang Mai with Dee and Terry Quill, and their children Tony, Keith, and Danielle. Afterwards, we went to Bangkok to visit other friends. We stayed with the Manleys in their house on Lang Suan Road, and we told everyone our immigration problem. Our friend Ed Kenny, now working in Thailand, suggested that we get a letter notarized by the former Minister of Justice, who was running a Laundromat in Massachusetts, saying that the issuing of a new birth certificate was the method of adoption in Laos. He wrote the letter and had it notarized by his daughter, who was a notary public. I also submitted an affidavit saying adoptions were processed like that in Laos. Years later Khounta asked me if I believed that was the adoption procedure. I had because he had told me it was. I said yes, and he laughed.

The process of getting the additional documents took another year. Finally, we sent the application in again. The INS wrote that they would send them to the Library of Congress for a ruling. After several more months, INS gave us an appointment in October 1978 for the final interview for citizenship. Khounta stayed in Tehran, and Peter, Alice and I took off around the world again. In Hawaii, the children and I went to the INS office. A very nice man invited us into his sunny office. We sat in front of his desk in comfortable chairs, and he interviewed the children, swore them in, and they signed their certificates. He issued them Certificates of Citizenship. Then, all smiles, he wished us a happy vacation in Hawaii. We shook hands and went to the passport office.

At the passport office, I filled out the forms and turned them in. The next day, when I went to pick up the passports, they were given to me, and I was asked to wait for a moment. A high counter with a thick glass divider on top separated the office workers from the applicants. In this barrier were holes for speaking and passing papers, just like at a theater box office or in a prison. However, the room was occupied by gray desks piled with papers and gray people trying to keep from being buried under mounds of documents

A woman came from the back of the office and asked to see the Certificates of Citizenship. I showed them to her. "How did you get them?" she demanded. She asked for them to show her supervisor. The woman's manner was harsh and threatening, and I didn't like the way she looked at me. I had worked hard for the documents, and I wasn't going to let them out of my sight for a moment. I didn't give them to her.

We left the passport office thrilled and excited to have passports that easily opened most port doors around the world, and I thought no more about it. It never occurred to me that the woman was going to cause trouble.

My mother, my sister, and her two children came to Hawaii for a vacation to see Peter and Alice and to celebrate their citizenship. We played on the beach, went to Pearl Harbor, visited the zoo, and had fun.

Peter, Alice and I got visas for Iran, Taiwan, and Thailand. On the way home to Tehran, we visited our friends the Suggses in Taipei and the Manleys in Bangkok. My brother was in Bangkok, too, and we had a wonderful Thanksgiving dinner together at the Manley's.

Tehran: the Last Days of 1979

When we arrived in Tehran on November 24, 1978, it was a very changed place. The Tehran American School had closed permanently. At home and in my office, we had electricity for only a few hours a day. All telecommunications into and out of Iran were blocked. *Kayhan,* the local English-language newspaper, was no longer published. There had never been any news in English on TV. We were isolated from the rest of the world.

BHI began to downsize. Since there was usually no electricity during the day, work at Amirabad couldn't proceed. We were wholly dependent on our electric typewriters and the photocopy machine. Besides, there were no lights and not much heat.

I had a second office at the Telemedia Language Center, which was closer to our apartment than the office at Amirabad. I had a car and driver and was not dependent on the BHI bus, so I chose to work at Telemedia. Many of the Telemedia teachers and staff had been evacuated so there was not much to do. Many days I just stayed home, packed our belongings, and made an inventory of everything in each trunk, right down to the last salad fork.

I found a Christian missionary school within walking distance of our apartment for Peter and Alice. Each pupil had a cubicle and workbooks for programmed learning. BHI wanted to send the children back to the States. I asked with whom they would stay, and who would pay for their accommodations. BHI had no answers. I told them I had recently been separated from my children for a year, and I was not going to be separated from them again. They were in school, and we would stay together as a family.

There was a nine p.m. curfew in effect now. We spent New Year's Eve at the Orbases. It was a fun time of food, champagne, and laughter. We had come prepared to spend the night because of the curfew. On New Year's Day, BHI called me. I was surprised people were at work. They informed me that the children had to leave the next day. Again, I refused.

Earlier in the year, Dick Russell, one of my assistants, had introduced me to Persian carpets. I had always found them too busy and too colorful, but now I loved them. I began meeting him at his house on Fridays, and he would take me to his favorite shop. It was about fifteen feet wide. Against the walls were stacks of carpets. The owner would throw them down, one by one. If we were attracted to one, we would get on our hands and knees, examine it and count the knots. If I liked it, I would take it home for a month or so to see if Khounta and I felt we could live with it for years. In this way, we had a steady change of carpets and eventually bought several.

One day in mid-January 1979, I went with my friend Janice Zewlenski, a Telemedia teacher who also lived near Medone Ektiarieh, to her boyfriend's carpet shop in the south of Tehran. It was a tense time, and we both wore scarves to cover our heads and be as inconspicuous as possible. I spent $3000 on two beautiful carpets. That was enough to make the day memorable, but it was also the day the Shah and his family fled the country. People in the street went crazy with jubilation. They turned on car headlights, pulled the windshield wipers away from the windows, and drove around in circles honking their horns. They put flowers on their cars and gave them to people on the street. The vision of the events remains colorful and noisy in my mind. It was very stirring to see their elation. We didn't stay on the street long but quickly caught a taxi home.

Over the next several weeks, BHI evacuated all but essential personnel. The children continued to go to school, and I kept packing. Khounta went to work. Houses and apartments in Tehran were heated with *naft*, that is, kerosene, and it was becoming hard to get. The petroleum industry had gone on strike in October. Fortunately, our neighbor Ahmad on the fourth floor was able to get a truckload for us, so our apartment was never cold.

The Ayatollah Khomeini arrived in Tehran on February 1.

On February 7, BHI said the children had to leave. I finally acquiesced. The next day we took them to the Hilton Hotel for out-processing and transportation to the airport. The place was in an uproar with Iranians occasionally coming in and threatening with guns, causing everyone to drop to the floor. Khounta wasn't feeling well. On the ninth, Peter and Alice got the last U.S. Military Transport flight (MATS) out of Tehran. They flew via Athens to Texas, then to California. My mother met them in San Francisco.

Khounta was in lots of pain. I took him to the nearest hospital, where they admitted him. He was having a severe bout of kidney stones. BHI wanted us to leave, but Khounta couldn't travel. Ron and Sallie Orbas were still in Tehran, but their kids, pet rat, and Abejo had flown out a few days before Peter and Alice. I wanted to take Pishey, but Khounta said I couldn't take another cat to my mother. She already had Jin-Jin. I visited Khounta in the hospital by blue taxi every day.

On February 11, the Shah's troops were defeated in street fighting. Now firearms were no longer guarded and were available for the taking. Men helped themselves. Khounta told me that when they took him for X-rays the emergency room was always full of Iranians who had accidentally shot themselves with their newfound weapons. It was scary to be out on the streets because men were riding around in taxis waving their guns out of the windows. That was how people were shot by mistake. I was surprised that the men were so unsophisticated with the automatics and pistols because, by law, every Iranian man had to be in the army for two years.

On February 16, the Iranian newspaper showed photos of three men whom they had interrogated and killed the night before. One was Major General Manouchehr Khosrodad, the Iranian general counterpart to the American Director at BHI in charge of Training at Amirabad. Their deaths marked the beginning of the interrogation, torture, and murder of more than 400 people in the higher echelons of the government and the military.

I went to the bank next to the Amirabad building to get our money out. The bank was closed and the doors locked. However, a bank clerk recognized me through the glass door and let me in. He let me with-draw all our money. Other BHI personnel were not as lucky at their banks. Another day, I went to the Tehran American School to return the French horn that Peter was learning to play. I wish I had packed it up and taken it with us! It is probably unused to this day. After that, I went to the Pars-American Club to get a refund on our membership. I was not lucky there. The driveway had a chain across it, and the guard indicated that the Club had closed.

BHI arranged for our belongings to be shipped to Piedmont. I was disappointed that the warehouse at ACE, the preferred company, was full, so our things were stored with a different company. Later, disap-pointment changed to euphoria. ACE burned to the ground. Had our boxes been there, not only would we have lost our possessions, but even more importantly, our documents.

There were no scheduled flights in or out of Tehran for ten days. Then the U.S. Ambassador, William Sullivan, was able to negotiate evacuation flights to Frankfurt on Pan American planes for BHI per-sonnel, and probably other American groups as well.

In the last days, as I walked around Medone Ektiarieh, I felt melan-choly when I thought about leaving Iran. Tears came to my eyes. That hadn't happened when I left Laos. In our apartment building and the shops we frequented, there were friendly faces. I remember the pharma-cist telling me that the Iranians were not angry with Americans, only the American government. He said he was sorry to see us go. It had taken more than a year to become familiar with where things were and how to get around. After more than three years, I felt at home and wanted to stay another ten years. As a family, I wanted us to explore more of Iran and take the train to Istanbul. The Orbases had visited Afghanistan, and I wanted to go there, too. Work, outdoor activities, school, climate, and the food agreed with us. Our family was thriving. We were discussing how to give Peter and Alice separate bedrooms. We were not ready to go.

On February 18, Khounta was barely well enough to travel. Our shipment of belongings was gone from the house. We had a stove, refrigerator, some furniture, and our ski equipment to sell. I had decided that downhill skiing was too dangerous. The speed scared me, and I was afraid of breaking a leg. I had already been crashed into on the slopes by a hit-run skier. After sliding down the hill on my back, I was able to stop but had severely sprained my left wrist. I invited the neighbors in and sold everything. We went to the Hilton Hotel again, where we had to spend the night. We stood in a long line to sign separation papers and to get some American dollars for traveling. Khounta was still feeling poorly and had to sit down whenever he could.

In the hotel, the doorframe to our room had been shattered, so we could not lock the door. We kept the curtains closed and were careful to stay away from the windows because men out front found it entertaining to spray the hotel with bullets.

We were bused to the airport. I hand carried the silk Isfahani rug that I had bought the month before through customs and onto our evacuation flight. After we had boarded the plane, Iranians came down the aisles for a final search. They wanted our BHI ID cards. I kept mine as a souvenir. We held our breath as the plane taxied down the runway. When the wheels left the tarmac, people cheered and clapped.

In Frankfurt, we met up with the Orbases, who had flown out on the plane after ours. We went to a restaurant and enjoyed a delicious farewell dinner of Kasseler Rippchen (special pork chops) and sauerkraut. The next day in the hotel, I was surprised to see the missionaries from the school Peter and Alice had attended. The Iranians made them leave with only what they could carry. I felt sympathy for them because they had to leave all their possessions and family heirlooms in Tehran.

From Frankfurt, Khounta went to Paris to see his sister and nephews who had recently been resettled there from the refugee camp in Thailand. I went to Bangkok for six weeks to recover at the Manley's.

CHAPTER 27

California: 1979

I went to California in April in time for Easter. Khounta didn't join us because when he arrived in France, he was still quite ill and spent a few weeks in the hospital getting medications to stabilize his diabetes and hypertension. He had to begin insulin injections three times a day. The children and I dyed Easter eggs, already a family tradition. I was the Easter bunny and hid the eggs in the garden.

My mother loved all the holidays and celebrated them with decorations, gifts, and traditional food served using her best china, silver, and glassware. She had Easter decorations, big and small paper eggs that opened with tiny hinges and fastened, baskets from my childhood, and some tin painted Easter eggs from hers. We added to them with lots of chocolate eggs from See's Candies, pink marshmallow rabbits, and yellow marshmallow chickens. For dinner, we had a leg of lamb, and my mother always baked a pink or white bunny cake for dessert decorated with shredded coconut, with long ears cut from stiff white paper. She used the Valentine heart-shaped cake pan turned upside down. I smile now remembering our holidays spent at my mother's house.

A letter from the Immigration and Naturalization Service had been waiting for me in California since November 1978, saying that they had issued the children's Certificates of Citizenship by mistake. I was to return them, and they would refund my money. I called the INS to ask what to do and said I would not return the Certificates. They insisted. I said I was sorry, but I would only return them when new certificates were issued. I had not asked for the Certificates of Citizenship, which had been issued to us by the very friendly, kind man at the INS office in Hawaii. I had filled out the forms for the children to be naturalized. I had never heard of Certificates of Citizenship.

I had to start the application process again, this time for Certificates of Naturalization. Fortunately, my shipment from Iran with the earlier application forms and birth certificates had arrived intact. I needed witnesses to say that I was a good mother and that the children had lived with me for some years. Who was going to do that? We had only been in the States a couple of weeks. In the end, my mother and our friend Jean Martin agreed to help. We went to San Francisco, without the children, for an appointment in a cluttered office in a tall, gray, impersonal building. My mother and Jean were interviewed. I received a refund for the previous certificates and paid higher fees for the new applications.

A month later, my mother and I went to a swearing-in ceremony to complete the naturalization process. About one hundred applicants and many of their family and friends gathered in the U.S. Court of Justice in San Francisco. With them, I raised my right hand for Peter and Alice and took the oath of allegiance. When their names were called, I walked down the long central aisle, received the new certificates, and handed back the first ones. The person handing out the Certificates of Naturalization looked at them. Then he looked mystified and a little irritated, shook his head, and muttered, "Why?" I shrugged and moved on.

A Year in Limbo 1979-1980

My mother was happy to have the children and me with her. She thought I was gone from her life forever when I married Khounta, but daughters have a way of coming back. My mother was the Dean of Admissions and Dean of Student Affairs at the San Francisco Art Institute (SFAI). Alice was in the third grade at Havens School, which was across the street, and Peter was in the seventh grade at Piedmont Middle School, which was across the street on the other side of the block. Peter's classmates knew he had come from Iran and thought he must be Iranian. Khounta had to stay in France for his health. Because he had diabetes and high blood pressure, he didn't qualify for private insurance in the U.S.

He was very discouraged about finding a job. He realized his engineering skills were rusty because he had been in administration for many years. He was fifty-three years old, and his English was difficult to understand. Consequently, he was determined to find a job in France. We would have liked to live together as a family, but without jobs, we didn't have any money or prospects for health insurance. The schooling in California was better for Peter and Alice, neither of whom spoke French, and they and I could live with my mother.

I was concerned about my future. What was I going to do? I had been living outside the United States for sixteen years, except for graduate school in Hawaii. I had never felt any desire to come back and settle down in America, but now I was trying to convince myself that I should be ready to do so. I received unemployment checks from Texas because that was where BHI was headquartered, but the cost of living in California was much higher than in Texas. I needed a job. I was a professional ESL teacher. Therefore, I decided it would be a good idea to take some professional development courses to make myself current with mainstream thought, and then look for a job.

TESOL, to which I had belonged since 1966, was having a Summer Institute at UCLA. I decided I would go. I telephoned my friend June Pulcini and asked if I could stay at her place in Hermosa Beach for the six weeks of the Institute. She was delighted and greeted me with open arms. They had a guesthouse behind their house where I could stay for as long as I wanted. From her house, it was a long bus commute to Los Angeles, but sometimes I got a ride with June's next-door neighbor who worked at UCLA. I took a course in ESL testing and another in school administration. I took up golf too, but I couldn't seem to hit the ball, let alone make it go in the direction I intended.

Peter and Alice came and stayed with me for a couple of weeks in July when the courses finished. During this time, Alice turned nine, so she planned a birthday party for herself, from games to party favors, and made a cake. It was a great success. June was very impressed with Alice's organizational skills. Alice knew what she wanted, and she made it happen. June and Marvin May, her partner, had a 27-foot Catalina sailboat moored at Port Royal in King Harbor at Redondo Beach on which we would picnic and go for an occasional sail. June and Marvin each had a daughter Peter's age, and all the kids and I had a lot of fun going to the beach and out in a Zodiac dinghy to catch mackerel in the yachting marina.

The children and I returned to Piedmont. I still didn't know what to do with myself. When I was a junior and senior in high school, I had taught sailing to adults on Lake Merritt in Oakland. Pa suggested I take the Red Cross Sailing Instructor course at the same lake. I completed the course, learning to sail and teach on a larger boat than I had taught on in the 1950s. Sailing took my mind off my employment difficulties.

Years before, John Beery, one of my former sailing students, had opened a business teaching sailing and selling boats at Berkeley Aquatic Park. His father had invited my father to live in the boathouse/sales office, which John rented from the city. By 1979, my father had lived there for about twenty years, and the business in the boathouse was going to close. Gene Harris, one of my classmates in the Red Cross sailing course, opened her own boat business in the boathouse, and we have been good friends ever since. My father continued to live there for another twelve years.

While I was studying sailing and thinking about my future, I was also looking for a job. I thought that perhaps a new career was in order. I didn't want to teach English as a second language in public schools in California. Besides, I didn't have a California teaching credential. I wanted to go back overseas where I felt more comfortable.

In Piedmont, I had been attracted to advertisements by the Computer Learning Center (CLC) where they taught computer operations and computer programming. I decided that computer programming sounded interesting. So, after the sailing course, I took out a bank loan and began a six-month course.

CLC was on Howard Street off Fremont Street in San Francisco. I commuted daily with Jean Martin, who had helped with the children's naturalization and was a computer programmer at Del Monte Company near Fremont Street, and my mother, who drove every day to the San Francisco Art Institute in North Beach.

At CLC, one of our teachers was a former data processing employee at BHI in Tehran. He taught the introductory course. We also had courses in Assembly, RPG II, and COBOL. The instructors would give us an assignment, and we had to figure out the logic and write a program to perform the task. In those days, we used keypunch cards, one for every line of the program. CLC employed one keypunch operator to punch the cards. Then, if the program didn't run, we would have to debug it until it did. I spent about ten hours a day going to class and writing and debugging programs. Sometimes Jean would help me with the debugging. I found the challenge all consuming. I wouldn't notice the passage of time. Fortunately, for the children and me, my mother was always there. Mama usually cooked dinner. Peter and Alice occupied themselves with school and their new friends. We all pitched in with feeding the cats and dog, doing household chores, and caring for the garden. Peter had my former bedroom, and Alice had my sister's room. I slept in the attic.

In May, the course finished. During the time that CLC was helping us with our résumés before we looked for a job, I received a call from my friend B. Ellen of Thailand days. She had already asked me if I would be interested in a job in Burundi, but it was a French-speaking country, and there would be no schools for the children. I couldn't work, learn French, and home school the children, so I had to decline. Then she called again and asked me if I would be interested in Karachi, Pakistan. I found out all I could about the city. Its proximity to the beach and its development and history were very inviting, but the country was very unsettled at the time. Deposed Prime Minister Ali Bhutto had been hung the year before. General Zia had declared himself president and martial law was in force. Not a safe place for us. So again, I declined. This time, she asked me to go to Madrid, Spain. I said yes immediately, and that was the end of my nascent computer-programming career. Spain! I had always wanted to go there, and now I would be paid to go.

CHAPTER 28

Spain

1980-1981

The United States Information Service (USIS) wanted a new director/director of courses for the bi-national center in Madrid. The USIS library and the English language program had recently been turned over to ACHNA, a Spanish organization. It had a longer name, too. *La Sociedad de las lengua y cultura de norteamericanos*. USIS maintained a Cultural Affairs Office, with a USIS officer and a display space in the building that they rented for the ACHNA library and language program. Because I knew many of the USIS English language division staff from my time in Laos and Tehran, and because they wanted someone whom they knew was familiar with the bi-national center policy and procedures, they approached me. USIS hoped that I could resolve the labor problems that ACHNA was having with the American teachers.

In Piedmont, we were all very excited that we would be going to Spain. We would be nearer Khounta, who was still in France living with his sister, and my mother, father, and siblings were interested in visiting Spain. My mother and I had fun shopping for new clothes. Peter and Alice would stay in Piedmont until school began in Madrid. Peter was doing very well on the swim team.

I wrote Khounta and let him know when I would arrive in Paris, and he met my plane. He had arranged for us to stay with Madame

Boulom, the former French wife of his friend with whom he had first gone to France to study. She lived in Chilly-Mazarin in Essonne near Paris. I knew her from when she came with her children to Vientiane in the sixties and again from when Khounta and I were married. Her children were grown and no longer living with her. Khounta and I were thrilled to be together again. We took up where we had left off as if we had not been apart for more than a year. He had to put mattresses side by side on the floor for sleeping because Mme. Boulom only had her children's old single beds. I could only stay for a few days, but we made plans for Khounta to drive to Madrid. Then I had to go.

On Sunday, June 22, 1980, the longest day of the year, I arrived in Madrid. Mano Villa, the business manager at ACHNA, met me and took me to a hotel within walking distance of my workplace. As it was Sunday, most of the shops were closed, but I was able to get some drinking water and food for the apartment with Mano's help. I unpacked and took a nap because I was still jetlagged. When I woke up, I decided to take a walk. The sun was high in the expansive blue sky, and the light was brilliant. I walked to the Palacio Real. Hundreds of people were walking, smoking, and kissing all around me. They were enjoying the freedom of behaving the way that they wished, free from the constraints of General Franco, the authoritarian dictator who ruled from 1939 until his death in 1975. From the Palacio Real, the largest royal palace in Western Europe, I walked and soaked in the buildings, people, and street activities until I arrived at the Puerta del Sol, a vast plaza in the center of Madrid. It was alive with people and stalls selling things. I felt fantastic. I looked at my watch for the first time thinking it must be around 3:30 in the afternoon. It was 10:30 at night! I thought, how can this be? It is late at night, and it is as light as day, and there are so many people walking around. I didn't know the Spanish dinner hour could easily be 10:30 or 11 p.m. and that some of the bars and dance clubs on the square didn't open until 1 a.m.

Khounta came for a week's visit. While I went to work, he drove into the countryside exploring. On the weekend, we went to Avila for the first time. It is a beautiful walled city. I later went there many times with the children. When my mother, father, sister, and brother came to visit, I took them there, also.

Very quickly, with the help of the American Embassy housing office, I found a lovely three bedroom, two-bath apartment just four minutes walk from work. It was in a large apartment building, and we lived on the fourth floor. All the apartment balconies overlooked a large garden with grass and flowers built on top of the apartment's underground garage, but no one was allowed to go into it. It was just a quiet, green place to look at. It was a foreign idea to me, to have a garden and not be able to go in it, but in that way, it stayed manicured, and no loud voices or barking dogs disturbed the peace.

It seemed that every second apartment kept one or two dogs. People took them walking, of course, but they didn't clean up after them, so one had to be careful where one stepped. Once a week, or thereabouts, a man came, and he sprayed lime on the building walls to neutralize the urine smell of the dogs' pee. Another custom that was new to me was that many people smoked while walking down the street, including young women. It was at this time that I gave up even the occasional cigarette. I could get plenty of nicotine just walking to and from work.

Alice and Peter arrived at the end of August, bringing our household belongings. I enrolled them in the American School of Madrid. The school bus took care of their transportation. Some friends of ours from Vientiane, Bob and Margery Myers and their boys, Robbie, Michael, and Christopher, lived about a kilometer from us. Robbie and Peter had birth dates a day apart, and Michael was in the fifth grade with Alice. In Laos, Margery was the den mother for a pack of Cub Scouts to which Robbie and Peter belonged. In Madrid, Bob was the den father for a pack of Boy Scouts, so Peter's scouting continued. Alice joined Girl Scouts.

On Saturday mornings, I got up early and went alone to the fresh food market a few blocks up the hill from our apartment. At each stall, people stood around waiting their turn. On arrival at a stall, you would ask the other customers, "*La ultima*?" That means, "the last one" so you would know when it was your turn to be served. You did this wherever people were waiting to buy things such as fish, cheese, meat, fruit, vegetables, etc. I appreciated this practice because there was not a line, just a gathering of people.

Peter and Alice would still be asleep when I got back. After putting the food away, I would start the washing machine. The children were supposed to have put their clothes to be washed in the kitchen the night before, but they always seemed to forget, and I had to gather the dirty clothes from their rooms. Finally, I told them that if they did not put their clothes in the kitchen to be washed, they would have to wash them themselves. They both ended up learning how to sort whites from colored and to do their own laundry. Alice earned a Girl Scout badge for her new knowledge.

On the weekends, we picnicked in Retiro Park, which is vast and green with many trees and paths, and grass that one cannot walk on. It has a pond where you can rent paddleboats. The children loved to be out and be able to run and walk in the freshness of the park. We went to the Prado Museum, delighted to see the huge, marvelous canvases of Velasquez, Goya, and other Spanish painters. Sometimes we took a bus to Segovia, Avila or Toledo and other times we just went to the Puerto del Sol or our neighborhood bar and had a *bocadillo de calamares*, our favorite baguette with deep fried battered squid. Peter was fourteen, so he and I drank beer. Beer and tea cost less than popular soft drinks, and I believed they were healthier to consume, so Alice drank tea.

At Christmastime, we bought a tree at the Puerto del Sol, and hot roasted chestnuts from the street vendors, a new delicacy for us. We celebrated Christmas following my family's tradition of Santa Claus coming on Christmas Eve and leaving presents to be opened on Christmas morning.

For most children in Spain, however, the gifts arrive on the evening before the twelfth day of Christmas, January 5, *El Dia de los Reyes Magos*, or Three Kings Day. In many Spanish cities during the afternoon or evening, there is a procession featuring the three kings dispensing gifts.

We would always go to the parade, and Peter and Alice would try to catch the candy or toys that the Kings would throw. On January 6, more presents were given and received. On January 7 school holidays were over, and businesses were open as usual.

Daily life continued as normal until one evening when the reception-ist at ACHNA called about eight p.m. and said there was a coup d'état in progress at the Congress of Deputies. I thought, my goodness, these things just seem to follow me around. The Parliament building was quite a ways from our school, and the school closed at nine p.m. I told her to stay open and act as normal. If students chose not to come, that was up to them, but I didn't believe that they or the teachers were in any danger. In fact, this attempted coup d'état, which became known as F-23 after Feb-ruary 23, 1981, the day it occurred, was over by the next morning. It was exciting and alarming for the people who had never experienced any-thing like that, but we couldn't even hear the few shots that were fired. No one was killed, and King Juan Carlos emerged with his position and power stronger than before. I learned a new word in Spanish, "*que verguenza*," meaning "what a shame." The wife of Lieutenant Colonel Tejero, the leader of the failed coup, was mortified by her husband's ac-tions, and we heard her say this on the radio repeatedly. After the at-tempted coup, the colonel spent fifteen years in prison. He was released in December 1996.

At Easter, we took the train to Paris to spend time with Khounta. We stayed with Madame Boulom. We went to the Eiffel Tower, the Pompidou Museum, the Louvre, Les Invalides, the Army Museum, Notre Dame Cathedral, Le Bois de Boulogne and many other places. At Notre Dame when we were across the street from the restaurant where Khounta and I had had our wedding-day lunch, I wanted to have a nostalgic cappuccino, but Khounta said it was too expensive.

One sunny day we picnicked on a park bench along the Seine. Peter and Alice fed the pigeons and chased them out of sight. Khounta kept after me to watch the children. He was terrified that they would be snatched from us if we weren't careful. I couldn't believe it and thought it was ridiculous, but he was dreadfully earnest. After that, I never let the children out of my sight.

We went to the Paris Opera on two evenings. Khounta got us fantastic orchestra seats in the tenth row. The Paris Opera is a beautiful building inside and out. The second time we went, Alice was so excited that she was ready to go an hour before the rest of us. From Madame Boulom's we took the E05 motorway to the end of the Metro at Porte d'Orleans, where we could park. Here we took the Metro in the direction of Clignancourt, and with one transfer, we reached the Opera Station. No car parking was available there. The Metro trip took about 45 minutes. Khounta had it planned so that we would arrive just on time and not have to wait. He hated waiting. As we got out of the car, Alice noticed that she hadn't changed from her tennis shoes to her party shoes. "We have to go back," she cried. "I have to change my shoes. I can't wear these shoes. Everybody will look at me and laugh," but it was too late. We didn't have time to go back. I told her that if she didn't look at her feet, no one else would either. "I can't go," she insisted. "You have to come with us," I said. "Stop looking at your feet." Finally, she stopped looking, and no one noticed.

My mother came to Madrid for a three-week visit in June, but I persuaded her to stay for an additional two weeks. She and I traveled around the country by bus to Merida, Algeciras to Ceuta, Cordoba, Barcelona, Avila, Toledo, and Seville. She had fallen and broken her ankle a couple of months before and needed to walk with a cane, but she didn't let that deter her. In a shop in Toledo, she fell in love with a birdcage with a porcelain base of delicate pastel pink, blue and yellow flowers and delicate pale green leaves. The top piece was of creamy plain porcelain. The wire cage was golden. One could either place it on a table on its feet or hang it from a golden chain. It was a meter tall and cost $150, but it was not a souvenir with which to travel! Sadly, she decided it was not a practical thing to buy, and it stayed behind, calling to her.

When my mother left, she took Alice to spend the summer with her in Piedmont. Peter went to a Spanish language camp. Khounta drove down from Paris where he had been unsuccessfully looking for a job. Our relationship was unchanged. He had never expressed his feelings or shown any affection. Ours was a peaceful and companionable existence with no questions asked, and no information volunteered. We enjoyed exploring new places and eating new food. We visited Peter at his camp and the windmills of Don Quixote.

1981-1982

In October of 1981, my father, who was 81 years old and had never left the States, came with my sister to visit us in Madrid. Fortunately, Khounta was with us, so they got to see him again. I put them on the train two days after they arrived to take the same circuit of cities that my mother and I had done by bus. I had made the train trip with Peter and Alice and found it a more comfortable way to travel. Khounta had to go back to France. I was disappointed, but he said he had some business he had to attend to. About the time my father and sister returned from their trip, my brother came with his Lao girlfriend. We were a houseful. The seven of us went together to Avila and some other favorite cities. My father, sister and I took the train to Lisbon too and visited palaces and gardens. All he saw captivated him. It made me disappointed and sorry that he had never wanted to come to Asia or to visit me in Laos. I believe he would have been equally fascinated.

The day after Christmas, Peter, Alice and I took the bus via Alicante to Calpe on the Costa Blanca. We stayed at a timeshare that belonged to my sister's brother-in-law. Dozens of apartment buildings and bungalows spotted the hillsides around us. Calpe is a favorite place for many English to retire. Every day we strolled on the beach, Peter flew his kite; Alice ran on the sand, and I nestled in the rocks and read. I had Anne Morrow Lindbergh's beautiful book *Gift from the Sea* with me. In the mornings, we watched the fishing boats come in with their catch. In the evenings, we enjoyed the sunset. For New Year's Eve, we got a kilo each of fresh octopus, calamari, and mussels. We spent the day getting the sand out of the suction cups of the octopus, removing the beak, ink sac and cuttlebone from the calamari and pulling the beard from the mussel shells. That night we played board games and ate until we could not swallow another mouthful.

In January 1982, John Berwald of Rescue Now, an organization in San Francisco that was interested in helping refugees, wrote and offered me the position of director. I wanted to stay in Spain because we were near Khounta, and it still wasn't possible for him to get health coverage in the States because of preexisting conditions. I liked my job and especially life in Spain. There were places to go and things to do. We had not toured the northwest, Burgos, Zaragoza, gone skiing nor stayed in many *paradores*, that is, castles and palaces used as hotels for funds to maintain them. It was a difficult decision, but, finally, I decided to return to California as I felt it would be better for the children. Peter was getting Cs at the American School of Madrid. Such grades would not get him into the University of California. I spoke to the school administrators, and they said a C at their school was the same as a B at another high school. I didn't think the Admissions Office at UC would see things the same way. Furthermore, Peter had to be a resident to avoid paying out-of-state tuition, for which I didn't have enough money. Also, neither Alice nor Peter had friends nearby to play with. We lived in Madrid, and most of their classmates lived near the school, which was in an outlying suburb. When I went to see Mano Villa to tell him I had been offered a job in San Francisco, he was up on a ladder in the storeroom, counting books. He came down and listened very intently. I am sure he was quite relieved. My salary and the school fees for the children were restricting profits for ACHNA. Moreover, I had not been able to resolve the labor problems of the long-term American teachers. I was part of "them," the administration, the enemy, to the teachers and they were hostile towards me, which was not pleasant. The Spanish staff and American personnel I had hired were very friendly. I loved living in Spain, but I was the family breadwinner, and I had a job to go to.

Over the Easter break, Alice visited a classmate she knew from Piedmont at the beach in Fuengirola. Peter and I took the train to Portugal. We stayed at a lovely pension on the hill of Castile. On our last day, Peter had his pocket picked on a tram, which was very inconvenient because he was safekeeping the rent for the pension.

In our last months in Spain, we revisited our favorite cities and discovered new places to visit and new delicacies to eat.

Khounta, his sister Kellie, Oudone and another friend came to visit. I should have taken time off work to be with them, but stupidly it didn't occur to me. I could have done it, but for some unknown reason, I felt I had to work. We got together in the evenings and had a dinner party once with Amy Wallace from my office. On the weekend, we walked up the hill to the swimming pool near the apartment. When it was time for them to leave, I went with them as far as Galicia where they dropped me off to visit Mano and his girlfriend on his farm.

In 1982, Spain hosted the World Cup. The country had prepared for this event for two years. Football fever filled the air. The government even minted coins with soccer balls on them. In June, Peter, Alice and I went to Santiago de Compostela on vacation. We watched the games on TV at local bars. One day we went to Galicia and watched the Cameroons play Poland. I have been an avid fan of the World Cup games ever since.

A week before we were to leave, we visited King Philip II's palace at El Escorial. We had snuck over a chain behind the palace into an area not open to the public. We were hurrying so we wouldn't be caught when the tip of my left boot caught between two cobblestones, and I fell face forward. The result was a broken big toe. The doctor offered me a medical excuse for two weeks off work. Unfortunately, I didn't have two weeks left, and I had lots of wrapping up to do in my office. I regretted not being able to take advantage of the opportunity, and I thanked the doctor and joked that it was not necessary, my brains were in my head, not in my feet.

With three workdays left, I received a letter from my mother saying that she wanted the porcelain birdcage from Toledo. I thought it was an extravagant whim. The cage was too big and fragile to be successfully transported to the United States. I decided to ignore her request. But her friend Anona Colvin surprised me with a call from Piedmont. She told me how much my mother talked about and admired the birdcage, and she said that I must get it for her. So I took a day off work and made a special train trip to Toledo to get it. Peter hand-carried it to her in August 1982 when he returned to Piedmont. It hung in her bedroom until she passed away in 2006. My initial exasperation at having to make the birdcage expedition evaporated when I saw how lovely it looked with a stuffed, blue paper bird in it. It was a beautiful and unexpected sight to see the cage hanging where it did, and we loved it.

Leaving Spain, the Trip Back

Finally, school was out. Peter and I put Alice on the plane in Madrid to my mother in California. Our Spanish cat Sootie rode in a box under her seat. I planned a trip to visit B. Ellen in Rome and Eileen Streich, my roommate from Hawaii, in Istanbul, stopping in Paris to stay with Khounta on the outward and inward journeys. Peter saw me off at the train station, then remained another eight weeks to go to Spanish language camp with his friends Robbie and Michael Myers before returning to California.

Khounta was living with his sister in Orly, a suburb of Paris. The French government had provided her and her sons housing in one of the many low-cost housing estates built for refugees and emigrants. Her apartment was on the fourth floor, no elevator. The whole complex was a bit scary with graffiti on the walls and smashed mailboxes. Khounta was always afraid that his car would be stolen or vandalized. He had a tiny bedroom, and at night in bed, we were like sardines in a can. Most of the time, we went out. We went to the Asian markets in Paris, visited his cousin Oudone and his sister's friend with whom she had been in the refugee camp. We drove to the palace at Versailles and picnicked in the park behind it. Picnics with bread, cheese, and wine were our favorite pastime.

After a few fun and relaxing days together, I left most of my luggage and my heavy single lens reflex camera and its attachments with Khounta, who continued to look for a job. I took the train to Florence. It was incredibly hot, as it always is in July. I loved seeing the sculptures, frescoes, and architecture. I was near Michelangelo's statue of

David in the Piazza della Signoria when the news came that Italy had won the World Cup. What a moment! The Italians turned their windshield wipers on and drove around in circles honking their horns and shouting. It reminded me of the jubilation of the Iranians when they heard that the Shah had left.

In Rome, I couldn't find B. Ellen. She had left without leaving me a message. I was disappointed, but I made my way to the catacombs, the outdoor opera, and the Coliseum. The next stop was Venice. I loved seeing the places that I had studied in art history classes in university, taking the water ferries, and watching the glassblowing masters.

Then it was time to go to Istanbul. I bought a sandwich and boarded the train. The seats were in small compartments with two padded, high-backed benches for six facing each other and perpendicular to the window. There was room for twelve people in all. Luggage was placed overhead and in a section that was actually over the aisle outside the compartment, but only accessible from inside by standing on the seats. My compartment was full, including seven or eight young men. On both sides of the border with Italy, the train stood for a long time as customs and immigration officials came through. During these stops, the young men jumped up from their seats and moved their luggage around frequently. I finally understood that they were smugglers. They reminded me of the ladies on the ferryboats going from Thailand to Laos. I nibbled at my sandwich when I felt hungry. I wished for something to drink, but there was no dining car on the train. We slept through the night sitting up in our seats. I thought, soon I will be in Istanbul. The morning seemed to drag on. I wondered when the train would arrive. Then a large man from my compartment beckoned me into the outside aisle. He pointed to a chain-link fence between Yugoslavia and Bulgaria and soldiers with dogs and guns patrolling it. I thought, what is this? We were supposed to go from Venice to Greece to Turkey. When I booked my train in Madrid, I didn't have time to look at a map and my knowledge of the geography of this area was very vague. We came to a station, and some foreigners were herded off the train to show their passports. I was one of them, and by sign language, I learned that I needed a visa for Bulgaria. Naturally, I didn't have one. I hadn't known I was going to Bulgaria! The next surprise for us in-transit passengers was that we had to pay for the visa in U.S. dollars. I had just enough. I was planning to dash off the train at this station in any case because I had found an empty Coke-Cola can in our compartment, and there was a fountain in the station yard where I could fill it with water.

The Bulgarian man knew some English, and we began to chat. He had been to Naples to visit his son who had previously lived in Los Angeles. He explained that his wife and daughter hadn't been allowed to go with him because the authorities were afraid they wouldn't come back. He said he was the soccer coach for the Bulgarian national team. We exchanged addresses. In Sophia, I met his daughter who had come to meet him at the train station. He told me I had to change trains for Istanbul, and he took me to the train and found a compartment for me. A cleaning woman was sleeping on one of the compartment beds. He told me to stay there, and that when she left, I was to lock the door and not let anyone in. I followed his directions. I was extremely grateful to him for his help. The station in Sophia is large, and I would not have known to get off my train and onto another without his help. We exchanged Christmas cards for many years after that until one of us missed a year.

When I arrived in Istanbul, 24 hours later than I had expected, I called Eileen, and she picked me up and took me to her house. I met her husband and her son Nedim briefly. They were on the way to the airport, going to New York. The next day Eileen had to work, so I took a city tour. Deniz, her daughter, was ten years old. We went together to their summerhouse on Princess Island, where there are no cars, only horse-drawn carts. We had an enjoyable time catching up on our lives. She had left Hawaii in June 1966 when I was on vacation on Kauai. We hadn't seen each other for sixteen years, and she never answered my letters. The scant information I had about her during all those years was from her sister Ursel. But we were always friends, and I understood from my experience with Khounta that some people just don't write.

They don't change much, either. We picked up from when we had last seen each other as if there hadn't been a myriad of life-changing events. After ten days in Istanbul, I made my way directly back to Paris. I was prepared with food and water this time.

I brought a Turkish tray-table for his sister in gratitude for staying with her, but Khounta liked it and kept it. We moped around for a few days, not knowing when we would see each other again. There was nothing to say. Khounta needed and wanted a job, but he couldn't find one. His language and education were French, and he felt he had a better chance of finding work in France. Besides, his residence in France gave him access to health services, which he wouldn't have in the United States. The children and I didn't speak French. Their school ages, our lack of funds and jobs didn't allow us to stay together as a family in France. We would have liked to, but our focus was on providing the best for our children. The situation wasn't a happy one, but long separations by family members were not uncommon for Lao. I was familiar with it through my Lao friends from when I first went to work for USAID. Lao husbands, wives or their children would go abroad for years to study or work. I found the idea very shocking and unnatural at first, but it was commonplace to me now. That's the way it was. People accepted it, and so did I. But it didn't keep anyone from wondering, worrying or missing the absent spouse, sibling or child.

After a few more days with Khounta, I flew to Bangkok. Since Rescue Now was interested in refugees, I visited the camp at Aranyaprathet on the Thai-Cambodian border. I went to Nong Khai where I met Sister Mary Hayden and two other Sisters with the Order of the Good Shepherds. They had just arrived to start a program teaching village girls how to sew. The purpose was to provide a means of livelihood to keep the girls in their communities rather than letting them look for work in Bangkok. Finally, in August, I was home in Piedmont with my mother and children, ready to begin my new job.

CHAPTER 29

California

1982-1983

In September 1982, Peter began his junior year at Piedmont High School, and Alice entered Middle School in the seventh grade. Alice was an excellent student, wanting to learn everything she could to do well on her tests. Peter, on the other hand, was more lackadaisical. His attitude was that a grade of C was good enough. Khounta and I knew he was capable of more, so I pushed him, and Khounta worried for both of us.

Every morning I carpooled to work and took the AC Transit C bus home to Piedmont at night. The Rescue Now office was in San Francisco in the Flood building on the corner of Market and Powell Streets at the end of the Powell Street cable car line. On the ground floor of the building was a large Woolworth's and across the street was the Emporium Department Store. Tourists always crowded this corner, waiting to catch the cable car, and people with loudspeakers ranted about some issue or another. It was never dull.

Over the next twelve months, Rescue Now proved to be a frustrating, disappointing experience. My job title metamorphosed from director to operations manager to fundraiser. At first, the title didn't make much difference. Because I was the only employee, the duties and responsibilities for which I had been hired — recruiter of medical

volunteers, trainer, bookkeeper, copy girl and general office gofer—
remained the same. But when they expanded my duties to include
fundraising, not only did I not get a raise in salary, but they also denied me professional development training because I had been hired
with, in their words, "adequate knowledge." In fact, I was never paid
what I had been offered over the telephone in Spain because, as I was
told when I arrived in California, "You don't need money. You live
with your mother." I was offended and shocked. Would the directors
offer that reason to a male employee? Wouldn't they think that perhaps such a situation was temporary until my husband and I could
afford a home of our own? In any case, living arrangements are not a
proper item for salary discussion.

There was another thing that upset me. The board of directors believed that people who dedicated themselves to ideals and worked for
non-profit organizations were naïve and lacked business expertise. I
knew it to be untrue. Also, the board had hired me because of my experience abroad, but they never consulted me on overseas issues, and
if I put forward suggestions, they were ignored.

I was able to negotiate a long, for the U.S., vacation break of three
weeks. However, I had been used to four weeks in Spain. In the spring
of 1983, I went to France, and Khounta and I took a trip through the
Loire valley looking at the grand villas and palaces of former aristo-
crats. It was good to be together, and we realized some of our often
talked about plans of traveling in Europe.

All too soon, I was back at work. As the year progressed, I became
more and more dissatisfied with my job, and in early 1984, I took the
first job that was offered to me at an insurance company. There I received a lot of training and was supported in my efforts for professional development. I received many awards and prizes for my work.
However, the hours were long, and the money I earned was inade-
quate for anything more than basic living expenses.

I was used to having many friends to go out with but had no success in finding anyone with whom I had something in common. My
work colleagues and I were too different in our backgrounds and in-

terests for more than an occasional lunch out together. As a working mother, I didn't have time to make friends with my children's parents, most of whom also worked. Furthermore, people had couples parties, but Khounta was usually away because of his health. In France, the government looked after him, but in the U.S. he could not get health insurance because of his prior chronic conditions.

Khounta continued to look for a job and even tried to start a business in France. It was one disappointment after another. The mayor in the suburb where he lived wanted to hire him. He had the perfect qualifications for the position. Then the mayor realized he was over 45, which disqualified him. We commiserated over the French laws. I felt for him. It was impossible to imagine the discouragement he must have felt, but he never complained.

1984-1987

In March 1984, Phanh was released from re-education camp in Viengxay after almost nine years and returned to Vientiane, where he went to live with Khounta's mother in SiHom. Nang Kellie and his sons stayed in France.

Peter graduated from high school in June and entered the University of California at Davis in September. Alice began high school. During the summer months, Peter escorted Alice and her friend Christian to Spain to the Spanish language camp that he had attended for two years. Khounta met them at the break between the two four-week courses and drove them on a sightseeing tour as far northwest as Santiago de Compostela.

Khounta was very pleased with Alice's academic success in school, but after the summer, he wrote me: *I am still a bit concerned about her — that she still runs after boys since that's what I observed in Spain. I know that it is what youngsters do and that it is the in thing in the United States. In my opinion, a little bit of moderation and another diversion such as cooking, sewing, sports, and music will make her think less about boys. That is only a suggestion on my part. I am still very old-fashioned and conservative, and I like to see young girls being more reserved and behaving well at home and in society.* He never wrote either Alice or Peter, and I never told them what he wrote me. I never spent much time reading his letters. He wrote in French, and his cursive was small and hard to read. I would just get the gist of what he wrote on the first page and give up on the second. It was receiving the letter that mattered—he cared and was thinking of us. Besides, Alice was behaving just like the other girls in her class.

The next summer, 1985, the Orbases gave Peter a job working with them building an earthen embankment at the U.S naval base at Point Magoo. After this experience, Peter decided to become an engineer.

Khounta came for the summer and wanted Alice to drive with him and her brother Deng to southern California to visit two of her older sisters Vongphet and Vongkeo. Alice resisted saying that she had promised to help a boy in her class organize a party and that she couldn't break her promise. Khounta told her that family was more important. It was a stalemate. Finally, she agreed to drive down if she could fly back after two days at her own expense. I thought it extravagant, but it was her money, she had earned it. Khounta agreed, and I thought the matter settled.

When Khounta returned from the trip, he called a family meeting. He was very stern and solemn. He explained that he was the father and children must obey their father. I didn't add that this was Lao culture. I thought they could figure that out for themselves. He asked them individually if they agreed. Peter did not hesitate. He already knew because he had lived with his Lao parents for seven years before he came to us. But Alice was only two and a half when she came. Now she was fifteen. Her experience was of American ways. She did not agree. The result was a permanent rift in the family. Alice wrote Khounta a thoughtful letter telling him she loved him, explaining why she felt the way she did and lectured him on teenagers' feelings and motivations. That did not sit well with Khounta. He wrote me: *Unfortunately, she forgot a very fundamental thing in her reasoning. You can remind her, that being 58 years old, I was once a teenager, and I traveled a lot, I know about culture and life, and as a result, I certainly have more experience and, of course, more than she does. Consequently, I do not need her advice. . . . What I want is that she listen and obey which is what I told her (twice in your presence).* Rightly or wrongly, I didn't intervene in this conflict of cultures. I couldn't take sides, so I said nothing. My hope was that time would resolve the problem, and the wounds of anger and sorrow would heal. Sadly, time ran out.

As for Peter, studying to be an engineer by playing basketball in the evenings and sitting around eating pizzas until one in the morning and then studying for an hour or so did not have good results. He failed several courses and had to go to summer school, which he hadn't planned to do.

Khounta came every summer and stayed for three months. We often took camping trips with the Orbases. In 1986 we went to the San Luis Reservoir. I put a tarp on the ground and our sleeping bags on it. Khounta asked where the tent was, and I told him we didn't need one. The Orbases hadn't arrived yet, but they came about one in the morning. Their car woke me up, and I looked around. Khounta was not next to me. Where was he? I found him in the car. He had never slept out before and was afraid there might be wild animals. It hadn't occurred to me. In my mind, I equated living in Laos with camping because most people didn't cook with gas or electricity, but with wood or coal on little hibachi-like stoves outside the house on the ground or in a shed. To me, they were always camping. But, of course, at night they slept under cover in their houses with the doors locked. The Orbases came with a camper trailer Khounta could sleep in, which he did.

Then in 1987 he and I went with the Orbases to Mexico and camped on a cliff above the ocean. We collected mussels from the rocks and Khounta spent hours cleaning them for dinner. He loved the freedom of camping, being outdoors, and seeing new things.

1988-1989

In June, Peter graduated from the University of California, Davis and came home to Piedmont to look for a job. Alice graduated from Piedmont High School and immediately began her studies at California Polytechnic State University in San Luis Obispo. Khounta and I had driven down the coast with her the year before to look at it as a possible place to go to school. My mother and I drove her down and helped her move into her dormitory.

In September Peter found a job as a Management Trainee with Woolworth's in South San Francisco and continued to live at home in Piedmont.

In 1975 when the new Lao PDR government closed itself to the Western world, Soviet aid and economic policies were instituted. Farms were collectivized, and the government set prices for produce. The people working the land could retain a specified portion of a crop, but the rest went to the government. The system didn't work. Traditionally, the Lao work for their family. As Noukham, Peter and Alice's birth father who visited us in California in 1985, told us, he wasn't going to work hard on his land and receive the same share of the crop and money for it as the lazy people in his collective nor give his harvest to the government. The farms began to produce less and less so that there was only enough for the people doing the work. Economic progress was stymied in the Lao PDR. The government re-alizing this instituted what was called the New Economic Mechanism in 1988. It opened the door for imports and business with other coun-tries. It became possible to get visas at Lao embassies abroad. There-fore, in late November 1988, Khounta was able to visit Vientiane.

Khounta hadn't seen his mother since our visit to the refugee camp near Nong Khai in 1977 when she was in Thailand to see the doctor. He was devoted to his mother. His mother's diabetes and high blood pressure were not as bad as Khounta's, but she was 81 years old, her joints hurt, and she had to walk with a cane. Khounta and his sister had been sending her medicine for years because it was unavailable in Laos.

When we had first met in 1965, Khounta told me that one day he would become a monk. It is traditional in Theravada Buddhism for young men to become a novice or a monk for a period before they get married. Under normal circumstances, Khounta would have already been a monk, but due to World War II and study in France, the time had never been right for him. He told me that at some point in the future, he would have to divorce his wife, if he had one, and give up all his possessions. Now he was sixty-two, his mother was ill, and he wanted to show his respect for her. His being ordained would bring her great merit. It might not be easy for him to follow the monks' routine because he was dependent on insulin, three times a day, and had difficulty walking due to claudication, severe cramp-like pain in his legs due to insufficient blood flow to the muscles. From Vientiane, he wrote, "I hope I can learn a little about Buddhism."

The day after Christmas 1988, Khounta became ordained as a Buddhist monk at Wat Khoua Leuang. That entailed having all the hair shaved from his head, including his eyebrows, dressing in orange robes and sandals, taking the five Buddhist precepts of not killing, stealing, lying, engaging in sexual pleasures or taking intoxicants, and promising to follow the 227 rules of monastic order. In his words: *I had two meals per day. Every day I would wake up at five o'clock for an hour of prayer before the big Buddha statue. After a little bit of exercise and a shower, we prepared ourselves for the tak baht. We walked with bare feet to ask for alms. We returned and ate from the tak baht (the big black bowl). After breakfast, we gave a prayer of thanks. Then we got ready for the work in the temple (on fence construction, on the chapel for the drum, the library, and around the property in general). We had lunch at 11:30 and after that a prayer of thanks. Then we rested for 1½ hours. We resumed work in the temple until 18:30. Then we showered and rested until 19:30 and had prayers before the big Buddha statue. After the prayers, we discussed philosophy and religion with the head monk, and then to bed between 11:30 and midnight. That was approximately my schedule during the seven days. In spite of only two meals per day and two injections, I didn't feel bad or hungry.* He told me later that he was disappointed because he hadn't learned much of anything about Buddhist philosophy. I forgot to ask him if he had to divorce me or if we had to get remarried. Later in March 1989, he wrote: *In Vientiane I paid strict attention to my food, but in spite of that I got a tapeworm.*

In addition to wanting to see his mother again after eleven years, Khounta wanted to get his property back. If he could, he could rent the houses, and we would have an income. Khounta had entrusted the deeds to our property, houses, and land to his Uncle Noukham, Peter and Alice's natural father. Noukham died in 1987, shortly before Khounta arrived, and the titles to the land couldn't be found. The houses and the land had either become occupied by squatters or been given by the government to people returning from re-education camp in Viengxay. Khounta requested restitution from the government. He hoped they would be lenient towards him and eventually return his land.

Khounta also spent many hours with friends and relatives, some of whom had returned from *semina* in Viengxay and some who had never gone. He wrote that his friends *are nationalists but not communist. The people have vegetables, fruit and fish (from the Nam Ngum Dam) in abundance, but pork and beef are expensive. All the necessities, except rice, come from Thailand or Vietnam. At present, there are a lot of changes, but there is still neither law nor a constitution. Martial law is strictly enforced. No one can predict the situation in Laos. This opening of the country is the big topic of everyone. Will it last or is it just temporary? No one can say.* Towards the end of January, Khounta returned to France.

In March, he wrote: *Since Laos opened its borders, all the little commercial shops opened their doors. Everyone is going into business. Small Thai merchants are coming to Vientiane looking futilely to make some fast money. More highly capitalized companies are not coming to invest in Laos. They are waiting for the protection of Lao laws and rules regularizing business and guaranteeing their interests.*

In November 1989, Khounta and I took a vacation. He was residing with his half-brother Chanbona in Argenteuil now. We drove from there to visit our friends Jennifer and Dennis Johnsen, who were living in Gingins, Switzerland. We had a wonderful time walking in the gardens in Geneva, strolling by the lake, and watching cheese making in Lucerne. It was grape harvest time, so we drove to wineries and vineyards to see the picking. We followed the grapes to be pressed and enjoyed the fresh grape juice. We drove to the Italian Alps, hiked, and ate delicious food. Khounta, Jennifer, and I went to the Matterhorn and spent the night. Jennifer and I walked up, and Khounta met us at a viewing point, having come up the mountain by cable car. Every night we had fun cooking, eating tasty cheese, and reminiscing about the good times we had together in Thailand.

On leaving Switzerland, we drove back directly to Argenteuil. It was evening when we arrived. We were relaxing in the living room at Chanbona's house with him and his wife when Khounta left the room to get a glass of water. While he was out, Chanbona told me that Khounta's mother had passed away and asked me not to say anything. He wanted to tell Khounta. Khounta came back in the room and, after a bit, I went upstairs to our mattress on the floor. Khounta came up much later. He didn't say anything, so in the darkness I said I was sorry about his mother. He was too unhappy to speak the words himself, but when he knew I knew, he was able to speak. He told me it was the fault of his brother in Laos that she had passed away because he had not gotten medical assistance quickly. We can never know in these situations. She was elderly and in poor health. I was thankful that Khounta had been able to see her earlier in the year and had spent time in the temple as a monk.

It was not until early in 1989 that I learned about NORCAL, the Northern California Peace Corps Association for returned volunteers, and went to one of their dinner get-togethers in San Francisco. We said our names and country of service, ate dinner, talked and laughed together. What I did now or where I lived was not important. Here was a group of people who had lived in different places all over the globe, and who had listened to Kennedy when he said in his inaugural address, "Ask not what your country can do for you—ask what you can do for your country." We believed we could make a difference, and we had. For the most part, we had all learned another language, about another culture, and we had lived and worked closely with the people in our assigned countries. At last, some people with whom I had something in common.

The next NORCAL event I attended was the annual picnic at Golden Gate Park in San Francisco. As I circulated on the grass from one blanket or mat of people to the next, tasting different ethnic foods and exchanging stories, I met a woman who asked me where I would like to travel next. Having reread Hemingway's *The Snows of Kilimanjaro* recently, I answered immediately, "Mt. Kilimanjaro." The mystery and romance of the word and the way it felt in my mouth captured my imagination. Much to my surprise, she said she would like to go there, too. It was decided.

She put an advertisement in *Connecting*, the NORCAL newsletter to see if anyone else was interested. George Ramstad, who had been in North Yemen, said he would like to go. February had the best weather for the ascent, so we planned to go in 1990. Jack Stoops, a colleague of mine from graduate school, came for a visit from Otsu, Japan. I told him of my plans. He said he was certain his wife, Fujiko, would love to go. He would let me know.

I bought good hiking boots and began to break them in. Elaine Winters, the woman from the picnic and a former volunteer in Fiji, wanted very much to go to China. She got a job shortly after the Tiananmen Square crisis and went. She began getting in shape, too, by hiking up and down the rock stairs behind her school. Unfortunately, she slipped one afternoon and came to in a wheelbarrow. She had knocked herself out and had severely chipped the bones in her knees and elbow. She would not be able to join us.

I worried about altitude sickness, so I signed up with a group of women for a seven-day trek to Mt. Whitney, the highest mountain in the contiguous United States at 14,250 feet. We hiked and camped and slowly gained elevation for five days before the final ascent. It was time well spent. On the sixth day, five soldiers passed us on their way down. They had not made the final ascent because of the altitude. However, we all got to the top, and none of us were sick. On the way down the next day, we saw people lying along the path, vomiting and ill. They had thought they would make a quick day trip to the top. Mt. Kilimanjaro was 4,000 feet higher, but I felt I had passed the test.

1990

George and I flew from San Francisco to Nairobi. Fujiko was to meet us the same day, but it had been snowing in Tokyo so she had to return to Osaka and would try the next day. When we were all together, we left our passports at the Tanzania Consulate for visas. We could get them the next day. While we waited, George suggested we go to Lake Naivasha. It sounded like fun and an opportunity to see more of Kenya. George found a local bus, and we squeezed in. The road was so full of deep potholes that the bus ran on the shoulder when it could.

At dusk, the bus deposited us at an empty campground on the shore of the lake. We were able to rent a large tent, which we put up with the help of our flashlights. Finally, we sat down inside the tent to relax and think about dinner. We had not brought any food, expecting to be able to get something when we arrived. Outside the tent, the moonless sky presented total blackness, and our eyes saw no lights signaling human habitation anywhere, and probably in the dark were hungry animals prowling for their dinner. Luckily for us, Fujiko had bought a pound of See's chocolates, my favorite, on her stopover in Hong Kong. It was our dinner.

The next morning we walked down the road the way we had come and found some shops where we got some bread and eggs for breakfast. Farther down the road was the entrance to what was purported to be one of Louis Leakey's digs. It would have only cost a few dollars to rent a vehicle to go to it, and we wanted to, but George was on a tight budget. We couldn't walk because lions and other carnivorous animals were on the prowl. Instead, we rented a motorboat and went out on Lake Naivasha. When the motor died, we were much too close to the hippos bathing near the shore. Fortunately, we were ignorant of the strength and speed of the hippopotamus or we would have been petrified with fear. George casually got the motor running, and we moved away.

The rest of the trip continued in the same vein. We knew where we wanted to go, and on an hour-to-hour basis, Fujiko and I trusted George to get us there. It worked out perfectly from Nairobi and back.

We took a bus to the YMCA in Moshe in Tanzania. At the border, George was in a sweat about currency because of some discrepancy the customs man caught him in, but he got away all right. At Moshe, we met two young Japanese men. George and I couldn't talk to them, but Fujiko could, and we invited them to go with us. At the Y, we were able to hire a couple of guides for Mt. Kilimanjaro. We left the next morning, stopping on our way for the guides to buy food at the local market. At Mt Kilimanjaro Park Headquarters, Marangu Gate at 6,000 feet, we paid the park fees and started off into a subtropical jungle. At one point I swung from a vine hanging from a tall tree over the road, like Tarzan. Another notch in the pole of childhood dreams nicked. Our destination was Mandara Huts at 9,000 feet, eight kilometers away. The guides carried everything. They had to take firewood besides our bedding and food for all of us. They were very strong men and walked in thongs rather than sturdy boots. We only carried our water bottle, camera, and lunch. When the guides would see me, they said, "*Jumbo Mama.*" I didn't like it because I was not jumbo-size and I was not their mama, but they were being polite. In Swahili, it just means "Hello Lady." George usually went faster than the four of us, and we would meet up at the huts. Going faster resulted in a longer wait for him, and every day he had a headache for going so quickly.

The second day our goal was Horombo Huts at 12,100 feet, 12 kilometers of walking. The vegetation was much shorter and scrubby-looking. Giant lobelias and huge groundsel decorated the land. It was a magical walk. On the way, a couple of guides ran passed us carrying a stretcher with a man who had altitude sickness. The way to survive the affliction is to get to a lower altitude as quickly as possible.

By the third day, we were above the tree line, and the landscape looked the way one imagines the moon's surface. Kibo Huts were at 15,400 feet, 5-6 kilometers more. On arrival, we ate and went to bed early because we would get up at one a.m. to start hiking in time to get to Gilman's point to see the sunrise. Fujiko was exhausted and stayed behind. Here the mountain surface is scree, and for every two steps forward, you would slip back one. It was switchbacks all the way. We were lucky that it was a full moon so that we didn't have to use our flashlights to see the way. I stopped to take a drink once, but the water had frozen in my bottle. At the top, Gilman's Point at 18,640 feet, I was able to take one photo before my battery froze. We were late for the sunrise, and disappointingly, clouds hid the view, but oh, the exaltation of success! Going down was easy. One of the guides took my arm under his, and we slipped and slid straight down in the scree. What took us hours to go up, took an hour to go down. We left immediately for Horombo Huts. We spent the night there, and the next day, twenty kilometers later, we were back to the Marangu Gate. We gave our guides our cold-weather gear and caught a bus to Arusha.

George continued to guide us—from Ngoro-Goro Crater to Dar es Salaam, from Zanzibar to Mombasa and finally back to Nairobi where he left us. Fujiko and I went horseback riding on the Karen Blixen estate. It was novel to ride along and see giraffe grazing in the bush. Unfortunately for me, when my horse was moving at a fast canter, I stupidly bent down to put my foot back in the stirrup and fell off. I landed on my right arm and shoulder, got up, brushed myself off, and pretended that it didn't hurt. We rode for several more hours. Fujiko left that afternoon and in the evening, I went to the Nairobi General Hospital for an x-ray. Nothing was broken, but I had multiple bruises and a severely sprained wrist. The doctor wrapped it with an Ace bandage, and the pain somewhat incapacitated me for several weeks. Try closing an overstuffed pack with only one hand!

The next day I flew on to Cairo. I joined an Adventure Center tour, which I had previously booked. We visited the Pyramids and then took the night train to Luxor. On the drive to Abu-Simbel, we saw great herds of camels being taken to market. One morning we took a ferry across the Nile where we got on little donkeys. With our feet dangling down almost touching the ground, we rode to the tombs of the Nobles, Valley of the Kings, and the Temple of Hatshepsut. The ride was charming, the ancient art and architecture of Egypt awe-inspiring. After a visit to Karnak, other antiquities and a camel ride in the desert, my group split onto three feluccas and sailed down the Nile for seven days and six nights. Each night we tied up at an island in the river and slept on the boat. The boatmen cooked our meals. I had imagined a leisurely and possibly boring run down the Nile. However, the wind came from the north, so we had to beat into it, tacking from one side of the river to the other, which necessitated our moving from one side of the boat to the other. The shore life and scenery made it impossible to be bored. Scenes drew my eyes to memories of pictures in my childhood Bible of bulrushes and a lone donkey being ridden by a man in robes, moving along the riverbank.

That trip accentuated how bored I was with life in America. It was routine, and I disliked it more than ever. In the spring of 1990, my father had an operation for prostate cancer. He had had one a few years before. After surgery, he was weak, tired, and seemed a little disoriented. His doctor suggested that he go to an assisted care home. I believed my father would rather go to his place in the boathouse, so that is where I took him. We made living adjustments, for example, a chair that would stand up and go down with the push of a button, making it easy to get out of. Khounta came from France in July to be his caregiver. Every morning he would pick up my father and take him shopping or to the doctor. He made him lunch and followed his directions for gardening at the Piedmont house. Then he would take him home.

We had a big party for his ninetieth birthday in August. My father designed the invitation himself and made the mimosas and coffee on the day.

Khounta assisted my father for six months, but he was anxious to go back to Vientiane to build a *taht* (stupa) in which to place his mother's ashes. He had been worrying about a design for it since she had passed away in 1989. Also, he wanted to pursue his case with the government for the return of his property.

He went back to France a few days after New Year's.

1991

My father died the first day of summer, just two months short of his ninety-first birthday. My sister and I had a small farewell gathering with some family and his close friends on the boat dock at Berkeley Aquatic Park. My father had lived in a room in the boathouse for over thirty years.

Mickey Akiyama, a good friend of my father's whom he had met at the Oakland Y.M.C.A., where he lived for a while after my parent's divorce in 1951, said some words of farewell and lit incense to send him on his way. We threw most of his ashes into the air to land in the water where the geese, ducks, and sailboats had brought beauty and joy into his life for so many years. We scattered more ashes around the trees he had planted in his garden. Then we went to his room and remembered him with his favorites: mimosas, coffee, and Danish pastries.

My sister and I decided to have a celebration of his departure in the Piedmont house for his friends of many generations. We prepared a special invitation on colored paper and sent it to everyone in his address book. My sister laughed and said I did not need to invite L.L. Bean, however.

I couldn't telephone Khounta to tell him of my father's death because I didn't have his half-brother, Chanbona's number in Argenteuil. In fact, I had no way of contacting him directly in case of an emergency. Chanbona was a hospital administrator in the daytime and his wife, Michelle, was a nurse on the night shift. Therefore, someone was always sleeping, and he didn't want me to bother them. He hated to ask anyone to help him or to disturb people in any way. I resorted to calling Khounta's sister and asked her to inform Khounta of my father's death. Khounta came immediately.

We worked in the Piedmont garden every day, clearing out the old leaves and weeds, cutting dead branches, planting colorful plants, and overall making the garden sparkle. The propagation and planting of flowers and trees had been one of my father's passions. He had recently received a mail order of five new fuchsias and had hung them in the big fruit trees. The begonias from the year before were flowering graciously. This year's ten hanging baskets of petunias that he had planted were hanging at the driveway entrance, in the fig tree by the patio, and around the verandah, spilling over with blossoms of purple and white, pink and blue.

I took down the John Cunningham paintings hanging in the downstairs room of the carriage house. John was a Carmel painter, primarily of seascapes and floral arrangements, for whom my mother had held an exhibition. Susan Ehrens, whom my father had helped with information about Imogen Cunningham and Anne Brigman, photographers, helped me. We put up a display of Pa's work: lacquer screens in black, gold and silver, multicolored sets of lacquered trays, a chair, small lacquered cabinets, a jewelry box, wood cuttings, art deco paintings of masks, furniture and set designs, and batiks. He had made these things in the 1920s and 1930s. However, most of his friends were from the 1950s and later, and had no knowledge of his talent as an artist and artisan. To them, he was just Gus, who loved beauty in plants, the arts, good pastries and good coffee. Someone you could always count on to be there for you, then to help you in any way he could. The celebration was a happy one and brought closure for most people.

After the celebration, Khounta stayed in Piedmont for another week. He was anxious to return to Laos to continue with the design of a *taht* (stupa) for his mother's ashes. First, he went to France, but he was in Laos by mid-September, staying until late December when he returned to France.

When I was in Africa, Alice met a former Peace Corps volunteer Mazen Fawzy, who had a work assignment on the slope of Mt. Kilimanjaro. That made a connection for her, and Mazen became her boyfriend. In September, when he needed a quiet place to finish his Master's dissertation, we invited him to stay with us. He settled into Peter's room. Peter had transferred to Oahu, Hawaii with Woolworth's in 1990. I lived in the carriage house and stable. My mother and I enjoyed Maz's company. He liked to cook, and he was very handy with fixing things, carpentry, and house painting. He put a sliding glass door in the stable, which was challenging due to the uneven shifting and settling of the walls over the preceding 100 or so years. It was cheerful to have a man around. Alice was in her junior year at Cal Poly but was doing an internship with a computer company in Santa Clara, so we saw her more often than we would have if she had been in San Luis Obispo. The four of us, Maz, my mother, Alice and I, enjoyed the Christmas holidays together and in January, Alice took a cross-country drive to Pennsylvania to meet Maz's parents. I asked Alice not to go. She had met Vincent Pannebakker, a Dutchman, in Japan during the summer when she was doing an agricultural internship that Maz had helped her get. According to the high telephone bills, it seemed that it was becoming serious. I told her that she was misleading Maz. She said that she liked them both and was not certain which one she felt more strongly about. Khounta would have been outraged. I felt sad, but she had to make her own decisions.

1992

Soon it was summer 1992. Alice declared that she had to go camping in Europe. Maz wanted to go with her, but she had other plans. She went to Holland to get to know Vincent better. She and Vincent, whom she later married, traveled to many places. She didn't try to visit Khounta when they went to Paris, but he wasn't there, in any case, because he was in Vientiane.

Khounta had stopped writing entirely. I used to get a letter or a phone call once a month or so, but now nothing. I wondered why. I had a booklet of postcards and wrote Khounta every Sunday at his brother's place in France about what I had been doing that week. I enjoyed receiving mail and thought he must, too.

I had begun to wonder where he was. Actually, in July, I had started to write him at his cousin's post office box in Vientiane because I thought he must be there by then. In fact, as I learned later from looking at the dates in his passport, he arrived in Laos July 31. In any case, I had never spent much time reading his letters. I had experienced long periods without hearing from him before. I had unconsciously trained myself not to think about Khounta when he was away. It was too painful never to know where he was or what he was doing. The weeks just crept by almost unnoticed. I was not concerned. My emotions were tied up in grief over my father's death.

His passing away had devastated me. Now fifteen months later, I was still living in a haze. Pa had been my best friend. We had gotten together at least once a week and frequently talked on the telephone. I stopped going to church because the music made me so sad that I couldn't keep from crying. I couldn't think of Pa or say his name without tears. There was no sympathy at home from my mother. She had divorced my father in 1951, but since the house was half his, he would come over most days to take care of the garden. Now she was happily free of him. My family and friends didn't expect me to cry. I was supposed to be strong.

On my way to and from work over the Oakland-Bay Bridge, I began to notice a billboard advertising group grief therapy at Kaiser Permanente Hospital. That was my hospital. In September, I couldn't bear my sadness any longer, and I called Kaiser and made an appointment with a psychologist. The offices were in a building up the street and around the corner from the main hospital buildings. I had never known they were there. This location offered some privacy to people who had emotional needs, and, as I felt at the time, to those who were embarrassed at not being able to cope on their own. The doctor recommended group therapy, and I began to go once a week. There were about twelve of us trying to manage the losses in our lives. We sat in chairs in a circle, and the doctor would ask questions. Sometimes they were general questions, and sometimes they were specific to an individual's problem. The questions he asked helped me to see my father's departure in a larger landscape, and the deaths the other members of the group were dealing with, also contributed to putting Pa in his flowerbed. After two months, I didn't need the group any longer and stopped going. That is not to say that the hole in my heart filled, but I could live with it.

In early December 1992, I received a letter from Khounta from Vientiane, in English, requesting $5,000. Now I knew for sure where he was. I sent money immediately through Air Chansomphou. I asked him how the design for the *taht* for his mother was coming along, and he sent me the plans. He also wanted enlarged photos made of his mother, one when she was young and another when she was older. He sent me the negatives. To have the pictures colored would have been very expensive, so I sent him 20" x 24" black and white enlargements.

In December, Alice graduated from college, and Vincent came from the Netherlands to spend Christmas and New Year's with her, my mother and me. Vincent's parents had insisted he be with Alice in Piedmont instead of mooning about her in Holland. He had to make a decision about their relationship during this holiday, and he did. Alice went with Vincent to Holland when he returned home in January.

In my wedding dress with Khounta, posing on our verandah in Vientiane,
February, 1969.

My wedding shower at June Pulcini's house, Vientiane, February 1969.

With Peter and my father in Emeryville, CA, December 1972.

Peter visits the Johnsens: *(left to right)* Dennis, Jennifer, Cyndy, Greg and Stan
at Ft. Baker, Sausalito, CA, Christmas, 1972.

With Peter, Khounta, and Alice, posing for Christmas card photo in front yard, Mekong River flowing behind, Vientiane, 1973.

Alice in front of the water purifying system behind our house, Vientiane, Laos, 1974.

With Alice, Khounta and Peter, Vientiane, Christmas 1974.

Khounta, Lisa, Margie, and Frank. Last picnic in Laos at Nam Ngum Dam with the Manley family, April 1975.

The Quills visit us in Tehran. *(in back)* Terry, Khounta, Dee, *(children left to right)* Peter, Tony, Alice, Keith, Danielle, June 1977.

Visiting family in Piedmont, CA. *Standing*: David Grill, Penny's mother Alice Erskine, nephew Jeff Grill, me, Penny's father Gus Breuer; *Sitting:* Melissa Grill, Alice, niece Teresa Grill, Peter, Khounta, Christmas 1977.

We visit family at Lao Refugee Camp near Nongkhai , Thailand. (*in back from left*),
Vongkeo, Deng, Vongphet. (*in front*), Alice, Peter and Joe, Vongkeo's son,
December 1977.

At *baci* ceremony for Khounta's mother. A *baci* string is tied around my wrist. Nang Im and Khounta watch. Lao Refugee Camp near Nongkhai, Thailand, December 1977.

*Eight brothers and sisters gather in Anaheim, CA. *(left to right)* Alice, Khemphone, Peter, Bounleua, Van, Deng, Vongkeo, Vongphet, December 1979.

Alice and Pa's birthday, with Khounta, Melissa and Peter, Spain, July 1981.

Mama and Toledo bird cage, Piedmont, CA, Christmas 1982.

Peter becomes an Eagle Scout. With Khounta and Alice, Piedmont, CA, 1985.

Khounta, Alice, and June Pulcini, Hermosa Beach, CA, 1985.

(back left to right) Ronald, Sallie Carol, Sallie and her mother,
(front row) Peter, Me, Alice, Christy, Mama.
The Orbas family visited us in Piedmont, CA, 1982.

Peter and Alice's birth parents visit the USA.
Alice, Peter, Bounthom, Noukham, Piedmont, CA, late 1985.

(left to right) Pa, Khounta, me, Wade, Melissa, Dave, and Mama, Piedmont, CA,
July 1986.

Khounta becomes a monk for seven days, Wat Khoua Luang, Vientiane, Laos,
December 26, 1988.

With Alice, Khounta, and Peter, a photo for our 1990 Christmas card,
below the Cliff House, San Francisco, CA.

PART 3

CHAPTER 30

The Nest is Empty:
January to May 1993

After Alice had left, I wrote Khounta to tell him that I wanted to come to the dedication of the *taht* and to ask him what he thought. He said the dedication would probably be in April.

That was the first time I had considered going back to Laos. I had never wanted to go back before. I remembered how happy we had been and how much fun we had had there. In contrast, Laos, when I left in 1975, was scary, solemn, bleak and lacking in dance and music. It had been eighteen years since then. When I left, I'd thought it would be forever. I thought I would feel angry and sad to see squatters living on our properties, which were located on main streets that I could not conveniently avoid. I would have to readjust my feelings if I were to go back.

It was like the Berlin Wall coming down. I had never thought it would happen in my lifetime. I had grown up with the Wall. The novels I read were spy novels centered on the KGB and the CIA sneaking around behind the Iron Curtain. Now, what in our house we called the bamboo wall was falling. If I could find someone to sponsor me, I could visit Laos. Khounta did not suggest anyone.

At home, it was just my mother and me. The children were gone, and I wanted to be with Khounta. I worried about my job, of which I was very weary. I wanted to do something else, but I always worried about money. Could I afford to leave work and visit Laos? My friend Sharolyn said, "Don't think about it. If you have plastic, you can do anything you want." On the other hand, my mother raised me saying, "Neither a lender nor a borrower be." How to decide?

My good friend Khamsouk Sundara, who had taught at LAA and stayed in Laos, was on a study tour in the United States. He was in San Francisco for two nights in January, and we met over coffee and chocolate cake in a shop near Fort Mason. I asked his advice, and he urged me to come back. His words helped me to decide to go to Laos. My family responsibilities were fewer. My father was gone. My brother had come to live in Piedmont in February, so my mother was not alone. Although she was a vibrant, and healthy 83 years, it is always handy to have a man to help with home maintenance and in the garden. Khamsouk helped me get a visa at the Lao Embassy in Washington D.C.

I learned that Khemphone Chansomphou, the sister born between Peter and Alice, was to be married in San Jose in early May. Since Alice couldn't be there, I decided to go to her wedding before I left. My mother, Peter, who just happened to be in town, and I drove down to San Jose for the Lao marriage ceremony in the morning and fabulous Lao lunches afterwards, first at a sister's house and then at her new mother-in-law's place. All the brothers and sisters were there except for the two in Laos and Alice. I remember sitting in the garden next to my mother. Deng, one of the brothers, was sitting behind us. Conversationally, he asked me about the house Khounta was building. I froze. What did I think? I didn't know Khounta was building a house, but his cousin knew. Why hadn't Khounta written and told me? I should have felt pleased, excited and grateful for the surprise he was preparing for me. Instead, I felt humiliated, hurt, and left out. But most of all I felt embarrassed. I should have laughed and said right out, "What house?" Why couldn't I? Other people knew more about what my husband was doing than I did. I wrote every week. I was going to Laos in a few days, but I didn't know that he was building us a house. Was Khounta just trying to surprise me and Deng had let the cat out of the bag? I answered, "Fine, I guess," as if I knew what he was talking about. In my American dream world, I still lived with the idea that significant decisions were made as a marriage team. I had had enough experience to know that was not Khounta's way. When would I learn?

CHAPTER 31

Trip to Lao PDR: May 1993

I left for Thailand later in May. I hadn't been there for seven years, not since I passed through Bangkok in 1986 on my way to visit friends in Sri Lanka. Margie and Frank Manley met me at Don Muang Airport. I was so happy to see them, to be back and smelling familiar smells—damp vegetation, coconut and garlic frying in pig fat—and seeing familiar sights. I stayed in Bangkok for two days. I walked the streets, smelling and eating the food in the street stalls. It was like a dream. Margie and I took an all-day boat trip on the canals of the Chao Phraya River. The noise of the long-tail motor boats, the houses over the water along the shore, the flow of air from the speed of the boat, and the sun on our faces combined to create a feeling of being carefree and at peace.

I took the familiar night train to Nong Khai, arrived at the old train station, and dallied. I was probably the last one off the train, and by then it had begun to drizzle. There was one *samlor* (pedicab) left waiting for a rider. The driver had to untie the plastic sheets rolled up on the sides of the buggy seat and put them in place for protection against the rain. He pedaled me to the immigration office on the Mekong River in the center of town. I had my passport stamped, walked down the steps to the ferryboat, crossed the river, and trudged up the stairs on the Lao side. The dry season was ending, but the river was still very low, and it was a long walk to the top of the bank. The train had been an hour late, and I was probably the last one to cross the river. Khounta had wondered if perhaps I had missed the train, but he was there, waiting. I almost didn't recognize him. He looked gaunt, and his hair was dark again. He wanted to know why I was the last one, and why I had not come immediately to Vientiane instead of spending time in Bangkok. I couldn't put into words the reasons for my reluctance, my expectation of being saddened by changes. He put my bags in the car, and we crossed the road to a coffee stall shaded by a big tree. He ordered two Lao coffees, black and strong with sweetened condensed milk at the bottom, which changed color to warm brown when we stirred it. It was strange to be back, but I didn't feel any different from when we had been there before. Everything looked, felt and tasted the same. It was as though I had only been gone a day or two. I began to relax.

After coffee, we drove directly to Wat Done Natong in Khounta's late '60s Land Rover. The temple was on the other side of Vientiane. We drove along Thadeua Road to SamSenThai Street. Venus Photo and all the old businesses were intact but seemingly unpainted for eighteen years. We turned right on Khoun Boulom Road and then left onto Khoua Leuang Street. We drove to the end of the road and turned right. That road does not stop there anymore. It is the ASEAN Road that cuts through the wetlands to the airport. The dirt road soon ran next to an irrigation canal built, I imagined, with Russian aid. With access to the canal, farmers now planted two rice crops a year. That was a sign of progress. We drove on the road on the left side of the canal because it was in the best condition. It was a lovely ride with rice paddies as far as you could see. Since that drive, the road on the left side of the canal has become overgrown, and the right side is paved. It is called Sitang. Today people are planting houses and businesses instead of rice on both sides of the canal.

At the *wat* (temple) was the *taht* that Khounta had built for his mother. It was lovely. Four sweeping curved legs supported a tall, slender, tapering column rising into the sky, topped with a golden finial. It reminded me of the Eiffel Tower. A waist-high wall enclosed the area around the *taht*, and a black metal gate opened onto the grounds. The headstone for Khounta's mother had her picture etched in a sheet of granite and sat under the *taht* on a three-step-high, red tiled platform surrounded by a metal fence with a padlocked metal gate. On another piece of granite below the headstone, her birth and death dates were engraved. On the back of the headstone, carved in cement and painted yellow, was the story of her family giving this land to the district to build a temple many years before. The ceremony of placing her ashes had taken place in late April. How could I know I would perform the same ceremony in less than a year?

There was only one old, toothless Chinese monk living at the temple. Smiling, he chatted over the wall with Khounta. Khounta had brought flowers, incense, and candles for me to place before his mother's headstone. I had never performed this Lao practice before, and I was not sure of the order of things. Do I light the candles first and place them on the stand or do I light the incense first and place it in the holder? The white flowers Khounta had given to me still had their roots. In my inexperience, I did not know that was how they were picked. Therefore, instead of laying them before the headstone, as is the custom, I planted them. As usual, Khounta never said anything. I asked him where his mother's ashes were, and he pointed to the top of the right front support. I asked him if he wanted his ashes to be placed here, too, but he didn't answer me.

On the way back to town, we stopped to see our Lao cousin Souvanh, who used to live behind us with his family in Ban Phone Sa'at. He was now a rice farmer. Instead of live buffalo, he had an iron buffalo, that is, a tractor for rice paddies. He said that because of the double cropping, there was not enough rice stubble to feed buffalo, and a tractor was more economical than live animals. I was surprised that Souvanh had become a farmer. He had been in the police force and was a genius with anything electrical or mechanical. When we arrived, he was tinkering with his tractor.

We continued to town to the "surprise house." It wasn't finished, but we had to stay there, for which I was glad. Khounta's brother Prakan was terrified to have an American stay in the SiHom house and wouldn't allow it. The authorities watched the movement of people closely, and he would have had to register my presence with the village chief. He might be suspected of being a sympathizer with the hated imperialist Americans. During the time Khounta was in Vientiane, he always stayed with his brother Prakan, who occupied the house where Khounta and I had lived when we were first married. We had moved out of this house when Khounta's mother had come to live with us, many years before. When their mother died, Prakan inherited it because he was the only offspring with Lao citizenship. Foreigners cannot own property in Lao PDR.

The new house stood on a red dirt plot on ten-foot wooden posts with walls made of woven bamboo. The main room was without a ceiling and rose twenty feet to the thatch roof, above. For the floor, Khounta used the wooden boards from his Uncle Noukham's house that had been torn down some years before. The floorboards had quarter inch gaps between them to let air in. At the time, they were filled with wood shavings. I was certain that mosquitoes would slip up and bite me, but they never did, only red dust rose through the cracks, and filtered through the woven bamboo walls from the un-paved road outside, laying a red coating on everything. The land belonged to Aunt Bounthom, Uncle Noukham's widow. She said Khounta could live there for the rest of his life.

A carpenter was at work putting handles and locks on the windows. Khounta had managed to move our bed from the SiHom house into the bedroom and rig up a mosquito net. That was all we needed. We had running water, not heated, but the weather was sweltering. The electric wires hung from above without light sockets, but we had flashlights. Khounta had furnished the house with the furniture from the house we had had in 1975. It was very familiar and comforting. I loved it. The kitchen had a refrigerator, but no stove. Khounta didn't want cooking smells in the house. He had a hot plate for boiling drinking water.

After nine days of being with Khounta, visiting friends and living in our new house, I knew I was going to return. At first, I thought my driving force was to open an English school, but on reflection, it was Khounta—to live, love and work together where our love began. We had survived revolutions, children, sickness, and months and years apart, and we had come together again with a stronger, more understanding, and compassionate and knowledgeable love. We wanted the same things, appreciated what each had to give, and understood what each one could not give. Leaving was difficult, and I was sorry that I had not hurried there on my arrival in Bangkok.

I remembered Air, Kim, and Deng at Kim's wedding wondering why I was going to stay in Vientiane more than three days. "There is nothing to do," they said. I told them I was not going as a tourist "to do things." I was going to be with my husband to live together as married people usually do. I didn't need to be entertained. The better question would have been, "Why aren't you staying longer?"

When it was time to leave, Khounta drove me to Thadeua. It didn't occur to us to reschedule the train and plane tickets. I expected Khounta to go to the train station with me, but when we arrived at Immigration, he explained that the border closed before the train left, and he wouldn't be able to get back that night. We sat silently on a stone bench until the last minute. He looked so solemn and sad. I wanted to hug him and kiss him good-bye, but Lao culture doesn't permit such an outward demonstration of feelings. We clasped hands tightly, and I left him, waving.

CHAPTER 32

California Interlude and Return: May to September

I was going back! I was on cloud nine. I had waited. Now it was going to happen. We would talk and love and laugh. I was tingling with anticipation.

Among the many commitments to wrap up in California was the pleasure of camping with my family during the Memorial Day weekend at the end of May. My sister had made reservations at Yosemite National Park for nine of us from four generations. Some of us took our bicycles. One day, Wade and Peter hiked to the top of Half Dome. Climbing to the top was something my father had talked about and done, so they wanted to do it, too. Melissa, Dave and I had gone up a couple of years before. When we were there, pockets of snow lay on the ground and a rattlesnake, which a squirrel alerted us to, leisurely wound its way off the path. It's a long, tough hike, especially the way down.

I gave my niece Teresa the baby clothes I had bought in Bangkok. I had spent hours shopping for them, but they didn't impress her. She forgot about them and left them in my sister's camping trailer, where they lay lost for several years. Perceptively, Teresa asked me if I was going back to Laos to stay. I told her I was. No one else asked, and I didn't say anything, not because it was a secret, but because in our family we were not in the habit of sharing our plans and discussing them.

One beautiful summer day, I invited my book group to lunch at the Piedmont house. The day was warm, the grass green, and the weather mild. We sat under an umbrella around a table on the back lawn. I made Vietnamese spring rolls and a version of green papaya salad with carrots and sticky rice. After more than ten years, I, at last, had some friends to say goodbye to. I wondered how long our friendships would endure after I left.

I now had responsibilities with NORCAL. I had taken office as an area representative and had made more friends. We had meetings and regularly got together for lunch or dinner. I was the co-chairperson with Dorrie Dodge for the Country-of-Service Groups at the 20th Annual Peace Corps Convention held on the campus of the University of California, Berkeley in June. We found local representatives for all the countries of service who arranged meetings, and we helped design T-shirts for different events. At the conference, it was fun to meet up with old friends, take walks, and eat together. Eventually, I had to resign from my position and sadly say goodbye.

Christy Orbas, our friend from Iran, got married on August 8. At the wedding, I was surprised to learn from Sallie and Ron that they had visited Khounta in May 1992 along with their daughter Sallie Carol. They assumed I knew this, but I hadn't heard from Khounta since he had left the previous August. I don't know why Khounta didn't write or telephone. It was a protracted emptiness for me. He took them to visit Monet's gardens in Giverny. I had always wanted to go there. They had had a lovely time. I must admit that it made me feel sad, and a little envious, too, that I had not been with them.

In September, I attended to some legal work finalizing some changes to Khounta's and my trust. I was ready to go.

On Khounta's part, he obtained a guarantor for me for a one-month visa. On July 1, the house in Vientiane was finished, and he went to France. The garden remained to be landscaped, and he wrote that he would take care of it on his return from Argenteuil. By the end of the month, he had found a trustworthy person to guard the house and keep it in good order. On August 10, he wrote: *I am really happy and very proud to learn your firm decision to open an English school in Vientiane. You can be sure you have my entire support."* A couple of weeks later he wrote, *"Thanks for the trust in our future in Laos . . . I will leave for Laos on Oct 4 – direct Paris to Vientiane (Qantas and Air Lao).*

I prepared my departure so that I could spend a few days in Bangkok with the Manleys before I took the train to Vientiane. My plan was to arrive in Vientiane on October 4, the same day as Khounta. I could hardly contain my happiness, imagining our future together. For the first time, I felt he had questions he wanted to ask me, and I expected finally to get some answers to my years of unanswered questions. My happy expectations were almost overwhelming.

On September 26, the plane landed at Don Muang Airport. Margie and Frank Manley met me and took me to their house. The next day, I followed Margie around while she did errands. I bought some birthday paper and a bow for Khounta's birthday present, a package set from Trader Joe's in Concord, California of a bottle of single malt Glenfiddich whiskey and two crystal whiskey glasses. We were going to celebrate!

CHAPTER 33

Coming Home: October 1993

On October 3, I took the night train to Nong Khai. After eighteen years, I was going back to resume our life in Laos. In our house, it would be just the two of us eating, playing, reading, entertaining, talking, laughing, and sleeping together. From outside would come the sounds of the cowbells in the morning, the dogs barking, the cicadas whining in the sun, the frogs croaking in the rain, and the roosters crowing all day and night. It would be hot most of the time and cool in winter.

I knew Khounta would arrive sometime during the day, and I wanted him to get to the house before me and arrange everything the way he wanted me to see it for the first time. I had called Somsai, a former teacher at LAA, and he met my train when it arrived in Nong Khai the following morning. I spent the day with him. First, we inspected the new Nong Khai Holiday Inn. From the rooftop, we could see that the section of the new bridge across the Mekong River that had been missing in May and was now in place. It was impressive to see one continuous span across the river. The bridge would open in April 1994. King Bhumibol would leave Thailand for the first time in about 20 years for this momentous event.

Then we went to see the Good Shepherd Sisters. I had met Sister
Mary Hayden in 1982, shortly after she and Sister Joan and Sister
Margaret had first arrived. From a small rented house, her dream had
come true. The Bishop had given the Good Shepherd Sisters a large
piece of property, and they had set up their quarters and a sewing
workshop for village girls. From there Somsai and I decided to go to
Tha Bo District, upriver from Nong Khai. We drove on a back road so
that we could visit one of Somsai's friends who had a couple of chick-
en farms. He had built the chicken houses on stilts over ponds in
which he was farming fish. It was a very efficient system. The chicken
poop and spilled seed from the chicken houses would fall through the
wire floor into the pond, where it would fertilize the vegetation in the
water for the fish. In Tha Bo Village, Somsai treated for lunch of crab
fried rice and tom yam fish soup. On the way back to Nong Khai, we
stopped at a temple that was undergoing archaeological excavation,
one of many temples that King Sethathirath, the king of Laos from
1548 to 1571, had commissioned.

At three p.m., it was time to leave before the border closed. I sat in the
ferryboat and thought. It is as though nothing has changed. The same,
but different. Water flows in the Mekong. The wooden boats look the
same. The people with goods bought in Nong Khai for resale in Vientiane
look the same. You still settle yourself in one boat and then sometimes
have to change to another.

I took a taxi to BounNyok's workplace. He took me to the house and
gave me the keys. Khounta had furnished and decorated the house
with all our old furniture, framed posters, pictures, and carpets from
Kashmir. The ceiling was a stretched, thick, brown cloth. I was surprised and disappointed that Khounta hadn't arrived yet. I spent the
next two hours dusting, washing, and making the bed. Dust was everywhere. I thought it would be endlessly dirty. It looked great, but I
didn't want to live in a veneer of dust. The border closed at five p.m.
Where was Khounta? I couldn't even imagine. BounNyok and his wife
came over at 6:30 and took me to dinner. They wondered where

Khounta was, too. I felt a little hollow inside. I had been stood up, but I wasn't worried. A logical explanation was imminent. He would come.

In the night, I had terrible diarrhea. Where was Khounta?

The next day, October 5, I wanted to telephone people, but I didn't know the code. Phone numbers were four digits. I had the numbers of people whom I wanted to call, but two new area codes had been implemented, and I didn't know where people lived. I was still sick, but I went out with the driver Somchit and changed money, came back, and dusted some more. Doran called, and I was able to set up an appointment at USIS with Mary Johnson. A truck came down the street and knocked out the electricity, so I decided to clean and defrost the refrigerator. Then I cleaned off the desk and found a chart for making phone calls. I made an appointment with Mark Gordon, a lead from Doran for some ESL classes. I ached all over, had slight chills and no appetite. My diarrhea continued. BounNyok sent over a couple of coconuts. I ate one and gave the other one to the driver. Somchit guarded and cleaned the house, watered the garden, and fortunately for me, knew how to drive. So he had many names: guard, cleaner, gardener, driver. He had his room with a bed and mosquito net under the house and a bathroom. When he wasn't working, he passed his time making fishing nets.

I went to bed early with a couple of Advil. Khounta called at nine p.m. His doctor had told him that due to diabetic retinopathy he could not leave for three months. He must have laser surgery to save his sight. I was happy to hear that his sight could be saved. I told him that I would come to France to be with him. He said, "No, stay there." He would be back in January. I was disappointed he hadn't said, "Come." The whole idea for me was to be together. It didn't matter where.

Upon waking on October 6, I felt much better. At the U.S. Embassy, Mary Johnson was rather discouraging about any ELT classes. In the afternoon, I met Mark Gordon at Saysettha Learning Center (SLC). It was an impressive school, clean and light. Mark said he would help me set up a school, or I could do something jointly with him.

That evening Khounta called to ask if I had any problems and, if I did, just to contact BounNyok for help.

I was terribly disappointed and depressed. My expectations had been bludgeoned. I wanted to be with Khounta, but I was alone in the house. I stayed home with a terrible headache all the next day and the day after that.

On Saturday, October 9, Khamthoune Butts, Doran's wife, came by in the morning and took me to a WIG meeting (Women's International Group). The purpose of the group was to support newcomers to living in Vientiane. About twenty-four women attended the meeting: Swedish, French, American, British, New Zealanders, Australian, Indian, and others. They discussed plans, projects, and events. Then lunch appeared, including two beautiful tortes. There were no bakeries in the city, so they were a special treat. One had fruit on top with a cream filling, and the other was of apples. Apples had been a luxury in the '60s and '70s, but I learned that many were imported from China now, and anyone could afford them.

I was feeling better already. Living in Vientiane was not easy for foreigners, of whom there were not many. I knew of only a few restaurants with Western food: Nam Phu, Le Vendome, and L'Opera. None was near my house. There were no restaurants on Setthathirath or Fa Ngum roads. For food, I needed to find Talat Thong Khan Kham, the market Khounta had taken me to, but I had no sense of direction or of how far it was from my house. I borrowed Somchit's bicycle to search the neighborhood for it, but I couldn't find it. Later, when I learned where the market was, I could drive there. Even so, many foodstuffs, cosmetics, clothes and other everyday household and personal products were not available. For example, I could get sardines in a can with tomato sauce, but not a can of tuna. Mayonnaise, forget it. It didn't matter to me, however, because I didn't have a stove. I ate fruit for breakfast and drove to one of the few small local noodle shops for lunch and dinner of fried noodles, noodle soup or fried rice. Additional variety came in the choice of adding pork, chicken or beef and flavoring with fish sauce, brown sauce, soy sauce, fresh lime, vinegar, sugar, chilies or, sometimes, chopped peanuts.

Later on Saturday, I met with Mark. He offered me the director-ship of his school, but I decided I wanted to open my own school. For the next two weeks, I continued my market analysis by visiting estab-lished English language schools, looking at potential school locations, and analyzing available materials and sources of teachers. I also began to teach a couple of classes at the SLC in the afternoons.

For a diversion, I started swimming at the Belvedere Hotel (now the Mercure). Only a few people stayed there. It hadn't been officially opened. It was idyllic. In the mornings, I had the place to myself. Ho-tel buildings surrounded the pool, cutting it off from the outside world. I would laze in the water or on a lounge chair and look at the blue sky with the fronds of a few palm trees gently moving in the dis-tance, marveling at how peaceful and otherworldly it was. I would read a book or sleep. In the silence, I imagined I could be anywhere. This water sanctuary was not Laos. Afterwards, I would take a hot shower and wash my hair. I didn't have hot water at home, and there were no hairdressers in Vientiane. Wednesday was movie night at the American Embassy. The ticket seller also sold popcorn and soft drinks. WIG was planning a bazaar and raffle, so I spent many days soliciting prizes for it. In mid-October, a calico cat jumped out of my bamboo grove. She was just a kitten and alone, like me. I named her Vita, after Vita Sackville-West. She became a source of comfort to me for fourteen years. In Laos, if a cat comes to you, it is considered very lucky, and you must keep it.

CHAPTER 34
Bad News: Late October

On Monday, October 25, Nang Sy, an old friend and my dressmaker from the sixties came to the house at 7:30 a.m. to tell me that my brother had called and for me to call home. When I called, my mother said that Khounta had been in a coma for ten days. I asked her what to do. Should I go to France? She told me to wait and do nothing. At noon, BounNyok came and gave me the same news. He said he would get an extension of my visa.

The next day, I wrote a letter to Prak Chanbona, Khounta's Cambo-dian half-brother in Argenteuil, and took the letter to Khamsouk to translate into French and mail for me. I wrote another letter to Phanh Inthavong, Khounta's brother-in-law in Orly, and gave it to BounNyok to translate into Lao and mail for me. I asked for specific information about Khounta's condition and if I should come and to please contact me by letter or telephone, if necessary. I worried about Khounta all the time: why is he in a coma, what caused it?

Two days later, BounNyok came across the field at the back of his house, waving a letter from Khounta. He had written it on the eighth and, after almost three weeks, it had only just arrived. BounNyok hoped it was good news, not realizing it was written before the coma. Khounta wrote, in French, as usual.

I am really sorry that I cannot leave Paris for Vientiane as planned (4 Oct). At the last minute, the doctor prohibited me from traveling. The last exam showed a proliferating retinopathy in my right eye. I risk becoming blind at any moment. Therefore, I need immediate laser treatment. According to the ophthalmologist, I need a minimum of 16 laser sessions that could last at least three months. Therefore, I can be in Vientiane at the beginning of Jan 1994.

Hoped to catch you before your departure to Vientiane to inform you about this unfortunate mishap. I called Bangkok on Oct 4. Mrs. Manley answered the phone. We talked a little about your trip to Vientiane. For the other sicknesses, diabetes, hypertension, etc… All goes well.

I am really sorry and sad to think that I am leaving you completely alone in a house hardly finished where nothing was arranged. I hope that you will manage properly and without trouble. Do what you think is right.

Khounta was a good man, always wanting to do the right thing and be correct. He provided opportunities for his nephews and was generous to them and his nieces when he could be. He gave up living with us in Piedmont so that there would be enough money for Peter and Alice to go to university, in the sense that money that could have been spent on maintaining a household in California was preserved for college. He saved what little money he had to take us to the theatre and have a car with all its expenses in order to take us places when we were in Paris.

October 30 was the last day of Buddhist Lent. Boats from the temples raced on the Mekong River. I went to the balcony of Burapha, a Swedish business that had its office overlooking the river. I met the owner Peter Fogde and others. Pat Stone, whom I had met at a WIG meeting, was there with her husband and kids.

Khamsouk came by and helped me get the telephone number of Mrs. Khamphou, the wife of a former general. She had just come from France. When I got a hold of her later in the evening, she told me that Khounta's eye had hemorrhaged, resulting in a blood clot on the brain.

The next morning I went to the PTT (Post, Telephone, and Telegraph) office to call Nang Kellie in France. I couldn't make international calls from my house. She said that Khounta's condition remained unchanged and that he had been transferred to a neurological hospital. "When are you coming?" she asked. I said I would come when his condition changed and asked her to call me. I went back to Burapha to watch the boat races. I explained my situation to Pat Stone and asked her what she thought. She recommended that I do what felt right. What felt right was to stay in Vientiane. Khounta never wanted me to visit him in the hospital. He had told me to wait.

The next day I learned from BounNyok that he couldn't extend my visa. It wasn't a tourist visa. I hadn't realized that I was on a business visa. I went to Somchith, Khounta's employer who had first sponsored my business visa. To stay longer, one needs an employer for a business visa or to be working for an embassy, a non-governmental organization (NGO) on a government project for some other specific visa or be a spouse of someone with such a visa. Somchit was very hesitant to extend my visa because Khounta was not back and he wanted the director of SLC to extend my visa, but the director couldn't do it. I took Somchith a couple of large chocolate bars, and he finally agreed. I continued to teach every day and solicit prizes for the WIG raffle. My market analysis regarding an English language school revealed that it wouldn't be worth the time or stress to start one. It would be easier simply to teach. Mentally, I was very distraught. I decided to leave as soon as I got my passport back.

On November 8, Khounta's birthday, I went to teach at the Comcenter from 10:15 to 11:45 as usual. As I got in my car, I suddenly felt so grief-stricken that I felt I would vomit. I sat in my car and struggled to breathe. I could not understand the powerful feeling that came over me, out of nowhere. It happened at other times during the day, too. I wondered if it was because it was Khounta's birthday. Perhaps I should have telephoned.

Finally, two and a half weeks later, on November 17, I got my passport. A course at ARDA that I had contracted for would end on the 19th. Then I would leave. Khamsouk would take over my classes at SLC and the Comcenter. Mary Johnson said she would have a class for me when I returned. I called Margie Manley and asked her to get me a ticket, leaving for Paris on Saturday, November 27. I said my good-byes. Sunday the border was closed, as usual, and on Monday BounNyok drove me to Thadeua.

I called Somsai from Immigration in Nong Khai, and he picked me up. My entire body ached the night before, and I was still not feeling well. I had dinner at Somsai's house, and he took me to the train. I fell immediately asleep at seven p.m.

In Bangkok, my fatigue and pain continued. I went to MD Travel by taxi and picked up my tickets to France. Normally I would have gone by bus, but I did not have the strength. I wanted to shop, but I was too sick to make any decisions regarding clothes. A street vendor persuaded me to buy a sweater. I went to the bank with my Visa card and got 20,000 baht, which I changed to $500. I took a taxi to Margie's house. In the afternoon, I decided to go to Bangkok General Hospital, which was next door. The doctor did some tests, but he couldn't find the cause of my weakness. He gave me some pills and told me to come back the next morning for a barium test. He thought I might have an ulcer. I spent most of the night in the bathroom.

The next morning, when I went to the hospital, the doctor took one look at me and admitted me for twenty-four hours of rehydration. He said I had an intestinal yeast infection. I called Margie and let her know where I was. The nurse put in an IV drip, and I slept until the next morning.

CHAPTER 35

Paris: November

I arrived back at Margie's from the hospital at noon and had a sandwich. Margie returned home from teaching English at A.U.A. around one o'clock. It would be seven a.m. in Paris, not too early to call my in-laws, so I called to tell them I would be arriving on Saturday and what time to pick me up. Nang Kellie answered the phone. She did not say anything but called Phanh to the phone.

"Khounta is dead. He had cardiac arrest last night at ten o'clock," Phanh intoned in his deep voice and precise English.

In a controlled, emotionless voice, I gave Phanh my arrival information. I hung up. An animal moan erupted from deep within me and tears coursed my face. I doubled over. Margie came from the kitchen and helped me upstairs to her bedroom, away from the maid's eyes and the windows open to the house across the lane.

Light came in from the high bedroom windows. I sat on the edge of the bed, moaning and crying. Margie kept her arm around me until finally I could speak, "Khounta died," I gasped in disbelief. "He died last night at ten o'clock." Phanh's blunt words made me think of M's telegram in Albert Camus' *The Stranger*, "Mother died yesterday." But when did Khounta die? It was Wednesday night in Paris, but it was four a.m. Thursday in Bangkok. He died while I was in the hospital. Did he die on the 24th French time or the 25th Bangkok time? Not that it mattered.

I finally stopped crying and telephoned my mother and sister. They both asked me if Khounta had regained consciousness and I said no. Somehow, this knowledge comforted me. I called Peter in Hawaii and Alice in Holland. I didn't know when the funeral would be. I would call them back when I knew.

It was Thanksgiving Day. I had planned to take the Manleys to a special dinner on Thursday and leave on Saturday. Since I needed some clothes for Paris, Margie and I went shopping and then had Thanksgiving dinner at Le Meridian in the President Hotel. I ate with the words, "Khounta is dead," quietly repeating in my head. The good food and Margie's talking helped keep me in control.

The next morning Margie had to teach. I went to Pratunam market, which has more than a hundred small stalls crammed next to each other selling all kinds of clothing, retail and wholesale. In California, whenever I had felt depressed in my job, I would go shopping. How many sweaters and jackets would I need? What should I wear to the funeral? It must be white. What was appropriate? The questions and choices of materials, colors, and textures filled my mind, leaving no room for other thoughts. I had never participated in a Lao funeral before. I felt obligated to dress correctly, that is, in agreement with Lao traditions. But what was correct? I had no one to ask. The day slipped away in small decisions of what and how much to buy.

I got back to Margie's just in time to pack, eat dinner, bathe, and get to Don Muang Airport for the midnight flight on Thai International.

My nephew Phonekeo, Kellie and Phanh's son, met my plane at Charles de Gaulle Airport. We went to their apartment. Khounta's cousin Oudone and other family members were there. When I came in the door, Oudone bleated, "Why didn't you come?" I looked at her not understanding. She told me that Khounta had regained consciousness after 24 days, the same day I had felt so sad in Vientiane. I believe Khounta was trying to send me a message. Hindsight tells me I should have telephoned. Oudone spoke in French and Lao. I hardly understood what she was telling me. Suddenly my throat felt constricted. I could not speak or cry. I listened in shock, thinking, Kellie didn't call me. Khounta came out of the coma. He was conscious. I never knew. Why didn't she call me? Years later, I asked myself, why didn't he call me? But, I know the answer: he was in the hospital, and it was not his habit to telephone or to bother anyone with making a call.

Oudone said that every day he grew stronger. He could walk and talk, and he laughed a lot. His sister made him the foods he liked. Oudone said they didn't call me because he was better every day, and they knew I would be in Paris soon. Why did they think that? In any case, I couldn't have left. My passport was with Immigration.

Oudone went on to say Khounta was anxious to leave the hospital. Chanbona told him he had three letters from Laos. Khounta didn't have his glasses, and he demanded that his brother get them immediately, but his house was too far away. The next day Chanbona brought his daughter to read the letters because she knew English. Khounta was pleased to receive my two letters and Grandma's card and $25.00. Khounta talked about returning to Laos where he could breathe the air, work all day, sleep well at night, and never be tired.

I arrived on the third day of the wake. As is the custom, friends and relatives came to Nang Kellie's all day and into the evening to pay their respects, eat and drink. They had removed all the furniture from the front rooms and placed mats on the floor to sit on. I sat in shock, unable to think or speak. I went to bed at ten p.m.

The next morning, Phanh took me to the mortuary. An attendant took us to a small, white-painted room. On a rolling table was Khounta's body in a casket. It was cold in the room, and we didn't take off our coats. Phanh asked me if I had my camera. I said it was in the car. He offered to get it for me, and left. I was alone with the body. My first thought was, what am I supposed to do? It was the first dead body I had ever seen. I had no feelings for it. I didn't feel like doing anything. I didn't want to be there. In books, in the movies and on television, the grieving wife throws herself weeping and sobbing on the corpse. But this was not Khounta. The body in the coffin was not breathing or smiling. Khounta had left. My second thought was that I should at least touch the suited body. I walked around to the other side of the casket. Eventually, I felt the gray hair on the side of his head, and I thought it is probably still growing. I remembered that I had heard that a person's hair continues to grow after they have died. I looked at the face. The lips were protruding as if padding were under them. Phanh came back and handed me my camera. I asked him why Khounta looked that way. Phanh explained that the hospital had lost his new dental plate, and the embalmers had fixed him that way. Because Phanh expected me to, I took some pictures. It was a strange idea to me. Why would I want photos of my husband's dead body?

The second morning, Oudone took me to the Lao temple to offer food to the monks for Khounta. We brought rice, fruit, and *khao phoun*, a Lao specialty. At 10:45, the chanting of prayers began and lasted for about thirty minutes. After that, we took the food and did *tak baht*; that is, we put some food in each of the four monks' bowls. People crowded the temple, and so the *tak baht* continued until noon, after which the monks ate and chanted again.

In the evening, more and more people came to Kellie's to pay their respects. The talk was deafening. The floor was wall-to-wall people. Wakes are a good custom to help alleviate the feelings of sadness, which are overpowering when one is alone. Friends cook, and the children serve and wash up. Friends also contribute to funeral costs in little envelopes. Nang Kellie graciously accepted them with a *nop* (palms pressed together as if in prayer) and words of thanks and best wishes.

Alice arrived from Holland by train on Monday. Peter flew in from Hawaii on Tuesday. Because of an icy runway, his plane was diverted to Holland. We had to go to the airport four times before we were able to pick him up.

The funeral was on Wednesday, December 1. I had not needed to worry about clothes. The family had hastily made sarongs of white cloth for all of us. We drove to the mortuary. The place was not heated, and it was bitterly cold. First, we went to visit the body in a little room. We stood around the casket, and some monks said some blessings. My relatives instructed me to put some coins in Khounta's breast pocket so that he would have some money when he arrived. Then we went to a vast funeral hall. The coffin was brought in and placed at the front of the room. We sat on mats in front of the casket but to the left side. Friends sat in rows of chairs to our right. I didn't know most of the people. Khounta had not introduced me to his friends. They had learned about the funeral from the Lao radio station. Some monks chanted, and my relatives gave them new robes.

People took many photos, but for the only one I wanted, the mortuary attendants signaled no when my nephew went to take it. He and I were the only ones at the oven. I wanted a photo of the incinerator flames consuming the coffin. It doesn't matter, however. Whenever I think I see Khounta on the street, I can visualize the orange flames, and I know it isn't him.

We had to stay at the mortuary a long time for the ashes to cool. When we finally got the urn with the ashes, we took it to the Lao temple, where we hid it in the back behind the big Buddha. Alice caught a train back to Holland. Peter stayed for a couple of days to help me sort Khounta's belongings. I left on Sunday for California. I had some work and things to sort out there before I would return for Christmas and New Year's with Vincent and Alice in Holland.

In Piedmont, I stayed in the carriage house, which is across the driveway from the house. I found phone messages from Khounta's brother and sister in France. Not knowing I was in Laos, they had called several times. My mother didn't know what to say to me. She told me she had baked a chocolate cake for my birthday. When no one was in the house, I went to see it, but I was too upset to eat it. Her boyfriend was visiting so I never went in the house when they were there, and she didn't visit me. I think she was always alone when faced with death and people dying and had no idea what to do or say. So she did nothing. We never talked. My sister, whom I found out later, was visiting my mother, never came to say anything, either. I wish Mama had tried to comfort me, but that was not the way in our family. My friends made soup, which sustained me through my visit. I was numb to my surroundings. Some friends telephoned with condolences, which were comforting. I had dinner one evening with my book group. I completed the job I had contracted for in San Francisco and left.

Holland was cold, gray, and rainy. I shared half the upstairs in Vincent and Alice's house in Leiden with Alice's college roommate Amy. Alice introduced me to her life in Holland and took me to her favorite places. Vincent's parents invited us to dinner one evening. We even went to the beach one day. I went through all life's daily motions, but I was still in shock. I don't know if Alice was aware of how I felt. She appeared to be unaffected by Khounta's passing. Other than to complain that I hadn't invited Vincent to the funeral, she did not mention him, nor did I.

After seeing in the New Year in Holland, I went back to Phanh and Kellie's apartment in Orly, a suburb of Paris. I still had a big lump in my throat, but I was able to ask Kellie why she hadn't telephoned me. Phanh misunderstood my question and said the cardiac arrest was on Saturday, and there wouldn't have been time for me to get to the hospital. I said no that was not what I meant. I wanted to know why she had not called me when Khounta regained consciousness. She simply said, "I didn't think of it."

We went to the Lao temple and found Khounta's ashes where we had hidden them. I gave the urn to Kellie, and I took the ashes home in a plastic bag. At the airport, we had a good conversation. I learned that Kellie and I shared the same birth date and that Khounta was famous with his friends for being very close-mouthed. They called him the "mystery man."

CHAPTER 36

One Hundred Day Ceremony: March 1994

Lao Buddhists follow many ceremonies after someone dies. After a vigil of a few days to a week beside the coffin at the person's home, monks, family, and friends form a procession to the local temple. Then, after a ceremony led by family members and blessings by the monks, the body is cremated. The cremation releases the soul to join other family and friends who have gone ahead. When the pyre has burned down, candy is often thrown to any neighborhood children who have come to watch. They scramble for it with shouts of joy, and that helps in the process of beginning to smile again. Other ceremonies of remembrance are usually performed after fifty days, one hundred days, and again after one year.

Khounta died in Paris, and so his funeral was there. I took his ashes back to Vientiane in a plastic bag and kept them in my house until March 4, 1994, one hundred days after he had passed away. Khounta's first cousin BounNyok made all the preparations for the *boun saj kraduk*, the ceremony to place the bones. He got the monks to the temple, arranged for an elder to lead the people in the ceremonial customs, got the food prepared and transported, bought the paraphernalia needed to conduct the rituals, and arranged for the placement of the ashes.

Although Khounta hadn't told me, I believed that when he died, he wanted to have his ashes placed in the *taht* he built for his mother. Fortunately, he had not only told one of his cousins that he wanted his ashes to be placed there, but had shown him where. He had had an urn-size hollow space built in the floor of the tile platform in front of his mother's headstone.

We arrived at Wat Done Natong at 7:30 a.m. The monks from Wat Inpeng were just arriving. Many family friends had come earlier to prepare the place for the monks and to fix the food. A friend of ours, Jack Stoops, a graduate school colleague of mine, had come from Japan and Rosalie Giacchino-Baker, whom I had met recently in Vientiane, came to support me and take photographs.

An important structure at every temple complex is an open meeting hall with a raised platform on one end where the monks sit. That is where ceremonies and activities take place, rather than in the temple itself. We sat on mats in front of the monks. I was sick with grief and could not talk or think. I just followed the directions of BounNyok. The ceremony began with the monks, eight from Wat Inpeng and the old Chinese monk at Wat Done Natong, chanting good wishes for Khounta. Afterwards, I led the *tak baht*, that is, we all gave food, sticky rice, and a treat to the monks by placing it in or near their bowls. I gave each monk an apple.

Then each monk was served a meal on a round, rattan table tray. There were nine different dishes of food on each table because there were nine monks. While the monks were eating, I took a tray of food to Khounta's mother at the stupa. Other family members joined me, and we placed flowers, lit incense, and candles and prayed for her.

On our return to the meeting hall, the head monk chanted best wishes over a long, embroidered yellow flag, a stiff, white paper bird, and the food the bird was to take to Khounta. The other monks continued with their meal. Then the head monk chanted good wishes while he poured water into an empty container symbolizing Khounta's empty spirit. He sprinkled some on the bird and flag, too. The water he poured represented the good merits of the people present that would generate thoughts of loving kindness and happiness and fill the emptiness in Khounta's soul. We would water the pole from which the flag and bird would fly with our thoughts and wishes. This merit would go to Khounta's spirit and shorten the time before the beginning of his next life. We went into the garden in front of the hall where the bamboo pole lay on the ground, ready for the ceremony. BounNyok attached the flag and bird, and Dam, Khounta's cousin, put some money in a plastic bag at the bottom of the hole where we would plant the pole. The money could help him get into heaven or with anything else that might come up, as necessary. Then we all took hold of the pole and helped raise it in place. Afterwards, we each poured a little of the water the monk had blessed onto the soil, and we lit incense and candles and put them, with marigolds, around the pole.

With the pole in place, we went back inside the hall. The monks were finishing their food. An elder cousin put a string around Khounta's photo, and it was extended to all the monks to hold in a *nop*. The head monk chanted a long sutra for Khounta. Then he poured water from a silver vessel into a silver bowl. BounNyok and I did the same. We had to pour the water slowly so that we would not run out while the monk chanted good wishes. We put this water on the earth around the pole, too.

After that, we ate. I nibbled at the rice and pretended to eat because I was sick and there weren't any bathrooms. When most people were finished eating, we went to the *taht*. I placed the urn in the hidden space under a tile in front of the marker for Khounta's mother. We offered flowers and lit candles and incense for Khounta, wishing him a safe journey and a place of peace and rest for his soul. His brother showed up while we were doing this. He said he had forgotten this was the day of the ceremony.

I set a large tile in place over the opening, and a worker spread cement over it and put six new tiles on top. Khounta was now at rest in his secret place.

The days, weeks and months turned into three years before I could stop crying and think rationally. I had let down my guard against disappointment. I went through the steps of living in a daze—eating, sleeping, bathing, and making decisions with my senses dulled. My spirit buried. But I didn't realize it at the time. My mind was wrapped up in my loss and Khounta's loss. I had been waiting since we had been married for the happiness of my dreams. We had anticipated so much for the coming years together that the loss was crushing and knowing that he was missing it, compounded it.

Afterword

Because I found I enjoyed writing, I began the recording of these stories that resonated and spiraled endlessly in my head, memories of memories that have undoubtedly changed through time. I read them now and wonder, who is this person? As a wife, I see I was very naïve, timid, and gullible, but those words are not descriptive of me. I would use the descriptors of enlightened, adventuresome but careful, and assertive.

Seven years after his death, I found a letter Khounta had written me. It was in French. I'd never read it carefully because I'd received it after my return from Paris, and I had put it in my safe and forgotten it. The letter was composed in the brief period between his coma and death. He tells me not to come to Paris. *Just wait,* he wrote, *I will come.* I regret not having been with him before he died, but I am consoled with the thought that he believed I had followed his final wishes and waited.

Most of my married life I was lonely, but now I'm not. I wasted time thinking about and wondering where Khounta was and what he was doing. Now it's not an issue. I can do what I want without worrying about whether or not Khounta would approve. His approval was important to me. I didn't want to make him angry. I wanted to be a wife whom he would be proud of, love, and respect. I loved him too much and subjugated myself to what I thought he wanted. He was my sweetheart, which is what I called him, and I still miss him every day.

Where are we now? Peter is in Hawaii, single. Alice married Vincent, and they live in Holland with their son and twin daughters. I decided to stay in the house Khounta built for us. I taught ESL at the Vientiane International School until 2003. Now I spend my time visiting friends abroad, vacationing in California, and volunteering with the Women's International Group to help improve facilities for Lao students and teachers in government schools.

I am blessed with children, grandchildren, many friends and satisfying pastimes. Nothing could make me happier. Well . . . maybe if my cat didn't nip my ankles.

Penelope Khounta
July 31, 2017

Khamsouk persuades me to return for a visit to Vientiane, San Francisco, January 1993.

Our new house on stilts in Vientiane, Laos, where I still live, May 1993.

Memorial *taht* for Nang Im and Khounta at Wat Done Nathong, Vientiane, Laos, 1994.

Noukham Chansomphou and Bounthom Inthavong

Here is some family history about your birth parents and family.

Your father Noukham was born on December 1, 1918. He was first married to Soy Philaphandeth. She died childless some years later. Noukham had a logging business, which he lost to his in-laws when she died. His marriage to your mom Bounthom was arranged in 1951, and according to custom, he moved into *Mom*[i] Thongla's house on the Mekong River in Vientiane.

Bounthom was born to Chinese immigrants on September 10, 1927, in Vientiane. Sadly, her mother was swept away by the Mekong River when Bounthom was just three months old. Her heart-broken father gave her to the doctor who had delivered her, and he went to Luang Prabang. The doctor Prince Kathinyarat[ii] and his wife *Mom* Thongla Inthavong had no children, and they immediately adopted her.

Prince Kathinyarat was the first doctor in Laos. He was educated in Hanoi and returned to Laos in 1916. Prince Kathinyarat practiced medicine in Vientiane. Sadly, one day when he was driving on Thadeua Road to see a patient in 1933 or '36 (date unclear), his car hit a horse, and he was killed. Bounthom's adopted mother *Mom* Thongla raised her.

Later, after Bounthom was married, she asked Noukham to bring her Chinese father from Luang Prabang. He came and lived in Noukham's office on Khoun Boulom Road until the family outgrew *Mom* Thongla's house on the Mekong River. Then they moved to the Khoun Boulom house where you and Peter were born. Bounthom's father passed away in 1968 and Mom Thongla in 1978.

Noukham and Bounthom had ten children: your brothers and sisters, BounNyok, Douangdeuane, Vongphet, Vongkeo, Van, Deng, Bounleua, Khemphone, and you, Peter Bounpeng, the eighth child and you, Alice Monepheth, the tenth.

Noukham passed away December 1, 1987, and Bounthom on October 1, 2007.

---

i *Mom* was the title given to Thongla because she was an ordinary person and was married to a prince.

ii He had several brothers and a half-brother who were leaders in the different Lao governments. His brother Prince Phetsarath was Prime Minister immediately after WWII in the French Protectorate of Laos. Another brother, Prince Souvanna Phomma was the Neutralist Prime Minister of the Royal Kingdom of Laos on and off from 1962 to 1975. His half-brother Prince Souphanouvong, the "Red Prince," was the first President of the Lao PDR from 1975 to 1986.

Khounta

Here is some family history about Papa and his family.

Papa was the first-born son of the Chansomphou grandchildren. His mother Nang[iii] Im had two sisters and three brothers. Her youngest brother Noukham was your birth father.

The Chansomphou's were born in Vientiane of farming parents. They grew rice and had the usual assortment of farm animals to help them, water buffalo, chickens, pigs and oxen. As farmers they also planted papaya, jackfruit, mangos, coconut trees, and raised vegetables.

Khounta's mother married Prak Praproeung, a Cambodian, in February 1926 and Papa was born on November 8 of the same year. Prak Praproeung was a civil servant employed by the French in the French Protectorate of Laos as a tax collector. He had been married before to a Lao woman from *Baan* Khounta, *baan* means village, in Vientiane, the French protectorate capital. Praproeung dearly loved his first wife, who had passed away childless, and he never wanted to forget her, so he named his first-born son after the village where she was born. A daughter followed who died when she was three years old, and then a son Prak Prakan and a girl Prakelie.

Prak Praproeung visited his family in Cambodia and Papa remembered taking a boat down the Mekong River to Phnom Penh with his father on several occasions. Prak Praproeung went to Phnom Penh alone in 1934. The dying wish of Prak Praproeung's mother Prak Kou, a lady-in-waiting to the royal family, was that her four children, including Prak Praproeung, be entrusted to her sister Thep Hoy and proposed the marriage of Thep Hoy's daughter Tep Srey Mom to her son Prak Praproeung before he returned to Laos.

In early 1935, Prak Praproeung returned to Vientiane. While he was back, a son Prak Chanbona was born to him and Tep Srey Mom in Phnom Penh in June 1935. The Cambodian family demanded he come back. Praproeung went back to Cambodia in September 1935 and never returned to Laos. His daughter, Papa's sister Prakelie was born in Vientiane in December 1935. I asked Papa many times how old his sister was, but he said he didn't know. After he passed away, in conversation with Kellie, she told me she was born December 7, the same as I was! Papa expunged Prak Praproeung from his documents after he abandoned the family. That is why he had only one name.

On his returned to Phnom Penh, Prak Praproeung continued to work for the French. After 1942, he was the governor of three provinces at various times. In 1951 he was the Director General of the National Police. He advanced in his career in the government until his death in 1962. He had a national funeral honored with the army corps, members of the government, the Queen Mother Sisowath Kossamack, and Prince Norodom Sihanouk, who gave the funeral oration and lit the funeral pyre. He was an honored and respected functionary.

Prak Praproeung's exit left Nang Im a single mother with three children, one as yet unborn. In the years that followed she worked selling vegetables in the market and her brothers and sisters variously brought up the children.

Papa attended French middle school at the *College* Pavie through grade ten, the highest level of education in Laos. It was not until the early 1970s that high school in Lao language was initiated by USAID with the FaNgum Comprehensive high schools.

In 1946, the French government sponsored him in France for his secondary education and university. He attended the *Ecole Spéciale des Travaux Publics* from which he graduated with a degree in civil engineering. On his return to Vientiane in 1952, he was appointed Director of Public Works for Vientiane. When we were married in 1968, he had risen to Inspector General in the Ministry of Public Works and Transportation, the position he held until we left in 1975.

---

iii *Nang* in Lao is a title and means Mrs. or Miss. I never addressed Nang Im directly by any name, but if I had, it would not have been with *Nang*. I don't know what I should have called her because no one told me. I always thought her name was Nang Im just as I believed my sister-in-law's name was Nang Kellie. It was Prakelie, and her friends called her Kellie, but, as she told me, at a meeting with her after Papa's funeral, I had embarrassed her by not calling her Ah Kellie. *Ah* indicating her relation to me vis-à-vis Papa and meaning aunt.

Lao people use their first names, and it isn't polite to use someone's name without an honorific indicating relationship unless you are very close friends. Lao people don't address one another by their last names. Even the prime minister or president is addressed by his title and his first name.

Lao New Year's Letter from Penny Breuer to her mother: April 17, 1965

NOTE: This letter has been included as it was written with any grammatical and punctuation mistakes I made at the time.

I went to Luang Prabang, the royal capital of Laos for New Years—13,14, &15. We (Dee and I) arrived in the middle of the morning by Royal Air Lao and went to stay with an I.V.S. friend. Her house was a two-story affair with the balcony opening onto a beautiful view of the Mekong. After we had lunched and napped, we took a boat across the Mekong to a sandbar where the week's first activity was to be held. All along the beach were hundreds of people building "Thats" of sand and covering them with lime to make them white ($\triangle\triangle\triangle\triangle\triangle$ ← the beach with little tent-shaped "Thats" about 3' high.)

Everybody was throwing water, and soon I was soaked through (I was dressed in a rag I was keeping for the refugees because I knew it would be messy). There was a bamboo shelter erected on the beach and several bands playing "lamvong" music. The instruments were all Lao—flutes, xylophone, two-stringed bow-played instruments and the bells you hit together like I sent home.

On the beach I met General Sarit — head of the first division of the Royal Lao Army, which is located out of Luang Prabang, General Ouphan, head of the army in Sayaboury, Chaw Y, the youngest son of the king, the *Chow Kouang* — Governor of L.P. province and many, many more people. They were making everyone drink *lao-Lao*, which is a rice whiskey of high potency and abominable taste, which burns all the way down. Nobody likes the taste of it including the Lao, and everyone regards drinking it with the same relish as taking some foul-tasting medicine. We danced, Dee, Betty and I with the above-mentioned men until about 4:30 when we decided to leave. By this time I was soaked, my shoes were gone, and my face had been blackened with the black, which had been scrapped from burned pots and mixed with some grease. We went to get in a boat and were followed by Sarit and his party who wouldn't let us leave. He said he would take us back, but when we went to get in the boat he still wouldn't let us leave. The band with a battery-speaker followed us down the beach, and we ended up throwing and pushing one another in the river. Once when we had managed to get in the boat, they just tipped the boat, and we were in the water again. Finally, we got across and went to a Chinese merchant's and drank beer. We were waiting for Sarit who had lost his keys on the beach. He never did find them, so the Chinese merchant drove us over to the Governor's mansion.

There it was more whiskey and beer, but we didn't have to drink it. We danced and sang some more. Dee, Betty and I were the only women and the only Americans there until some other USAID and I.V.S. people came. They had gone home and changed, but the Lao wouldn't let us leave. For hors d'oeuvres they served river moss, which had been dried and flatened (sic) into sheets. Then it was cut in rectangular pieces and heated over charcoal. It tasted just like you would imagine. I couldn't eat it. After the governor's we walked down to Sarit's where it was more of the same: drinking, singing, eating and dancing. One terrible little man — a known Communist, a tailor in town, asked me to dance and afterwards insisted on rubbing the black on his cheek onto mine. Once I got away from him, I never got near him again. Besides seaweed, Sarit also served strips of dried squid, which had been heated.

From Sarit's we went to General Ouphan's, and it was more of the same. Then we went to the Percival's, a French couple in town that teach at the lycée. There I could switch to Pernod to settle my stomach after all the 'lao-Lao.' They had a record player, so we began to twist and do other dances than the 'Lamvong.'

We finally piled into the cars again and went and ate noodle soup in a restaurant downtown. It was only 9:30 when we got home, but I was dead and slept till nine the next morning.

We had been invited to a picnic by Dr. Somphou (Director of the Lycée in Vientiane) and his wife for eleven a.m., so we went to the bungalow to meet them. We picnicked at his uncle's farm, which was 6 kilometers out of town. It was a very beautiful place. Luang Prabang itself is set in a valley surrounded by mountains. Two sides of the city are bordered by rivers. And in the middle of the city is Mt. Phousi, which is a least 1,000 feet high. Dee and I had climbed it that morning to see the *Wat* up there and look at the view. "Meanwhile back at the ranch . . ." We had to cross two streams from the road to get to the house. In the garden was a small grape arbor and rose bushes. They started pouring 'lao-Lao' again, and you just have to drink it. They never give you more than a swallow, but it's really vile stuff. Lunch was spread out on the table on banana leaves freshly picked from the garden. It consisted of all kinds of greens and at each end of the table was a charcoal hibachi with a pot of boiling water on it. In the water we held thin slices of beef with our chopsticks until it was done to our taste, and then the meat was placed on a lettuce leaf with a piece of peppermint, a raw banana slice, onions and other unknown leaves, then a bit of delicious sauce was spooned on and you popped it all in your mouth as fast as you could. It was very, very good. There was also sticky rice if you wanted it and the 'lao-Lao' came round again. Lunch was finished off with tea made from freshly picked citronella leaves and bananas. Then the water throwing began again. Our faces were blackened, and the men had their shirts ripped. An interesting sideline for me was that both Dr. and Mrs. Somphou, although Lao and with Lao friends, only spoke French to each other. They both went to school in France.

After the picnic, we piled in our jeep and army truck driven by some soldiers and went back to town. We threw water on everyone we passed and went directly to the Governor's Mansion. Everyone there was dressed to go to the *Wat*, but our friends rushed in and poured water on the first person they saw; it was the King's brother. They soaked him, blackened his face and tore his shirt in shreds. Then the governor came along, and they got him. I never thought it possible to tear a tee shirt to pieces, but they manage. After leaving there, we roared around town throwing water and ended up at a *Wat* where the procession was to end that day. As I was sitting on a sawhorse waiting for the people to arrive, over the Wat wall, which was about 5' high, two feet from me came General Ouane Rattikul, Chief of Staff for the Lao Army. He was being chased by his friends, but on the top of the wall he caught his foot and belly-flopped onto the ground. The general is a very fat man, and that ended the day for him.

Then the procession arrived. About five different *wats* came. The head monk from each one was being carried in a gilded chair-litter on the shoulders of twelve men and followed by other monks. A couple of men dressed as monkeys prayed and danced and the people were afraid of them. I don't know their significance (the monkeys) though. Following this, we went to another Major's to eat and drink beer and roast pig. We left as soon as we could because there was a party that night at the Cercle Sportif of which General Sarit was president, and he had invited us.

The party began at seven and was held on the covered basketball courts. Souvanna Phouma was there, and so was Phoui Sannanikone, ex-prime minister of Laos. The dinner was Lao food with a very good chicken curry. We stayed and danced until about 12 when we went for a nightcap. General Sarit bodily tried to keep us from going, but the party was folding. When we drove by two hours later, the lights were still on on the courts, and Sarit was the only one dancing, out in the middle with his arms around another man. Don't think he's queer though because men here do hold hands and dance with each other. There is no stigma attached (maybe only if you didn't) because they can't often dance with girls due to the segregation of the sexes here.

Thursday we decided to take it easy because of the ball given at the palace by the king that night. In the morning I went to take pictures at the *wat* where we had been the day before because it was decorated very differently. The walls were painted black, and gold figures had been stenciled and/or painted on. There were also mosaics made of glass. On the way, we passed a shop where a major from Vientiane was sitting, and he invited himself to show us around.

We were going down the alley that led to the *wat* and there on our right was a little bamboo shack, and the men and women were whooping it up. They made us drink some lao-Lao and we danced and sang till we could politely leave. Then I got my pictures, and the major said that the people next door to where we first stopped had invited us to lunch. We had planned on a quiet lunch and nap, but the afternoon procession was to start at one, which was in a half hour, so we decided to stay. Lunch was sticky rice, lahb (a Lao dish, made with peppers and chopped intestines, etc.; it is usually uncooked and tastes vile, besides being hot) and some awful tasting soup. They came again with the lao-Lao but we flatly refused. We sat on the floor in the house with the food served on an army poncho for a tablecloth. All the while old men and women were drinking and singing, and dancing on the front porch. They were really high. As a matter of fact, they carried a man away so we could sit down for lunch. The women sang lewd songs and the men kept poking each other, but they were deriving an immense amount of pleasure out of almost nothing. Everyone let themselves go, not caring about what anyone thought. Of course, there was no one to think ill because everyone participated in accepted behavior. By this time we found out the parade started at two and not one, so we still decided to wait. At this point, we were invited to drink coconut milk at a house around the corner, where we then proceeded. The milk was served with thinly sliced raw mango, which had been marinated in salty fish water. It wasn't really too bad. The old woman of the house was fixing the waist-length hair of the young girls who were to walk in the procession. It was fun watching her make a tight knot on the top of their heads. The major left then to put on some old rags as he had already lost 4 shirts. When he came back, he suggested we go to the prince's house for a drink, which we did. The king has five children, 3 boys and two girls. We went to the youngest son's house. His brother was also there. The Crown Prince was away on a State visit to Japan at the time. The youngest son is a big fat fellow with glasses He drinks too much, and I would never seek out his company. I wouldn't have gone to his house, but the major and he are apparently good friends. The prince's house was rather bare. We sat in 3' square chairs and drank 'lao-Lao' out of crystal glasses. The middle prince said he had made it and I will admit it was the best I'd ever had although it still tasted vile. He said it was only 60% alcohol, but I wonder. They lit a match to it, and it burned immediately. They also stuck their fingers in it, and it burned as if they had lighter fluid instead. The prince also served beer and some awful undercooked, sliced hard-boiled eggs. He had on his table a very old Lao weaving of silk. It is something that is no longer made and impossible to buy. Dee and I were admiring it, and he pulled it off the table as we grabbed for our glasses and gave it to her. Then we left for the *wat*. On the way out we walked past the walls of an old house, and the prince said it had been that way for five years as there was no money to finish it.

We joined the procession down to the *wat*, clapping and dancing. Someone this time had a bottle of Haig's Gold Label, which at least is better than 'lao-Lao' and I got away with only two swallows. The Governor joined us dressed as a Chinese cowboy in a farmer's shirt like I sent Wade and Bermuda shorts to match plus an army hat. I danced through most of the procession with the King's son-in-law, but I didn't find out who he was until the ball. We stopped for a while at one of the *wats* and Dee and I left to get our hair done.

The ball began at eight p.m., and it will probably be the most fantastic function I ever go to. The King's palace backs on the Mekong River, and the front is opposite the stairs down from Mt. Phousi. All the women wore beautiful long gowns except me because I don't have one, and the men wore white dinner jackets. The party was on the cleared, sandy area in front of the palace and all the tall tress had colored lights dangling in them. Several trees were heavy with mangos, which seemed like Christmas ornaments among the lights. The King came in with his entourage about 8:30, and as I was in the front row, I got to shake hands with him and the Queen. I said, "Good evening" to them both but neither spoke.

The entertainment began with a procession of small boys carrying candles in colored painted lanterns down the winding steps of the mountain. They were led by a transparent paper maché snake about 20 feet long, and by the time the snake entered the palace grounds, the last boys were leaving the top of the mountain, so it looked like one long snake curling down.

This was followed by a young girl carried in on a facsimile of a pig, which is the animal of the year. Men preceded her playing long drums, cymbals, and flutes. After her came rows of men dressed alike. When that procession left, three rows of girls in beautiful Lao costumes with gold headpieces danced in with silver bowls filled with flowers which they presented to the King and Queen.

They were followed by two columns of about 25 men each. The men were dressed in black with red hats like skullcaps with four flaps. The men each carried 2 lanterns made of watermelon colored parchment made into a lotus shape. All the lights were turned off, and they danced for at least 20 minutes in the classical style to the music of bells and xylophone. (A xylophone is about 3 ½' long and in a crescent shape. A man sits before it to play it.)

After the dance, we had an excerpt from the Ramayana for 2 hours and 10 minutes. I loved it and felt very fortunate to see it. I'm enclosing the script we received, so you'll know what part we saw.

This was followed by some final dancing by about 50-75 girls.

Finally, we got to eat at about 12:30. The usual Lao food was served. Then most of the guests left. Only the generals, the ambassadors, and our party stayed to dance. One man apologized for not attending to me more but it was an unusual circumstance for the King to stay after the entertainment and he was very busy. He asked me if I remembered him and I said yes, of course, although I hadn't. He was the man I danced with through the streets that afternoon—the King's son-in-law.

For the first time, the King stayed and received every minister and ambassador that attended the ball. He didn't leave until 4:30 a.m., and we all followed him out.

The next morning Generals Sarit and Udorn Sananikone (Assistant Chief of Staff) joined us for breakfast. They both mentioned that the excitement and spontaneity of the previous year were missing. The King's brother had said the same thing the night before. No champagne had been served as last year, but we figured that was because Phoumi wasn't there to pay.

There is a tension in the air, and everyone is busy playing politics. Phoumi is gone, and no one knows who to trust. All are jockeying for a better position. Rumors fly all the time. I don't hear them in Savannakhet, but in Vientiane, people spend their time creating and spreading them. Everyone expects another coup this year. I don't know what to think.

Phoumi's men are still at work in the country with sabotage and small incitements. Perhaps you read that they took over Thakhek for a few days last month.

I received the book on Laos yesterday, and I am so glad to have it. Did you read any of it? (Enclosed is the money to cover it.)

Love,
Penelope

Acknowledgements

First and foremost I am indebted to Janet Tan. She was my instructor at a writing class for teachers in Pattaya, Thailand in 1998. First, we had to write a short piece about one of the other students in the class. Second, we had to write about something of our choice for the course. I wrote "A Son, A Daughter." I found it to be so much fun that I wrote two stories. Her course and what she taught us inspired me to continue writing.

When I returned to my school in Vientiane, I formed a writers group with Bruce North, Lesley Hilts, and Janet Helmer. We wrote and encouraged each other. Then they moved away. A few years later, I joined another fun and motivating writers group with Angela Dickey, Susan Aiken, and Kit Norland. Then, they, too, moved away. I struggled to write on my own without a writers group, but things went slowly.

In 2010, I stayed at Jim Lehman's Ohana in Bangkok and finished writing the book, but I needed feedback for the new chapters. A new friend Jenny Owen whom I met in Vientiane helped me immeasurably with encouragement and editing, which she continued doing after she returned to Australia.

Oubolvady Rajasombat gave me invaluable assistance helping me translate some of my husband's letters.

In 2012, I joined another writers group with Joanna Ledbetter, Patty Parker, and Renata Da Silva Dee, until it too, dissolved. Then I printed out a couple of manuscripts and asked two friends Laurie Morris Younger and Joan Bossart to give me feedback. They very kindly and quickly edited and proofed my writing, but it took me a few more years to finish the book, using their excellent queries and suggestions.

I am also very grateful to my brother-in-law Prak Chanbona for providing me with family information about his and Khounta's father and families, and to Vongphet Chansomphou for information about her family.

And a special acknowledgment to my many other friends who have helped me. I appreciate beyond words the feedback, suggestions, and encouragement that you have given me through the years without which this memoir would never have been published. Thank you.

INDEX

216, 221, 233, 242, 244-245,
264-265, 279, 289, 327
Thakhek, 5-9, 15, 20, 27,
33, 43, 63, 155, 326
Thao Ma (Manosith), 167-168
That Luang Fair, 151, 186
Thongla Inthavong, Mom,
313-314

U
Udorn Sananikone, 326
United States Agency for
International Development
(USAID), 8, 19-20, 23-24, 27,
28, 34, 39-41, 47-48, 50, 52,
61-62, 64-65, 77, 115, 118, 153,
164, 179, 181, 235, 316, 320
United States Information
Service (USIS), 29, 31, 89-90,
123, 129, 133-135, 140, 178,
179, 181-182, 196, 223, 291
United States Peace Corps, 5,
8, 20, 49, 68, 81, 90, 117
University of Hawaii, 61, 123

V
Vieng Ratry Night Club,
43-45, 49, 50
Viengxay, 175, 185, 239, 244
Villa, Mano, 224, 230

W
Ware, Bob, 43
Wilder, Bernie, 19-20, 79

Women's International Group
(WIG), 292-293, 297
World Cup, 231, 233

Y
Yao, Shen, 61

Z
Zewlenski, Janice, 213

CPSIA information can be obtained
at www.ICGtesting.com
Printed in the USA
LVHW022316200423
744982LV00014B/960

9 780692 927298